A Revolutionary
ROGUE

For Madeleine and Stephen
Who knew the power of love

A Revolutionary
ROGUE

Henry Marten and the English Republic

Sarah Barber

SUTTON PUBLISHING

First published in the United Kingdom in 2000 by
Sutton Publishing Limited · Phoenix Mill
Thrupp · Stroud · Gloucestershire · GL5 2BU

British Library Cataloguing in Publication Data
A catalogue record for this book is available from the British Library.

ISBN 0-7509-2304-0

Typeset in 10/14pt Times.
Typesetting and origination by
Sutton Publishing Limited.
Printed in Great Britain by
Biddles Limited, Guildford, Surrey.

Contents

List of Plates and Maps

Plates

Between pages 116 and 117

1. Sir Henry Marten
   By permission of Trinity Hall, University of Cambridge
2. Map of Surinam
   By kind permission of the John Carter Brown Library, Providence, Rhode Island
3a. Margaret Onely
   By permission of Sudbury Hall, The Vernon Collection (The National Trust) and the Photographic Survey, Courtauld Institute of Art
3b. Edward Onely
   By permission of Sudbury Hall, The Vernon Collection (The National Trust) and the Photographic Survey, Courtauld Institute of Art
4a. Leominster Priory
   Photograph by the author
4b. Pervin Farm
   Photograph by the author
5. Sir James Croft
   Photograph by the author, by kind permission of The National Trust, Croft Castle
6. Marten's almanack
   By permission of Berkshire Record Office; photograph by the University of Reading Photographic Department
7. *Terrible and Bloudy Newes*
   By permission of the British Library, BL E462(28)
8. *A Plea for the People*
   Photograph courtesy of Sotheby's. This manuscript is now part of the British Library, Additional Manuscripts

Maps

Acknowledgements

It has been a pleasure to research into and write about Henry Marten. There can be few characters so colourful, entertaining and stimulating, who grow rather than shrink under the close scrutiny that academic study demands. The more one learns about the man, the more one wants to know. If communing with the dead were a valid historiographical technique, I could have felt less embarrassed about invoking his ghost to resolve ambiguities or to complete the drafts of manifestos that he left infuriatingly undone.

Over the last forty years, Marten fascinated two people to the extent that they spent their lives following his trail. C.M. Williams and Ivor Waters have since both died, and it is sad that they did not live to see a major study of Marten in print. Williams' work survives mainly in his Oxford doctoral thesis, completed in 1954; Waters' in two privately published volumes, which explains their slimness. Waters' knowledge of Marten could have produced a much more substantial study.

I began this research by working my way through the vast quantity of otherwise neglected Marten-Loder manuscripts, held by the University of Leeds. My thanks are due to Christopher Sheppard and his staff at the university's Brotherton Collection for their help and for making me welcome over a considerable period. I should also like to thank the staff of the other record offices – particularly Derbyshire, Berkshire and Barbados – whose collections contribute to a knowledge of Marten. The British Library and, prior to that, Sotherby's have been generous in giving me access to the recently acquired Marten manuscripts, formerly in the collection of the Lords Fairfax. My department at Lancaster University has been understanding in providing access to material otherwise difficult to consult.

A number of colleagues have contributed comments, advice, information, references and support over the years. In particular, I should like to thank David Norbrook, Nigel Smith, James Holstun, David Scott, John Morrill, Stephen Pumfrey, Angus Winchester, Sue Wiseman, David Shotter, David Smith, Tom Lofthouse, Anthony Phillips, Austin Woolrych, Kate Bennett and Manfred Brod. Others, including these, have been supportive in a wider sense. I should like to thank cartographer Chris Beacock, in the Department of Geography of Lancaster University, for producing three excellent maps which make sense of the diverse holdings that made up Marten's estates.

The publication of this monograph was assisted by a grant from the Scouloudi Foundation, in association with the Institute of Historical Research.

One of the greatest joys in compiling this work has been meeting others around the country who have shown such a spontaneous and wholehearted interest in Marten's trail and my own work, and my final thanks go to these enthusiasts. I arrived unannounced on their doorsteps, and they were open, friendly, generous and as spirited about a dead republican demagogue as I was myself. They could have been cautious and suspicious, but instead they showed me around their homes, passed on the oral history of their villages, and helped me to practical and scholarly information. There are – encouragingly – far too many of these good people to name, but I should like to mention Elizabeth and the late Johnnie Parker Jervis, Diana Uhlman, Rose and Leslie Wiles, Richard Price, Miles Drew, James Healy, and Ephraim Norville. I hope that I have used the knowledge and wisdom of everyone named here wisely. What error remains is my own. Of me I hope, and of them I know, that 'Honest Harry' Marten would have approved.

Introduction

This is an evaluative account of the life of Colonel Henry Marten MP. It was a long life, but his family was of short lineage. Marten was born in Oxford in 1602. His father was Sir Henry, Dean of the Arches, Judge of the Admiralty Court and a High Commissioner. Sir Henry was wealthy and important. When he died in 1641, his son inherited the wealth and proceeded to build an important political career. Little more than ten years later, both the fortune and power were spent. It was Henry, by repute, who destroyed the family legacy. He squandered the wealth in loose living. He frequented the stews, had many mistresses, drank to excess, and treated important matters shallowly, in the company of his libertinistic friends. His lifestyle was deemed to be the cause of his political demise. Since he appeared not to take life seriously, frivolity must have subsumed his politics.

Within Marten's lifetime, politics was so serious as to be deadly. In middle age, Marten lived through the storm of civil war, political crisis and social upheaval in Britain. This book opens with an account of Marten's political career in Westminster, from his election to the Short Parliament in 1640, to the execution of Charles I and the foundation of England's republican Commonwealth government. In 1640 Marten was a minor political figure – just another county gentleman in politics. By 1649 he was a notorious extremist, a demagogue of popular sovereignty. Throughout the 1640s he was a consistent enemy of monarchy, the leading republican, and not only a regicide but, with Oliver Cromwell, the one considered to have organised the signatures of the men who signed the death warrant of their King.

In chapter two, we trace Marten's years in power, and his fall. Marten was one of the stoutest defenders of the republican Commonwealth regime. He designed its emblems and mottos, wrote its constitutional statements and was a stalwart committee man. The fall of the regime – more commonly known by its pejorative nickname, the Rump Parliament – signalled his personal and political collapse. The marriage of the personal and the political was continued in the period of Cromwell's rule. Marten bore an implacable hatred towards Cromwell (and vice versa) which far outweighed any hostility that the royalists could direct at the Lord Protector. Marten's ability to damage Cromwell's reputation, however, was lessened by his own decline in fortune. For most of the later 1650s he struggled to satisfy a whole array of creditors, previously kept from the door by the shield of personal power. In 1654 he was spectacularly bankrupt. Imprisoned first by the Protectorate for bankruptcy, and subsequently by the triumphant royalists for regicide, he was denied a martyr's death at the Restoration, but instead drifted into obscurity in a series of remote prison castles.

Chapter three suggests, however, that Marten's personal reputation for licence and his protracted demise have obscured his serious opinions on the best form of government. Although he was poor at completing political tracts, he did produce an interpretation of republicanism. He was radical, populist and anti-hierarchical, and his view of republican government – the direct expression of the will of the people, or the rule of the many – was at odds with that of Harrington, Milton and Vane, for whom it was the senatorial rule of the few.

The way in which moderately minded people in the early-modern period came to terms with extremism within their midst was to attribute to those with extreme views on one issue, similarly extremist views on many. If one lived an amoral life and was a republican in politics, one was often accused of atheism. Marten was certainly unorthodox in his religious views, but he was not an absolute unbeliever. Instead, he carried extreme scepticism into his everyday life, in which he held it a lordly obligation to promote tolerance towards the religious opinions of others. A chapter is therefore devoted to explaining the intellectual and practical consequences of what is here described as his Epicurean epistemology.

The practical application of Henry Marten's personal philosophy can be analysed through his role as a landed gentleman. He inherited vast estates in Berkshire and the Commonwealth awarded him others in Derbyshire and Herefordshire. He was therefore a landlord in three very different parts of England. The grand themes of republican politics, religious heterodoxy and indebtedness were reflected in the microcosm of his estates. In the end, all three were lost to the tandem forces of royalists' and creditors' revenge.

The Marten family fortune was floated on the seas. Sir Henry practised the civil law in the Admiralty courts and had close ties with London and Bristol merchants. Henry and his younger brother, George, took on maritime roles as owner and captain of their barque, the *Marten*. When the civil war ended, George took a ship and several merchant friends, and sailed to the Caribbean. First in Barbados, and then in Surinam, he attempted to rescue the family's spent fortune by harvesting sugar. So unsuccessful was he that his debts, for which Henry was liable, brought the family low. The main subject of chapter six is therefore George Marten, but understanding the younger brother is a key to understanding Henry.

We therefore have two images of Henry Marten. One is that of a libertinistic, high-living rake, every aspect of whose life was unmeasured and expressed in ribald joviality, shared with his adulterous partner, Mary Ward. The other is that of a serious politician and thinker, whose views were, by his own admission, not widely held, but they were unusual, influential and feared. The two faces of Henry Marten worked together. One could undermine or reinforce the other. The way in which the two sides of Marten were symbiotically connected and the reputation that developed around his name are the subject of a final chapter. A postscript traces the reputation of Marten to the present day. The man who emerges from this study is fascinating: in fact, the more one studies Henry Marten, the more interesting the personality that emerges. A sceptic and a republican, he was a landed proprietor who took risks and was prosecuted for debt, an adulterer who practised charity, and an ideologue who preserved a sense of humour.

I
The Rise of the Republicans

The background of the Marten family was obscure, and in the 1620s and 1630s Henry Marten was described merely as a farmer of Hinton Waldrist in Berkshire.[1] The political storm, brewing in the late 1630s, rocketed Marten to sudden prominence. In April 1640, when King Charles was forced to call a parliament, desperately short of funds for the war in Scotland, Henry Marten was elected for the county seat of Berkshire and joined his father in the Commons. It is perhaps surprising that he managed to secure a return for the county, maybe because he had earned considerable popularity for refusing to contribute towards the loan for the Scottish wars. His family's estates lay to the north and west of Berkshire, close to Abingdon, the county town, which undoubtedly aided his return. When MPs gathered on 13 April, Marten was joined by his brother-in-law, Sir George Stonehouse, the member for Abingdon borough; the two members for Reading, Edward Herbert, the Solicitor General, and Sir John Berkeley; and the MPs for Wallingford, Edmund Dunch and Unton Croke. Sir Arthur Ingram and Sir Richard Harrison sat for New Windsor. A member of an old-established west Berkshire family, John Fettiplace, was his fellow representative for the county. Henry Marten junior made little impact on his first venture to London, whilst his father continued to steer a moderate course through increasingly choppy debates. He argued, for example, that should the tax of Ship Money be proven lawful, there should be a certain amount of give and take between parliamentary demands and the King's requirement for supply.[2]

On 5 May the King instructed the Keeper to appear in parliament and dissolve its sitting. The war in Scotland, which had necessitated the calling of the Short Parliament, was temporarily brought to a halt by the Treaty of Ripon, signed on 26 October 1640. Edward Hyde was quite baffled by the King's decision to dispense with the services of such a sober, respectable and moderate gathering. It was becoming clear that it would soon be necessary to call another and there would be little likelihood of such 'grave and unbiassed men' being re-elected.[3] Hyde advised Charles to remain with his army, rather than take the impetuous and ill-judged decision to call a second parliament. He counselled that the most prudent thing the King could do was to surround himself with men 'more afraid of dishonour than danger'.[4] But prudence was not the King's muse any more than it would be Marten's, and a new parliament was called to meet in November. Whilst the younger Henry Marten was quiet throughout its early months, his father increasingly emerged as a maverick, nobody quite sure which way he would jump. Sir Henry Marten sat on the Commons' committee to examine whether, once the Short Parliament had been dissolved, it was legal for convocation of the Church of England to continue to sit. It was formulating a new set of canons for the Church, which it was hoped would determine the religious controversies surrounding the nature and definition of the Anglican communion. When the canons were presented to the new parliament, Sir Henry complained long and loud, although it was cynically observed that, as a civil lawyer, he objected to an increased role for clerics because he would be 'going to the funeral of his profession'. A higher profile for canon law would reduce the status of civilians.[5] Sir Henry also sat on committees that sought to curb religious innovations and to codify and strengthen the privileges of parliament.[6]

Despite Sir Henry Marten's increasingly reformist stance, by 1641 the pressure for change was directed towards him. In August he was among nine High Commissioners ordered by a committee of the House of Lords to pay damages to John Ekins, because Parliament declared that the Commission had lacked the authority to fine him.[7] Neither was Sir Henry's neo-reformism sufficient to save him from being indicted as a member of the High Commission in the case brought by the puritan controversialist John Bastwick. Seven years after their prosecution by the prerogative courts, Bastwick and his supporters sought reparation.[8] Sir Henry was subsequently ordered to lend parliament £13,000 towards the relief of the northern garrisons at Carlisle and Berwick. The following weekend, as the parliament went into recess, he rode down to his country house at Bray, where he died on the Sunday night, at the age of eighty-one.[9]

Sir Henry Marten's son had played no recorded part in the Short Parliament, but began to be named to committees in its successor. He started in a small way with those concerned with the American colonies, customs' farming, and Dr Montague's case for a pardon.[10] In March 1641 his involvement increased, being named to the committee of twenty-four that conferred with the Lords on the impeachment of Thomas Wentworth, earl of Strafford. The trial of Strafford represented the most concerted effort to rid the three nations of an 'evil counsellor', one held guilty of a desire to impose arbitrary government and divide the king from his people.[11] Marten was also a member of Commons' groups that unsuccessfully called for the clergy to be disabled from temporal office, investigated the 'popish hierarchy', and prepared a bill to require new applications for tonnage and poundage every three years.[12]

In May 1641 Marten was named to the Commons' committee that was to 'prepare a Declaration of the unanimous Consent and Resolution of this House, for the Defence of the Religion established, of the King's Person, and the Liberty of the Subject', in the face of rumblings of discontent within the English army. Marten therefore sat in the Inner Court of Wards with men of greater stature, such as John Pym, John Selden, John Hampden and Lucius Cary, Viscount Falkland, whilst they prepared the document known as the Protestation. It complained of the changes that had occurred since 1629: popish innovation in the Church, arbitrary government, and the absence of parliaments. The Protestation called on subjects to swear an oath to 'maintain and defend His Majesty's royal person and estate', though as Russell points out, '[i]n an ironical, but thoroughly English fashion, they were defending established authority against its lawful king'.[13]

As the numbers of committees proliferated, Marten was named to several, ranging from day-to-day administration to matters of considerable moment. He dealt, for example, with the deliberations against Strafford and Archbishop Laud. He was put in charge of preparing the Heads of the Directions to the Lord General for the disbandment of the army.[14] From the first meeting of the Long Parliament on 3 November 1640 to the first recess, during which his father died, Marten was named to a total of forty-six committees. Some of these were constitutional; most were administrative. He also found his way onto the committee that held discussions with the House of Lords in order to report on the 'affairs of the kingdom' and was named one of the seven reporters on these conferences. By August 1641 this group had acquired the name of the Committee of Both Houses for the Defence of the Kingdom. A committee of forty-seven MPs from the Commons continued to meet with the Lords during the recess, when they assumed powers to discuss the ceasefire with the Scots, take action against delinquents, disband the army, suppress riots and examine the King's accounts.[15]

The Rise of a Republican

On the death of his father, Henry Marten was thirty-nine years old. The seeming coincidence between the death of Sir Henry Marten and the start of people taking notice of his elder son reveals a man who recognised the point at which human agency could twist fate to its own advantage. Shortly after Sir Henry's death, political affairs took a turn for the worse. When rebellion broke out in Ireland in late October, Marten was placed on the committee to examine its suppression. He was subsequently one of four MPs ordered to collect the contributions of his fellows towards the relief of Ireland, though he contributed only £200 himself.[16] On 18 November he was asked by the Commons to tap into his network of contacts among London's merchant community in order to discover the true nature of the safety of the House and the nation. His findings looked grave. The following week he was given charge of drawing up the agenda for a conference on safety, and, showing an early penchant for the rhetoric of representativeness, he emerged with the statement that the Commons,

3

being the Representative Body of the whole Kingdom, and their Lordships being but as particular Persons, and coming to Parliament in a particular Capacity, that if they shall not be pleased to consent to the Passing of those Acts, and others, necessary to the Preservation and safety of the Kingdom, that then this House, together with such of the Lords, that are more sensible of the Safety of the Kingdom, may join together, and represent the same unto his Majesty.[17]

Despite his relatively obscure background, Marten was named to the most important constitutional committees. The death of Sir Henry released the heavy hand of the sober but dourly cautious patriarch, and delivered a vast fortune into the hands of a man who equated danger with honour. One early – and, in view of his later anti-Scottish prejudices, ironic – example of the largesse that Marten's inheritance could bring was 'the free Offer . . . to accommodate the Scotts Commissioners with a House, at the Rent of One hundred Pounds per Annum',[18] and he was also in control of the purse-strings when it came to sending money to Sir Adam Loftus, treasurer of the wars in Ireland.[19] On 1 February 1642 Marten offered £2,000 as a loan to the 'service of the Commonwealth', a figure double that offered by Lord Capel or Sir Gilbert Gerrard and one which completely overshadowed the £300 committed by Oliver Cromwell.[20] At the end of the month he put his merchant vessel, the *Marten*, at the service of parliament for the defence of the kingdom, 'upon the same Terms as the other Ships are'. His offer was accepted by the Lord Admiral, who nevertheless declared himself unaware of any need for further sea defence.[21] It was another week before both Houses saw fit to put the kingdom into a defensive posture, at which point Marten attempted to deny Charles Stuart the right to his flagship, the *Prince Royal*.[22] He was not so much pre-empting events as making sure, by dint of the lavish expenditure of his fortune, that should matters deteriorate, he seemed both prescient and ideally placed to offer a solution.

Men were called to arms to defend parliament from the perceived threat of popish insurrection, and Marten was at the forefront of the manoeuvring, both in Berkshire and nationally, as 'treasurer' of the Committee for the Defence of the Kingdom responsible for directing the action.[23] In February 1642 he received promises of armed men to be raised for Colonel Philip Hill's regiment, then in Calais, and in July he passed money to Hill to cover his expenses whilst defending the magazine at Hull.[24] Also that month, Marten supported Ann Stagg of Southwark, who presented a women's petition calling for political reforms, required because of the decay in trade.[25] Richard Whitby, possibly one of his London merchant connections, undertook to pay for the training of sixty soldiers.[26] Marten financed troops under the command of his Berkshire neighbour, George Purefoy, who was acting as a deputy lieutenant to the Earl of Warwick, enabling him to take part in the relief of Hull. He supported them in money and kind, by supplying 200 coats, breeches and shoes. Marten's servant, Thomas Whitton, ran messages to the fleet, delivering 1,200 soldiers' uniforms for captains Fairfax, Bushell, Drake, Owen, Holman and Bullows, which cost Marten nearly £1,000.[27] After March 1642 Marten was active in distributing parliament's militia ordinance throughout Berkshire and in countering the responses of the court. When the king attempted to muster troops under a commission of array, the sheriff of the county, Tanfield Vachell, was ordered on Marten's motion to send the King's messages to the Commons.[28] Marten was said to have stood in front of his tenants and ripped the king's commission, an action which stirred them in his support and lent credence to his reputation as an incendiary.[29]

In the summer Marten rented a house and garden in St Anne's Street from Thomas Fauconbridge, Receiver General of the Revenue, putting himself at the very centre of Westminster's political machinations.[30] From here he masterminded the gathering of intelligences. He was the parliament's spymaster. Marten kept several receipts for information: to a George Combes or Tombes, employed around Sherborne in Dorset; £20 in August to Thomas Trotter for delivering a ship to the Earl of Warwick; and more to George Perrier and James Noel.[31] At the same time, Lord Willoughby of Parham, who had secured the south bank of the Humber during the siege of Hull, applied to Marten for compensation for the county officers who had acted under his authority.[32] Marten paid the informants and passed his receipts to John Pym. His brother George's expenses as captain of the *Marten* also came out of this money. The younger brother ran up considerable debts, which Henry was expected to cover. In fact, the committee paid Marten £500 towards intelligences.[33] In view of the levels of his expenditure during the spring and summer of 1642, it could not possibly have covered his outlay: he was subsidising parliamentary policy out of his own, not inconsiderable resources.

Throughout the events of the spring and summer of 1642, Marten lit fires under issues that others preferred to dampen down. Sir Simons D'Ewes, no revolutionary, invariably pitted himself against Marten in debate, and seems to have had good cause to describe Marten, and the small group with whom he acted in the House – such as William Strode or Sir Henry Ludlow[34] – with terms like 'agitation', 'asperity', or 'fierceness'. These were the 'violent spirits', though Marten countered, disingenuously, that it was not unlawful for 1,000 men to assemble and beat a drum.[35] When Charles answered the Commons' actions in March 1642, a majority in the House wished to call his response 'causeless Imputations'. Marten was more straightforward: the King's answers were a 'scandal'.[36] On another occasion, having taken action citing the militia ordinance as his authority, he was reluctant to see a bill for the regulation of the militia introduced. Having already framed the militia ordinance and declared its legitimate authority, to subsequently introduce another piece of legislation, with a different procedure of legitimisation – the agreement of King, Lords and Commons, rather than just the two Houses – would bring parliament's action in framing the ordinance into disrepute. Marten needed to establish the legitimacy of legislation by ordinance. He was in a tiny minority, 'there being scarce any negative besides the said MR. MARTEN himself'.[37] Throughout July the King and a majority in parliament struggled to prevent war, anxious to come to some form of accommodation. Marten and his allies, such as Strode and Alexander Rigby, fought against it. For Marten, the peace conditions were worse than war and 'though the King be King of the people of England, yet he is not master of the people of England'.[38]

Most of the committees that prepared impeachment proceedings during 1642 had Marten as a member. He was keen to see men such as Henry Killigrew ejected from the House for statements which seemed to support the actions of the King, and once the war officially began, he enthusiastically disabled delinquent members.[39] Local officers hauled before the House for implementing the King's orders were disproportionately from Berkshire: these included the deputy mayor of Reading, who had proclaimed the commission of array, and Marten's neighbour in Buckland, the High Constable, John Southby.[40]

In August 1642 Marten pronounced that the kingship was forfeitable: a statement unambiguous enough to exclude him from royal pardon.[41] Once there was no chance of amnesty, Marten's career was set. He had to be a participant in a glorious military victory, for to be on the losing side was to sacrifice his life on a charge of high treason. Hexter's study of Pym 'would not hesitate to select Martin [sic], Rigby, and Vane as leaders of the war party'.[42] Whilst the negotiations for a peace were underway at Oxford, Marten was the most frequently cited radical in opposition who made the propositions deliberately unacceptable and was ungracious about monarchy.[43]

Williams calculated that Marten sat on eighty committees before the end of 1641 and 150 during 1642. It is certain that his contribution was considerable, though Russell disputes whether his presence was 'positive', arguing that if Charles was unable to come to an accommodation with men like Marten, 'the blame might as well be theirs as his'.[44] If he was so far on the radical wing and had no patronage from aristocratic sponsors, why would a man of such known violent opinions be so often included in the counsels of those at the centre of Commons' politics and so often sent to consult with the Peers? The answer lay in Marten's connections and his ruthless enthusiasm to exploit them. His links with the merchant community enabled him to thrust his own ship into the naval coup, and provide a fleet for the purpose, which was to be important during the siege of Hull. His merchant links gave him valuable contacts amongst the monied men of the City. He borrowed huge sums from them, they earned massive interest rates from him, and he used the money to burrow into the political core, whilst the men at the centre called on City financiers for political and monetary support.

The Commons exploited Marten's connections with the City during the autumn of 1642. He advised Warwick on the apprentices ready to be armed in the capital.[45] The following day, when the House nominated six of its members to accompany six peers to inform the City of the progress of the peace negotiations, the six Commoners were surprisingly radical. It sent Marten, Henry Vane the younger, Thomas Lord Grey of Groby, Sir Peter Wentworth, and 'middle party' stalwarts Robert Goodwin and Sir John Evelyn. Marten chaired both committees, which negotiated the resulting offers of support from the citizens.[46]

In the summer of 1643 the radicals moved to assert the autonomy of the Common Council by calling for the City militia to commanded by an *ad hoc* committee – the London Militia Committee, meeting at Grocers' Hall – rather than being under the direct command of the Earl of Essex.[47] Opposition to Essex's command was growing, fanned by a powerful lobby of citizens who proposed a general armed rising. All Londoners would be enrolled in a militia, recruited by trade, with its own self-regulating body of 'agitators', six or eight men drawn from each trade to monitor the political temper of the recruits. The Londoners had already presumed to choose a committee, of thirteen members of the Commons, to oversee the new London army. Isaac Pennington, the Lord Mayor, was the only one with direct connections with the capital. Of the others, Bond, Bainton, Strode and Rigby had close personal and political connections with Marten, also named as a member; John Blakiston, Herbert Morley, Thomas Hoyle and John Gurdon were also of a radical temper and the remaining members were Sir William Masham, Henry Heyman and William Ashurst.[48]

Marten emerged at the head of the movement, chairing the committee for a General Rising, which met at the Merchant Tailors' Hall.[49] In the account given by Hexter, the threat posed by the movement for a General Rising was reflected in the numbers of Londoners it claimed to be able to raise; an armed force that well outnumbered the troops already under Essex. Hexter pulled back from his conclusion and sought to minimise the potency of the movement by making light of Marten's military abilities and much of his personal reputation for licence.[50] However, Marten organised the London citizens, raising contributions and forming them into regiments, whilst at the same time continuing to sit on committees to raise cavalry regiments in London and the surrounding counties.[51] On 28 July 1643 the Earl of Manchester announced to the assembled citizens that the Lord Mayor would have control of the forces in the Home Counties and that Sir William Waller would command the militia raised by the City. Parliament had stolen the thunder from the radicals by appointing Waller to head the forces raised by the Militia Committee, reducing the ability of the Committee for a General Rising to act with any autonomy. Pym read a proclamation to the same audience, claiming that the King sought to bar trade between the City and the rest of the country, on account of the appearance of the citizens at 'the head of that traiterous faction, and the receptacle of all such as are disaffected to our Government'. Pym, by demonstrating the danger that the King posed to the peace and livelihood of the City, hoped that they would approve the appointment of Waller.

Marten gave the third speech. His task, as a representative of the Committee for a General Rising, though also as a member of parliament, was to congratulate the citizens for securing Waller's charge of a London force. Despite the rousing language, which was to become familiar as that associated with Levellerism, Marten's speech was essentially that of a mediator between parliament on the one hand and the London agitators on the other. The House of Commons conceived

> that if there shall be a generall and unanimous rising of the people both in this Citie, and in other parts of the Kingdome, it will take downe the partition wall betwixt the well-affected, and ill-affected . . . It is desir'd you would all joyne in saving your selves, if it please you to give your best assistance and furtherance, to that work under the hands of that Committee, I presume they will be very faithfull, and they have beene very dilligent in the worke, but certainly I am of opinion, that either you must goe forth all, and meete the Enemy as Vassalls with Ropes about your neckes, or like men with swordes in your handes.[52]

In fact, despite the different backgrounds and political standpoints of the three men, the speeches were a co-operative exercise in the announcement of policy, and showed how far the radicals' bid for autonomous action had been nipped in the bud. The key speech by Pym, including the reading of the King's proclamation that had threatened the City, dressed up the threat to the state in his favourite language of papal conspiracy. The Londoners, thus alarmed, were grateful for Manchester's first announcement of Waller's command of the City forces, and further reassured when a representative of the Committee for a General Rising reminded them that they had achieved their aim and reinforced the message of unity. It was, in effect, a united opposition to the moves towards peace at Oxford. Although Hexter saw the Committee for a General Rising as both dangerously subversive and laughably ineffectual, the movement was, in fact, rather effective. It replaced commanders in a way that was least destructive to the overall war-effort, undermined the Oxford peace negotiations, and had a temporarily unifying effect on London. Marten seemed quite efficiently to have made 'the important transition from loud talk and fine phrases to effective action' and his speech seems quite restrained, not at all 'grandiose' or 'full of the very best bombast'.[53] The fact that London did not rise is surely not the point.[54]

Marten subscribed £1,200 to the parliamentary cause, undertook to raise a regiment of cavalry and was appointed governor of Reading, a post which he ignominiously abandoned in the face of the royal army marching on Oxford.[55] Nevertheless, the

Commons was indulgent as he raised another regiment the following year, perhaps unwittingly providing him with some of the means. In February 1643 he was named to the chair of the committee for sequestrations and was part of a radical group given the right to seize the personal property of anyone at war with the parliament.[56] In March he paid Silvester Reine £10 17s. to repair and re-line three suits of armour,[57] and set himself up as colonel of a regiment. He was most commonly known by his military title. Some were scathing about the appropriateness of the rank or the military conduct of the regiment, even though Thomas May congratulated the private gentlemen of the west of England, including Marten's neighbour, Alexander Popham, for their sterling work in opposing the royalists.[58] But Marten sailed close to the wind. He was ordered to give reparation to Lancelot Luke, and to the 'lady' whose coach horses he had seized. The earl of Manchester, recently appointed commander in chief of new regiments of horse and foot, was scandalised that Marten's Quartermaster, one de Luke, had stolen two of the king's horses from the royal mews.[59] On this last occasion, Marten brazened it out, and obtained the protection of his fellow MPs, by pointing out that he had been given authority to take 'the King's Ship, and Forts, for the Defence of the Kingdom, and might as well take his Horses, lest they might be employed against us'. The House was even more indulgent when he seized the plate and goods of two royalist colonels, allowing him to sell the goods and use the money towards his regiment. He was also permitted to use money from the Committee for a General Rising.

By July 1643, however, the Commons were determined to rein Marten in.[60] A mere fortnight after Marten had spoken with Manchester and Pym, he supported the sentiments of a sermon by puritan divine John Saltmarsh, who let drop words to the effect that it were better that one family should perish than the whole nation. When openly challenged in the House, Marten confirmed that he and Saltmarsh referred to the royal family. Marten was ejected from the Commons, imprisoned for fourteen days and banned for three years from representing his constituency.[61] Williams argued that Pym deliberately overreacted to Marten's statement, having been looking for an excuse to have him ejected from the House. The radicals caused him too much trouble. However, Marten's speech to the Common Council did not seem at odds with that of Pym and there is no evidence that Marten had done something to alienate him during the following two weeks. Marten's radicalism certainly made him something of a dangerous and unknown quantity, but he was a hard-working committee member, had successfully kept the fractious Londoners on board and was a major financial contributor to the parliamentary cause.

If Pym masterminded Marten's ejection, it was a move of Machiavellian cunning on his part. It may have been at the request of more conservative masters in the other House. In most respects, Hexter's argument seems convincing. Although Pym had doubts about the Oxford proposals, he could not be seen to dismiss them out of hand

and thus slapped down the radicals when they overstepped the bounds of acceptability. Sir Henry Vane the younger's attempt to root out peers who were not on the right side of the religious debate led Pym to support the honour and integrity of the Upper House. He defended the Committee of Safety against attacks from Marten and Rigby, and justified his own statements that the King's answers to the Oxford propositions were 'gracious'.[62] Marten was indulged when he treated the King's answers with 'scorn', but when he supported Saltmarsh by making *ad personam* attacks on the royal family, this was too much for the House to accept. One of the mainstays of the House's continued opposition to Charles was that nothing it did was to the detriment of his person. Implying that the King might be 'destroyed' to save the nation – that it would be well to 'extirpate the royal family and utterly to subvert monarchical government' – was well outside the bounds of acceptability.[63] The House acted swiftly to fill the gaps that Marten's military and parliamentary absence created, placing his regiment under the authority of the Committee of the Militia and having him replaced on key committees.[64]

The Campaign Outside the Commons

Marten's expulsion taught him a valuable lesson: it had highlighted the power that he could exercise inside the Commons' chamber and his relative powerlessness once he stepped outside. In a system in which both Houses were revered, Marten could not be seen to put their reputation in jeopardy. He needed to build up support outside the Commons, but would only be able to use extra-parliamentary action as a lever, not as an alternative source of power. He could be leader of a pressure group, but not as yet a leader of parliamentary opinion. More powerful men in parliament could use him in ways that contributed positively towards their own aims and successfully discard him once he got in their way.

The degree to which Marten's influence relied on his place within the Commons cannot be any more eloquently illustrated than by the absence of records relating to his activities during the mid-1640s. He signed the Solemn League and Covenant, reluctantly, he later claimed.[65] His brother was active in France during 1644.[66] Henry commanded a troop of trained bands, the infantry at the siege of Donnington Castle, and was governor of Aylesbury. His rehabilitation began on 6 January 1646, when the House decided to erase from the *Commons' Journal* the parts about the Saltmarsh affair that related to Marten and he retook his seat. He seems to have been restored to the county membership but, coincidentally, the following piece of business that day was the disabling of his brother-in-law, Sir George Stonehouse, whose royalism lost him the seat for Abingdon. The 'recruiter' elected for the county town was fellow radical, William Ball of Barkham.[67]

In the period that Marten had been out of the House, the exchanges between peace and war party members had sharpened. Whilst the former drew up and presented the propositions for peace at Uxbridge, the latter were providing a greater focus to the military effort by steering the passage of the New Model ordinance past first the Commons and then, amended, the Lords. By the end of February 1645 the Uxbridge Treaty had foundered, primarily over its religious clauses, which called on Charles to take the Solemn League and Covenant, abolish episcopacy and establish a national Presbyterian Church. On the other hand, the formation of the New Model Army, and the Scots' continued presence in England after Charles refused the Covenant, turned the tide in favour of the parliamentary forces. In a breathtaking piece of disavowal, the Commons resolved in May that the military help of a Scottish army within England was no longer required, and that it should be paid off. The following month, after the decisive battle of Naseby, the English played down the role of the Scottish forces and attributed victory to Providence and the New Model Army.[68] The King eventually surrendered to the Scots, who took him to their garrison at Newcastle-upon-Tyne, where he was offered peace terms in July 1646.

The Commons, released from the discipline of maintaining unity for the sake of military survival, became prey to factionalism. Dividing the House into 'Presbyterian' and 'Independent' parties is now seen as a misleadingly simplistic and anachronistic way of viewing the politics of the mid-1640s, but the one faction that had the discipline, vigour and commitment sufficient to make it recognisable was the one that was the most violently anti-Scottish. Many of the men of this faction – Marten, who had offered his house to the Scottish Commissioners, and Thomas Chaloner and Alexander Rigby, both of whom had landed estates that had witnessed the presence of the Scots – had been supporters, albeit cautious, of Scottish intervention in 1643. Then, England had needed additional arms if its parliament was not to be overrun, but the Scots exacted a high price. They were anxious to see their style of Calvinism in England and, in the northern counties in which their army was quartered, were overseeing its implementation.[69]

Most galling for the radicals, with their new-found anti-Scottish zeal, was the continuing demand by the Scottish Commissioners that they be part of the peace negotiations in which they promoted Charles' demand to be allowed to return to London. Thomas Chaloner stated his anger openly in the House in what became known as the 'Speech without Doors'. Marten supported his friend in print.[70] He did so anonymously, an unusual habit for a man so outspoken, though he had been chastened by his expulsion and was anxious not to repeat the experience so soon after his return. His public contribution was one of several tracts, both pro- and anti-Chaloner, to be published in London in a feverish rush of press activity. Marten's was called *A Corrector of the Answerer to the Speech out of Doores justifying the worthy speech of Master Thomas Chaloner a faithfull Member of the Parlement of England.* The style was unmistakably Marten's and a nicely sarcastic, Martenesque touch was the bogus imprimatur of the King's printer in Scotland, Evan Tyler. He practised the same conceit as the author of *An Vnhappy game at Scotch and English.*[71] Without doubt, Marten was the author of a further contribution – a reply to *An Answer to the Speech without Doores: or, Animadversions* – a draft of which is extant, written in his own hand.[72] Another did not reach the presses, but ribaldly lambasted 'jockey' for his presumption.[73]

Parliament continued to drag its heels in the peace negotiations and the New Model Army regiments grew fractious and militant. When the soldiers presented a list of their grievances, in late March 1647, Denzil Holles, by this point a convert to moderation, called them 'enemies of the state and disturbers of the public peace'. His phrase, the so-called Declaration of Dislike, rankled for years.[74] Both the radical faction in parliament and the dominant Presbyterian moderates felt the political impetus slipping away from themselves and towards Fairfax's army. The reason was, ironically, that the army was still in existence, even though it was no longer engaged in fighting. Without a war to manage, the Committee for Both Kingdoms lost its *raison d'être* and was replaced by the Committee for Irish Affairs, meeting at Derby House. This group could claim that the fighting was far from over and that there was necessary work to be done in restoring Protestant honour across the water.[75] Marten had taken an active part in overseeing Irish affairs during the early 1640s. Although, later in the decade, he was no longer at the centre of the parliamentary decisions being made about Ireland, Irish affairs had an impact on the future direction of radical thinking.

Ireland provided a counter-image to the majority of English parliamentarians' obsession with the Scottish Commissioners. Scotland was a nation of ostensibly sympathetic Protestants, which had chosen to intervene and exercise leverage over English affairs, but Ireland was a nation of rebellious Catholics, and a majority of the English saw it as part of their interest to crush them. Whilst even the most committed Presbyterian in the English Commons had become wary of the sense in which it was manifested by his Scottish brethren, Ireland was an excellent opportunity to be avenged of innocent blood, shed by the forces of antichrist. It was also a way of finding employment, a long way from London, for an under-resourced, unpaid and uppity army. However, the same concerns that made Marten nationalistically internalist about England's politics made him wary of his nation's alarmist, conditioned response to affairs in Ireland.

The new person chosen to oversee the imposition of English will in Ireland was Philip Sidney, Lord Lisle, whom parliament created Lord Lieutenant of Ireland. He was perhaps an unwise choice: he had been the commander of an ineffectual but ruinous slash and burn policy in Ireland in the autumn of 1642.[76] In the end, Lisle never took up the post, but his appointment offered the opportunity to readdress Ireland as a debating issue, through which Marten could express his concern about the direction of Commons' policy. In part, this was because parliament was unsympathetic to the soldiers' grievances at home and unrealistic about their mission in Ireland. It was also because Marten could not justify such levels of armed intervention. He penned a declaration for Lisle to carry to Ireland, granting the rebels twenty days – or longer if their delay was justifiable and not contemptuous – to respond to the fresh arrival of English forces. There were overtures for peace, for, as the 'Rebells hands [had] been ye first in shedding blood, so ye first motion for staunching it should arise from hence'. Marten stressed that Lisle's original mission should be diplomatic and not military. Any messages from the Irish were to be conveyed to the parliament with all convenient speed and only if the Irish refused all offers of negotiation could the agents of the English parliament 'apply themselves to a more vigorous proseqution thereof by other courses'.[77] In his justification, Marten denounced the levels of slaughter and devastation in Ireland and the failure of either side – discounting any negotiations between Sir Phelim O'Neill and Charles Stuart – to offer terms to halt it.

Although the English were then in a position to turn all of their force on the Irish, there were several reasons why Marten believed it was not in England's interests to do so. Domestically, the royalists were defeated, but Marten warned they were merely waiting for the opportunity to rise again. Besides, the nature of the King's actions against the parliament in 1642 quite overshadowed the seriousness of the Irish rebellion:

> The Kings rebellion in England was farr more high then that of ye Irish rebells . . . much more daungerous (being within our bowells) more uniust (in that hee could not pretend to ye shaking off a yoak from his own neck . . .) more chargeable, & if not altogether so bloody, that [it] is to bee imputed to Gods mercy, not to his, upon whose account must bee layed a great part even of that blood which hath bene spilt in Ireland.[78]

The English parliament should not intervene whilst it was so dangerously divided amongst itself, between Presbyterians and Independents. '[T]hose who seek to force all their brethren into one way of worship, & those who would pressure their own liberty in opinion & practise so as none be iniured thereby', provided a difference potentially far more damaging than the fight between king and parliament. Neither were the English on good terms with the Scots, especially in Ireland, where the latter were in control of the north-east. Overstretched English taxpayers should quite rightly question the legitimacy of assessments levied for the reduction of 'other Kingdomes', especially those separated from England by sea and thus expensive to supply with fighting men and war machines. Marten's summation was one of the most remarkable English statements about Ireland in the period of conquest:

> Upon yᵉ wholl matter, I conceive it most acceptable to God & Christ, most agreeable wᵗ common iustice, most consistent with yᵉ rules of policy, if not to graunt them almost any termes for peace, at least to hearken to their demaund . . . which for ought wee know may bee reasonable, or if wee think they cannot bee worn continue some propositions of our own, & admitt of peace upon them . . .
>
> Hee that would state yᵉ quarrell in Ireland upon religion & thinkes this way to make all Christendome a protestant is descended sure from those gallant ancestors that ly buryed in Palestine whether they were carryed with a fervent desire to recover yᵉ holy land, & beat yᵉ wholl world into Christianity.[79]

Marten did not publish this piece; possibly because Lisle did not sail for Ireland, or because it was so contrary to the direction of government thinking. He did cap his sense of alienation from the Presbyterian hegemony by reiterating his belief in religious toleration for Catholics.

Marten's concern with the interlinked issues of Ireland, the soldiery, and religious toleration was heightened by his emergence as a speaker for extra-parliamentary lobbies. Once limited to being a voice in parliament, financially necessary but ideologically marginalised, he was now able to speak more open extremism and back it with support from outside the House. A body of evidence, albeit tantalisingly circumstantial, goes to show that Marten was in contact with a number of groups acting outside parliament. He was close to the original, accredited agitators of the New Model Army – Sexby, Allen and Lockyer – and also to the new agents, whose emergence was the result of Leveller influence within the ranks. When Noel Brailsford wrote his study of the Leveller movement, he claimed that the key to the code with which the agitators of the army wrote to each other was found in Marten's desk. This has now surfaced in the manuscripts previously owned by the Fairfax family and now held by the British Library.[80]

Marten was certainly already close to civilian Leveller John Wildman during the 1640s. Both married into the Lovelace family and lived in the same area of Berkshire.[81] The code amongst the agitators was the first evidence of the initials by which Marten and Wildman came to address each other throughout their lives. Wildman was A and Marten, O.[82] The cipher listed the allies, Maximilian Petty (E),[83] Marten, Wildman, army colonels, Robert Overton (V), Thomas Rainsborough (W) and the Leveller, William Walwyn (B). There was also specific mention of William Eyres (AA), a close ally of Marten in Berkshire in the later 1640s, and it is interesting to see him named earlier. Friends in general were known as AF. Most of the written evidence showing Marten collaborating closely with several leading agents and Levellers dates, however, from the 1650s, but it seems that close personal and working relationships that existed by 1650 were the product of friendships and alliances formed in the years before. Marten probably already knew the Leveller Edward Sexby, who in 1652 wrote that 'as in time of old you were estemed truths soliciter [and] Libertys champyon so att p^rsent you are still Judged by me'.[84] Sexby had met Petty when both were apprenticed in the Grocers' Company during the 1630s.[85]

Marten, along with like-minded MPs such as Chaloner and Rigby, did have a close working relationship with the quadrumvirate of men known, clumsily, as the Leveller leadership. Marten had been involved at an early stage in the travails of John Lilburne, whilst Lilburne mounted a continuous campaign against figures of authority.[86] The quarrelsome Lilburne was in and out of prison during the 1640s and Marten was appointed to chair a committee to look into his case. Lilburne continuously called for the right to be tried by his peers – that is by his own peers and not by the Lords. This was a view with which Marten sympathised, but Lilburne was a hard man to please. It seems that Cromwell was probably the bar to Lilburne's better treatment, though the firebrand took out his frustrations on his old friend.[87] Marten was deeply hurt by Lilburne's anger, expressed in a reply to one of Lilburne's written bombasts about Marten's committee:

> First S^r I would not bee mistaken for one that goes about to assert ye iustness of all that even they [the committeemen] have said & done. I acknowledge (& so I presume they will themselves) they are but men, & have their faylings, & their true fancy to your self a man that alwayes dwelt upon a hill in a house of glass . . . Next, I for my part cannot take so much offence at my neighbour when he treads upon my toes in a crowd, as I would if hee should do so (when I meet him) walking leysurely by mee & having opportunity to think what he did.[88]

Despite several reports by Marten in Lilburne's favour, first Cromwell and then the Commons held up his case, until finally he was allowed a certain measure of freedom, supposedly in exile, until his case could be settled.[89]

However, although the arrival on the scene of extra-parliamentary lobbyists with views similar to those held by Marten was a boost to his political profile, for over two years after the collapse of the Speech without Doors campaign, Marten was careful to leave the activism outside Westminster to others; his forum was still inside the Commons. Gardiner perhaps overstates the case when he says that early in 1647 the Independents in the Commons split into two 'fractions': a traditional wing, still struggling to come to terms with Charles, and a new wing, 'which may fairly be styled Republican, aiming under the guidance of Marten and Rainsborough at the abolition of monarchy'.[90] Nevertheless, in September 1647 Marten began tactics that were to result in republican agitation and which provided a link between the anti-Scottish campaign of 1646 and the ultimate parliamentary triumph over Charles Stuart. On Wednesday 22 September 1647 the House voted on whether to turn itself into a grand committee to discuss the entire issue of the King. Cromwell and Evelyn, telling for the yeas, defeated the radicals, Sir Peter Wentworth and Thomas Rainsborough, by eighty-four to thirty-four, and the House proceeded to discuss the parliament's peace proposals. The debate continued the following day. Starting earlier that month, the newly formed General Council of the Army had been called to meet every Thursday in the church at Putney. After the first vote, on Wednesday 22 September, Rainsborough and Cromwell were therefore forced to return to their regiments and were replaced as tellers by Marten and Haselrig respectively. The radicals then lost a subsequent vote, by seventy to twenty-three, when they tried to block moves that the House should once more make a direct address to the King.[91] These votes highlight a radical minority, a small but increasingly coherent group that had pursued a series of campaigns and debates around which it gradually coalesced. Even though on this occasion it was defeated, the debates on the so-called Personal Treaty and the Vote of No Addresses provided a foundation for its republicanism.

A committee of the Lords selected four central elements from the Newcastle Propositions that it could continue to offer to the King. When these were presented to the Commons, to be turned into Bills, they were accepted by nine votes, with Morley and Marten telling against. The King was unable to come to any agreement with the English army. On 14 December 1647 the Four Bills passed and were sent to the King at Carisbroke. Charles, however, was negotiating with the Scots and he signed an *Engagement* with the Hamiltonians on 26 December.[92] In return for military help, the King agreed to confirm the Covenant, provided that no one was compelled to take it, to establish Presbyterianism for three years and to join with the Scots in stamping out all manner of dissidents. A pact against 'Anti-trinitarians, Anabaptists, Antinomians, Arminians, Familists, Brownists, Separatists, Libertines, Independents and Seekers' and those who could be netted by the following catch-all definition of heresy, was a gift to those looking for a way to unite the politically disparate strands of parliamentary opposition.[93]

A Second Civil War

Charles' rejection of the Four Bills presented the Commons with a chance to make a statement threatening to construct a peace settlement without any further addresses to the King. Sir Thomas Wroth was chosen to test the water, calling for Charles to be impeached, a move now supported by Oliver Cromwell and his son-in-law, Henry

Ireton. As a result, the radicals tried again to introduce a Vote of No Addresses, which now passed by 141 votes to 91. Marten headed the committee nominated to draft a justification: the committee comprised Thomas Chaloner, John Lisle, Humphrey Salway, Herbert Morley, Grey of Groby, Edmund Prideaux and William Pierrepont, as well as Marten himself.[94] The declaration, penned either by Nathaniel Fiennes or by John Sadler, rehearsed Charles' faults over the whole of his reign, rather than concentrating solely on his personal culpability for the war.[95]

Marten returned to his campaign against the role of the Scottish Commissioners in the personal treaty. He issued two more tracts, justifying parliament's actions and asserting 'England's independency'. The former, possibly written immediately prior to the Vote of No Addresses, charged the Scottish Commissioners with the hypocrisy of wishing to be part of the peace process when they had done most over the previous six years to prolong the fighting. Marten, the patriotic Englishman, was no more inclined to take the advice of foreign Scotsmen than that of 'Spaniards, Indians, or of the most remote Region of the Earth'.[96] This independence was defended by Marten's associates in the army, 'the greatest Bulwark, under God, of our Liberties', who would end the war by conquest rather than negotiation.[97] England's liberties consisted of being 'sole judges . . . what Religion they will set up, what kind of Lawes they will have, what size, what number of Magistrates they hold fit to exercise those Lawes, and what offenders to be tryed by them'.[98]

Following the Vote of No Addresses, Marten wrote a similar piece, for a wider audience than his 'late endeavours of this kind, . . . bestowed upon a few Strangers', called *The Parliaments Proceedings justified, in declining a Personall Treaty with the King, notwithstanding the advice of the Scottish Commissioners to that purpose.*[99] Marten continued the metaphors of the former piece, calling on the English people to assert their autonomy.[100] Marten took the nature of the proposals demanded by the Scots – '[t]hat there be a treaty upon all the Propositions, and that a personal one, & that for that end, the King be invited to come to London, with honor, freedom, & safety, as the most equal, fairest, and just way to obtain a well grounded peace' – and sarcastically poured scorn on the appropriateness of terms such as 'honour', 'freedom', 'equal' and 'fair'.[101] How could propositions between King and parliament be equal and fair, 'for he deals but for himself and perhaps for some of his own Family or Posterity; they for two whole Nations'?[102] The parliament had to settle the nation without Charles, for he had had chances enough, and had set his heart on giving them only one choice, between 'absolute Tyrant over us, or no King'.

The compact that Charles signed with the Hamiltonian Scots, in December 1647, hastened a complete breakdown of communications between the English Parliament and the King. There were also outbreaks of unrest in the south-east, south Wales and elsewhere, from people tired of war and the heavy taxation required to pay for it, who manifested their traditionalist politics in calls for the return of the old monarchical order. A combination of these spontaneous uprisings and the clear threat of a Scottish invasion of England signalled a second outbreak of civil war in the spring of 1648. The officer-MPs were compelled to return to their military commands and others to scurry to their country seats to defend their homes. This left the conservatives once again in power in Westminster. By this stage, however, opinion was polarised, with popular feeling for 'God and King' at one end of the spectrum, and a movement calling for the final defeat of Charles at the other.[103] In particular, pressure of this kind came from the rank and file soldiers, who had, in the years leading up to the second civil war, been under the tutelage of Leveller civilians and their own agents. Henry Marten returned to Berkshire and repeated his actions of 1642: that is, raising a regiment to defend his own corner of England, aid the war effort, and provide himself with the leverage to ensure that he could have some influence over policy. He used the same tactics, commandeering horses from travellers and picking up men and arms wherever he could find them.[104]

The difference between Marten's cavalier behaviour in 1642 and that in 1648 lay in the degree of threat that it posed to his ostensible allies. In 1642 he had been potentially a loose cannon, but a necessary one; he was in a minority, and his troops were useful, if not distinguished. The parliamentary army was under so much pressure that it was prepared to countenance a certain amount of rule-bending to achieve a viable fighting force. In 1648 the army was new modelled, well disciplined, if irregularly paid, and both parliament and the grandees were conscious of their need to keep its potentially revolutionary tendencies in check. Marten was now a fully fledged popular hero and he recruited his forces on this understanding.

Men were drawn to his force by their commander's citation of republican principles. They were also, to an extent, friends and tenants from Marten's estates in Berkshire. Two such were William Eyres, probably from Pusey, who was frequently mentioned in dispatches as an unruly extremist, not only at the regiment's formation but well into the 1650s, and Captain-Lieutenant William Yate, probably Marten's kinsman.[105] Another recruiter for the regiment was Captain John Waldron.[106] Although the troops raised by Marten startled God-fearing, moderate people by sheer dint of the colonel's reputation as a libertine and atheistical republican, there does seem to have been a close correlation between undisciplined behaviour and radical politics.[107] It comes from a hostile source, but the report of Marten's regiment in *Mercurius Pragmaticus* is worth quoting in full:

> The precious Saint Harry, is extream angry that the Houses should presume, contrary to his liking, to proceed so farre as they have done in order to a treaty, for which cause he is resolved to declare against them, in as high terms as ever he

did against the King . . . And therefore he and one Eires are busy in drawing up a manifesto both against King, Lords, and Commons, as confederate to the enslaving of the people; and having already *borrowed a sufficient number of Horse*, on which he hath set riders, who display their imbellished colours beautified with this misterious motto, 'For the People's Freedom against all tyrants whatsoever,' hee is now imployed about listing of foot; the rusticks of Berkshire resorting to him in great numbers, being mightily taken with [the] novell doctrine, that the supreame power & authority is inherently in the people, & to them doth Harry daily preach in the habit of a Leveller, proposing unto them that they ought not to acknowledge any power above them, or doe homage or yeeld obedience to any, they being free people subsisting of themselves, & that they ought to pay no tithes, and to confirm them in these opinions, hee hath already forbidden his owne tenants & souldiers, not to yeeld him any manner of reverence.[108]

Marten's only commission was the 'right' and 'duty' to which he was born as an Englishman.

Marten's was not the only unofficial regiment raised by a country gentleman during 1648. Lord Grey of Groby and John Pyne did likewise in Leicestershire and Somerset.[109] These regiments were one way in which republicanism in the 1640s could be demarcated.[110] The statements that they issued boldly asserted the brand of isolationist patriotism which began to form during the mid-1640s in response to the intervention of the Scots. David Underdown has noted a parallel phenomenon in the propaganda of the 'honest radicals in the counties',[111] but the auxiliary forces of 1648 augmented parochialist sentiment with the force of arms. Men claimed to be fighting alongside their regular, professional comrades towards a common end, but were at the same time a parallel and separate force. Those who raised such regiments threw attention onto the fact that they were fashioned at the private cost of the commander. They made a public statement of commitment to the common cause, but also reminded outsiders that they had a stake in their colonel's favoured outcome and that private money meant, ultimately, their autonomy. The money these men expended could only be recouped if military victory produced a state sympathetic to their cause. Marten's financial role in 1641 and 1642 found its ultimate expression in his auxiliary force in 1648.

Marten's claim to require no greater authority than his patriotic fervour and his zeal to serve the public with the aim of defeating all forms of oppression, meant that he could chose to define what constituted oppression as inclusively as proved necessary to achieve his ends. He could accuse the House of Commons or the New Model Army of exercising tyranny with almost the same ease as he had attacked repressive clerics, the Scots or the King. He could thus afford to be coyly dissembling when asked to explain himself to the House, by claiming that his efforts on behalf of the commonwealth had received 'strange obstructions . . . from those that owed their country as much assistance as my self'. He hoped that the Commons would 'consider that ye extraordinariness of ye occasion in this iuncture of affairs may excuse a little over-acting in a service of this nature, for which I do not doubt . . . but I shall receive ye happines of being favourably understood, if not well accepted by ye House'.[112] The militia regiments were a tangible expression of the radical revolution's two rallying cries: '*salus populi, suprema lex*' and 'necessity is the only law'.

Gentrymen were protecting what was left of their own patrimony and, in order to do so, were prepared to see their most radical tenants in arms. In 1648 *Mercurius Pragmaticus*, in a confusion of terms, there having been a number of more official means by which parliament had mustered auxiliary forces, railed against 'a *Bastard* kind of *Militia*, called the *County Troop*'. These shows of force were justified using the rhetoric of Levellerism. The people laid claim to their liberties and liberty could only be guaranteed by their sovereignty. From a tactical point of view, the regiments alarmed not only the royalists and the Presbyterians in the Commons, but undermined the discipline, unity and politics of the New Model Army. Whilst both parliament and army attempted to disband his force, Marten treated them with contempt.[113] His own allies chased him around the country, from Berkshire to Oxford and north to Leicestershire, where Grey of Groby was in charge of the garrison at Ashby de la Zouch.[114] The military usefulness to the New Model of any of these county troops is doubtful, but when the second civil war had been won and the radical minority in the Commons emerged triumphant, one of its earliest actions was to propose that Marten's band be regularised.[115] The real value of these auxiliary troops was to contribute to a developing republican ethos, both amongst parliamentarians and between county representatives and ordinary people. The official war was won by the New Model and especially by Cromwell's victory at Preston.

Parliament, particularly after the officer-MPs had returned to the fighting, was dominated by those who wished to continue to negotiate. Commissioners to treat with the King, then at Newport on the Isle of Wight, were chosen in September.[116] Parliamentarians who opposed a personal treaty with Charles, and army officers, convinced that Charles must answer for the blood spilt in the wars, urgently needed to find common ground to put an end to the negotiations at Newport. Edmund Ludlow reported that he favoured purging the parliament of delinquents willing to negotiate and managed to win agreement from Ireton for the army to intervene directly to achieve a political solution. The role of the King became a crucial sticking-point. Ludlow demanded immediate intervention, before the royalists had an opportunity to rally popular opinion behind the King. He argued that if the army wait until the King and parliament had come to a treaty, its delay would withhold real peace from the people. Ireton, on the other hand, was convinced that if they waited until a treaty had been signed, popular opinion would run with the army. The people would be sensible of the way in which the treaty threatened their liberties.[117]

Negotiations were also underway at army headquarters, where grandees, junior officers, soldiers and civilians were discussing a second draft of an *Agreement of the People*. The previous draft, a simple statement of fundamental principles, which had been presented at the debates of the General Council of the Army at Putney in October 1647, had not been overtly republican but had expressed the sovereignty of the people whilst making no mention of either king or monarchy.[118] In November 1648 the Levellers sent word to Cromwell for a meeting at the Nag's Head Tavern at Blackwell Hall.[119] According to Lilburne's account, the Levellers, represented by Lilburne and Wildman, favoured 'an equal distribution unto all men' together with a statement of constitutional principle to be established before the magistrates who would administer it were chosen. The 'Independents' wanted to purge the parliament and bring Charles to trial. It was decided to chose a committee of sixteen from four interest groups, who would hammer out an agreement of the people. The four Levellers – or, as Lilburne termed them, 'Londoners' – were Maximilian Petty, Wildman, Lilburne and William Walwyn, although Lieutenant-Colonel William Wetton had been involved in the organisation at an earlier stage. The four Independents were Colonel Titchborne, Colonel White, Daniel Taylor and John Price, though, again, Samuel Moyer had been involved before the final four were decided. They were joined by four parliamentmen, Henry Marten, Alexander Rigby, Thomas Chaloner and Thomas Scot, and four army grandees, Henry Ireton, Sir William Constable, and any two of Colonel Tomlinson, Colonel Baxter, Lieutenant-Colonel Kelsey and Captain Parker. Of the MPs, only Marten attended.

Lilburne's account focused on Henry Ireton, accusing him of being 'the cunningest of Machiavellians' for having taken the agreed statement and having it further amended by the Army Council at Whitehall, dismantling and changing it to suit the grandees. Barbara Taft has reconstructed the officers' debates and shown Lilburne's account to be self-serving. Taft's argument, however, relies on our acceptance that what should have been aimed at was a constitutional statement that could achieve two ends. Firstly, it had to be a statement of gradual and moderate constitutional change such as would persuade conservative sections of the English political nation. Secondly, it needed to show the practical steps whereby constitutional reform would be achieved, by spelling out structures and the extent of the franchise. Whereas the first *Agreement* was a simple, short statement of fundamental principles 'above law', the second *Agreement* emerged as a blue-print for pragmatic amendments.[120]

It was Lilburne's contention that the Levellers disagreed with the idea of purging parliament, believing the remaining members would lack the authority of representativeness. The radicals in the House were anxious to purge parliament in order to prevent an alliance of the King and moderate MPs from outweighing the so-called 'honest' party of minority MPs, soldiers and civilian activists who claimed to represent the people. On the other hand, Lilburne worried that a purged parliament would tip the balance of power in favour of the grandees, and that, as such, it was better to retain the King whilst his power could be used to balance the potential tyranny of men like Ireton. It is clear, however, that Lilburne's position did not command a majority, even among his potential supporters. On 5 December 1648 the House voted that the King's answers to the latest overtures for peace were sufficient to continue to negotiate. The following morning, detachments from the regiment of Colonel Thomas Pride lined up at the door to the Commons' chamber and barred entry to all those MPs deemed to have been implicated in this decision. Grey of Groby was at the door of the chamber to identify supporters of negotiation so that Pride knew whom to bar.

Despite a purge, of which Lilburne claimed the Levellers disapproved, and debates at Whitehall in which Ireton moved the *Agreement* away from a statement of fundamental principles, Lilburne's Leveller allies, Wildman and Walwyn, were prepared to continue to discuss its terms. It is quite clear that in December 1648, Marten supported the purge and shielded the army when an angry House demanded to know why some of its members had been detained by the sword.[121] Retrospectively, Marten saw Pride's Purge as the point at which the civilians allowed army power undue influence in civil affairs, though he could not accurately recall the date of the fateful day on which Pride's regiment abused the honour of the House, by 'what they did upon the 4th December 1648'.[122] He nevertheless accepted the purge because it established the sovereignty of the people. The House then called on members to register their dissent to the vote of 5 December, by which the radicals kept a check on the views of those returning to the Commons. Marten may have signified his dissent. He may not have needed to make such a public statement of his support for the revolution. Another Leveller, Richard Overton, was most scathing about Marten and his ally John Wildman. He accused them of complicity with the army grandees because their principles had been bought; Marten with a commission for his regiment, Wildman with the offer of preferment.[123]

Only one month after the event, Marten unambiguously supported the army's role in purging parliament. 'I honour Parliaments so long as they Act in Order to the publique good', he told William Prynne, one of the most vocal of the members who had been imprisoned.[124] He also rejected evil counsellors theory, claiming that it had always been known to be a lie.[125] 'Had they [the parliament] had but so much courage', he argued, 'as to have informed the Common wealth of the Kings guile, and that his owne faults might have been written on his owne forehead, not an evill Councell (a thing without body or soule, an empty name, the old grave mens harmlesse bugbear)', the king would not have rallied such wide support and the parliament would have been more speedily victorious.[126] He had always known the parliament to have contained men of dubious loyalty, and by 1648, Mr Prynne and his allies had been exposed serving the 'common enemy', and not their constituents.

Marten and Cromwell returned to the House together, and the former launched a vote of thanks to the Lieutenant General.[127] Despite this show of solidarity, Marten's attitude to the army grandees, especially Cromwell, was generally hostile. The Hamiltonians believed that Marten hated Cromwell so much that he would be prepared to lend his auxiliary regiments to their and the King's cause, rather than see Cromwell rise to sovereign power.[128] Along with Ludlow and Grey, Marten acted as a bridge between the grandees, the parliament and civilian lobbyists. On one side of the debate that followed was the grandees' desire for 'a speedy Prosecution of Justice, and the Settlement formerly propounded by them'.[129] The long-suffering soldiers wanted the opportunity to be the instruments of divine vengeance on the man of blood. On the other hand, the parliamentarians who remained in the House claimed to be believers in equity, representation and the liberties of the people. Whilst they felt they were the best, and possibly the only people to implement this, they were only in a position to do so because they had finally achieved power at the hands of the army, and could act out parliamentary sovereignty so long as the army saw them as its best vehicle. The failure of the grandees, Independents, radical civilians and MPs to agree a common programme – an *Agreement of the People* – meant that the Rump was 'an Heterogenial Body, consisting of parts very diverse from one another, setled upon principles inconsistent one with another'.[130] When the second, 'officers'' *Agreement of the People*, was presented to parliament on 20 January 1649, it was dismissed by the MPs, who thanked the army for bridging the 'gap' in sovereignty and now counselled them to return to their role as military servants of a civilian state.[131] Marten supported the purge in print – though not appending his name to the tract against Prynne – but this cold repudiation of the army was very similar to the way in which he had dismissed the Scots in 1646 when their army was no longer required.[132]

Marten was absent from most of the sessions that planned justice against the King. During the first half of December he was taken up with discussions of an *Agreement of the People*. It was not until 23 December, when the House nominated members to sit on a committee 'to consider how to proceed in a way of Justice against the King, and other capital Offenders', that Marten reappeared, though as the last named on a committee of thirty-five.[133] At committee stage, however, he re-established his position, reporting its deliberations to the Commons, whilst Grey of Groby carried its messages to the Lords. When a High Court of Justice was set up to try Charles Stuart, Marten was named one of its commissioners and attended regularly, though not assiduously.[134] Several of his allies in the Commons were named as commissioners but did not attend at all, including his kinsman, Sir Edward Bainton, Sir Peter Wentworth, John Corbet, and Alexander Rigby. Sir Thomas Wroth, who had tested the water during the debates on a Vote of No Addresses, saying he did not care who ruled, provided it was not a king or a devil, only attended the session of 15 January.

Marten's position at the head of the republican faction in the Commons was secured on 4 January 1649, when he chaired a committee that structured Commons' debate and penned the pivotal statement of Rump republicanism:

That the People, are, under God, the original of all just Power.
That the Commons of England, in Parliament assembled, being chosen by, and representing, the People, have the supreme Power in this Nation.
That whatsoever is enacted, or declared for Law, by the Commons, in Parliament assembled, hath the force of Law; and all the people of this Nation are concluded thereby, although the consent and concurrence of King, or House of Peers, be not had thereunto.[135]

Having been the man who had secured a goldsmith to forge a Great Seal for the parliament's use during the war, Marten was given the task of commissioning another for the Rump Parliament. He provided an image of a commonwealth that was a geographical entity, defined by its (lack of) loyalty to a king. The whole would have included Scotland, as well as Ireland and offshore islands, but, by definition, the new commonwealth consisted of communities that accepted as law the writ of the House of Commons. It was thus to be engraved 'with the Addition of a Map of the Kingdom of Ireland, and of Jersey and Guernsey, together with the Map of England; and, in some convenient Place, on that Side, the Arms by which the Kingdoms of England and Ireland are differenced from other Kingdoms'.[136] On the reverse was an image of the Commons in session and the legend 'in the First Year of Freedom, by God's Blessing restored, 1648'. He subsequently chaired the committee to prepare measures that tried to prevent local government officers proclaiming Charles II.[137]

Marten emerged a popular hero, champion of the ordinary soldier and the oppressed commoner. He was the dynamo behind a constitutional package for which the route to power, the actions necessary to sustain it, and its constant supervision, meant unpopular measures to implement it. Henry Marten bridged the position of army officers and radical MPs. He was a symbol of the form of peace that was secured in December 1648 and thus a model for a consequent constitution. For all his disagreements with Marten, it was John Lilburne's belief that '[t]he true lovers of their country in England, were more beholden to Mr. Henry Marten for his sincerity, uprightness, boldness, and gallantry, than to half, if not all, of those that are called conscientious men in the house'.

II
Liberty: Restored and Forfeited

To all intents and purposes, the group that met as a 'parliament' on 7 December 1648 formed the government; around fifty active MPs, shackled, in the public mind as well as in the public purse, to an army, the voracious appetite and opinions of which had previously been unknown within the political experience of the English. The country had suffered seven years' upheaval, which continued in Scotland and Ireland, draining England's resources. Unprecedented levels of taxation were required to maintain a state that was still at war and to rebuild the economy. The English political nation, well practised in fiscal dissent but less so in maximising tax revenue, wound up a catalogue of complaints. The purge of parliament had been unpopular, even with those who shared the government's aims, but shocked conservative elements even more. To both, it reflected badly on the Rump's claim to speak for the people. On the positive side, there were a number of millenarians, buoyed up with hope, for whom the overthrow of king and lords signalled the probability of the imminent rule of the saints. Likewise, the constitutional republicans, who had, with some difficulty, established themselves in supreme authority, were optimistic about the success of republican administration.

Marten was bombarded with requests from those who believed that they were entitled to a share of the limelight. During the first year of the new government's life, his time was filled with petitions from people from every strata of society who shared a faith that Marten's influence would bring them preferment. They flattered that he was a man 'unfit . . . to meet repetitions, especially of requests; the first being an injury to your understanding, and the other to the goodnesse of your Nature'.[1] A number of entreaties came from Marten's local city of Oxford, which in 1650 petitioned for a contribution to a collection to help its citizens, impoverished by a fire in 1644. The author, Thomas Kirby, renewed an old plea on his own behalf that Marten or another Commonwealth worthy would see fit to find him some small employment.[2] The former sheriff of Buckinghamshire, Henry Beck, claimed for his lands at Haddenham, all other holdings having been plundered, because they had been sequestered 'by ye late Kings sequestrator' at Oxford in June 1646.[3] Marten's neighbour, John Bowles of Marcham, who was renting Oxford Castle from Christ Church College, petitioned for compensation when the Commonwealth saw fit to garrison the old royalist stronghold.[4] Soldiers who had fought with parliament turned to Marten to secure their arrears or compensation.[5] Royalist politicians regarded Marten as the quickest route to lenient treatment. Thomas Tailor, a lawyer of the Inner Temple, sent several pleas on behalf of Lady Arundel, who was claiming wrongful sequestration.[6] In response to a barrage of lobbying from Sir William Davenant, who would 'rather owe my libertie to you than to any Man', Marten was prepared to go to the House and argue that his life be spared. Having sat on the High Court of Justice that tried Charles, Marten was reluctant to continue the court or extend its remit as far as lesser royalist prisoners. Davenant was 'an old rotten rascall' and unfit for the purity of sacrifice.[7]

The greater proportion of petitions Marten received concerned decisions about crown land. Soldiers' arrears had reached levels at which the government could never satisfy them in coin, but Marten's part in redistributing crown and church estates gave him a role in linking the issues of land and army. Prominent members of the army looked to Marten to prefer Major Richard Hill to a place in civil service, with the imminent sale of delinquents' estates. Hill could claim to have been faithful to the Commonwealth through two civil wars to the tune of £2,000.[8] Anne Windsor wrote on behalf of her husband, who had been the farrier for Marten's troop and was still following his trade in Colonel Okey's regiment in Scotland, but had as yet not received any money from two debentures that Marten had signed.[9]

Government by the Many

The language, ethos and administration of a system that had been dependent on the will of one was gradually replaced by a system supposed to 'restore' the will of the people as a whole. When Sir Henry Vane questioned what it was that had been restored, Marten's response indicated that he knew that the Rump's actions were unprecedented. He essayed one of his characteristic allegories: a man who has been blind from birth suddenly has his sight restored. The nation was that man. The man should have sight, as the nation should have had liberty.[10] Liberty was intrinsic, so it could not be traced to a point at which it had been instituted, though it could be traced to the point at which it had been wrested back from a tyrant. For the blind man, it was the ability to see which was so important, though no one questioned whether the scenery had changed as a result of a new-found ability to perceive it. Marten may not have approved of the manner of terminating addresses to the King, but it had fulfilled the aim which he had constantly espoused during the 1640s. He was consequently named to a committee to prepare the Commons' debate which confirmed that the vote of 5 December 1648 was 'highly dishonourable to the Parliament, and destructive to the Peace of the Kingdom; and tending to the Breach of the Publick Faith of the Kingdom'.[11] He was one of thirty-one members named on 29 December to the committee that registered the dissents of others.[12]

It was not necessarily the case that those members at the heart of the coup were among the earliest to register. The first full session of the Rump after Charles' execution was held on 1 February 1649, during which it was made compulsory for members to register their dissent before they could resume their seats. By this date, fifty-two MPs had registered. These included Daniel Blagrave of Reading and Edmund Dunch of Wallingford, John Blakiston, Oliver Cromwell, Henry Ireton, Sir John Danvers, Lord Grey of Groby, Cornelius Holland, John Jones, Isaac Pennington, Alexander Rigby, and possibly Sir Thomas Wroth. The lists of signatories illustrate the mixture of motivations that induced members to make a public declaration of their support for the Rump, and more importantly, their connivance at the Rump's route to power. Grey of Groby clearly supported the purge. He had been the chief agent of censorship. Soldiers such as Cromwell and Ireton may not have known about it until afterwards, although it was an unfortunate but necessary means to a desired end. Pennington and Rigby, who had long been associated with Marten and could be described as radicals, were anxious to be included in the new regime. There was a high correlation between the county of Berkshire and early registrations, but there is little evidence that Marten, as the county's member, listed his own dissent.[13] In a hierarchical system of registrations, those who were considered loyal to the ideals of the republic leaned on others who could be persuaded to register, and their names were reported to the House. As such, it may well have been the case that men like Marten and Thomas Chaloner did not need to make a public statement;[14] their loyalty was taken as read.

The most famous stand-off between men who supported constitutional change, but who bitterly differed about the means to the end, came between Lord Grey of Groby and Algernon Sidney. The two were rowing about a second issue, which was a measure of both the radicalism and potential for disagreement within the Rump. Since war continued in Scotland and Ireland, and the threat of royalism in England had not abated, the supremacy of a representative chamber of Commoners was further undermined by the need for an executive committee to manage the fighting. Thus a council of state was proposed, and set up on 13 February 1649.[15] It had forty-one nominated members. These ranged from the republican stalwarts – Marten, Grey of Groby, and Ludlow – to soldiers such as Cromwell and Fairfax. Independent stalwarts William Heveningham and Sir William Armyne provided stability in government. The continuity of the rule of law was ensured by its officers, Whitelocke and Rolle. There were peers who were prepared to owe allegiance to the new state, such as Denbigh, Mulgrave, Grey of Warke and Pembroke. However, there was no place for Ireton or Harrison.[16] The Council of State met in Derby House, and was similar to the wartime committee that acquired its name from the venue.

Together with the Council of State went an Engagement of loyalty to the republican form of government. An early version of the oath, proposed for the Councillors, called on them to 'approve of the late acts of the Commons of England assembled in parliament, erecting an high court of justice for the trying and adjudging of Charles Stuart, late king of England'.[17] Algernon Sidney opposed the clause and possibly the whole Engagement, with the inflammatory comment that it would 'prove a snare to many an honest man, but every knave would slip through it'. The hypersensitive Grey believed he had been branded a knave for having taken the oath, and it was left to Marten to try to maintain unity by pointing out the conditional in Sidney's expression. Knaves might slip through the oath's net, but not everyone who did so was (necessarily) a knave. The oath was not watertight, but was not designed to be definitional.[18] Cicero had instructed the political nation in the utility of oaths because they were effective in encouraging consent.[19] This oath for the Council was introduced to the House by Thomas Scot. Marten and Ireton attempted, unsuccessfully, to reintroduce the retrospective clause, which bound signatories to approve of the purge, trial and execution, as well as the form of the resultant government. The earliest signatories were the hardliners in the new government. The ten radical republicans had an average age of forty-nine. Leaving out Grey, who was a fresh faced twenty-five, the average was even higher, but even Grey had sat in the Long Parliament since its first session.[20]

Marten had a key part in the measures to establish a rhetoric and practice of revolution. He was responsible for the design and manufacture of a new Great Seal, was put in charge of drawing up the act that prohibited the proclamation of Charles II, and was one of five MPs who prepared the retrospective justification of the High Court. He sat on the committees to discuss the constitutional role of the House of Lords, having been the author of the declaration of 4 January 1649, which announced their lordships' concurrence was not a prerequisite of law, and which now declared them 'useless and dangerous'.[21] The same sub-group, with the addition of the equally republican Lord Grey and Thomas Chaloner, turned its attention to the kingship, declaring that 'it hath been found by Experience . . . That the Office of a king in this Nation, and to have the Power thereof in any Single Person, is unnecessary, burdensome, and dangerous to the Liberty, Safety, and publick Interest of the People of this Nation; and therefore ought to be abolished'.[22] This definitional phrase of republicanism was repeated when the act passed into statute on 17 March.[23]

Aubrey credits Marten with the declaration to explain the act that changed England from a monarchy into a republic, and its early phrases were certainly republican.[24] It reiterated the position outlined in the campaign against further addresses. The kings of England had, in some mythical and unstated past, been elected by the 'agreement of the people', but, with the reign of Charles Stuart, this particular king had sullied his office by the events surrounding the death of his father, the fiasco of La Rochelle, the seven offers of addresses from parliament that he had rejected, and his alliance with the turn-coat Scots. As such, 'the same Power and Authority which first erected a King, and made him a publique Officer for the common good, finding them perverted to their common Calamity, it may justly be admitted at the pleasure of those whose Officer he is, whether they will continue that officer any longer, or change that Government for a better, and instead of restoring Tyranny, to resolve into A Free State'.[25] The acts that had changed kingly to republican government were the same as those that had existed before 'the Norman slavery' and were clearly consistent 'with the present Government of a Republique, upon some easie alterations of Form onely, leaving intire the substance; the name of King being used in them in Form only'.[26] Since a free state would grant freedom for all of the people, the poor would enjoy the benefits of an unshackled economy. Marten paid only a nodding acquaintance to the saints and the agency of God and credited parliament with the change of government.

The so-called Leveller leadership, and in particular the new quadrumvirate of Lilburne, Overton, Walwyn and Prince, railed against the new government as much as the old. The institutions established to govern England as a republic appeared as corrosive of England's liberties as monarchy had been, and they suffered depression born of high expectations suddenly deflated. The Council of State, to which the Levellers' friends Marten, Grey and Ludlow were nominated – but not Chaloner and Rigby – was the target of particular vitriol.[27] Although, according to Marten's legend that graced the new Great Seal of the republic, liberty had been 'restored', many found it difficult to determine its nature. The year 1649 was, according to three soldiers who had supported the Levellers' large petition of 11 September 1648, 'the first year of the Peoples pretended Freedom but intended Slavery'.[28] William Eyres, Marten's loyal servant in his regiment of 1648, was a leader of the Leveller army mutiny at Burford in May 1649, as troops marched towards embarkation for Ireland.[29] Nevertheless, the villains whom the Levellers picked out were the army grandees, possessors of 'their own mock Parl. at Windsor'. In response to the threat of a revolution aborted, the Levellers proposed another conference, akin to the committee of sixteen that had attempted to reformulate the *Agreement of the People* in December 1648. Cromwell, Ireton and two others would debate with four Levellers, whilst four MPs would act as referees, two chosen by each side. The Levellers trusted to Henry Marten and Alexander Rigby.[30] They then went on to argue that the present government was merely a 'Notionall, Nominall, [and] Circumstantiall' republic, and would remain superficial until a fundamental, inclusive contract was made between the government and the governed.[31] The statements that Marten made in the declaration establishing England as a republic, would seem to bear out the concerns of his Leveller allies.

Although strained by Pride's Purge and the regicide, the link between Marten and Levellerism was not entirely broken. He continued to tread a delicate path between the grandees on the one hand and the Leveller leaders on the other. Marten's relationship with the 'rank and file' of both the army and the Leveller movement was more unequivocal. Several of those who had been active during the later 1640s formed an integral part of Marten's personal and political career during the 1650s. In 1650, Marten was awarded Duchy of Lancaster lands in Herefordshire and Derbyshire, choosing Leveller activists to administer his estates.

The first of these was William Wetton, from Bradley in Derbyshire. Wetton was a gentleman in his own right, with a town house in the newly developed and rapidly rising area of Covent Garden. A local man was an ideal choice to administer estates in the county, although Marten also occasionally employed him in Herefordshire. He had reached the rank of lieutenant-colonel in the army, possibly in the regiment of Colonel Gill. Wetton had offered to raise troops for Ireland during 1648, and was to be sent as part of Colonel Gill's regiment. He was convinced he was of better service, both personal and public, in rebuilding Marten's estates at home, and applied for help to get him out of such an onerous task.[32] One of his co-administrators in Derbyshire was his 'comrade', Maximilian Petty.[33] Petty is always described as a civilian Leveller at the Army Council debates at Putney, but the term evidences a close relationship between the two, possibly within the army, or as part of a Leveller language that aped military discourse.[34] John Wildman, who would become Marten's nephew by marriage and was his close neighbour in Shrivenham, was Marten's closest friend and confidante. Although Marten's own marriage to Margaret Lovelace was unhappy, he was close to Wildman's wife, Lucy Lovelace, and together with Marten's lifelong partner, Mary Ward, the group addressed each other with touching familiarity. John and Lucy were 'A' and 'a', and Henry and Mary, 'O' and 'o', cipher letters that also had their origin in the army agitators' code of 1647.[35] Wildman was involved in administering all of Marten's estates, especially around Berkshire. He built up a huge fortune for himself by combining legal training and insider knowledge of the land market, but Wildman was as helpful to Marten during the latter's financial crises as he helped himself during the sale of delinquents' estates.[36]

Marten also kept up political links with the Leveller movement. Levellers were anxious to see him make an explicit statement in the House in favour of the abolition of tithes. He had supported their abolition in committee, but many of 'those that love and honour you' pressed him to speed it through the House.[37] One of the Levellers who had the highest hopes of Marten's support was Samuel Chidley, who, in the early 1650s, sent his schemes for reform of the Commonwealth to a man whose 'howers [were] soe uncertayne', because numerous petitioners sent letters, appeals and propositions to someone who they believed had influence in government. Samuel Chidley sent Marten his 'Humble proposals of an easy & effectuall means both for making this Nation a glorious & flourishing Commonwealth for riches & defence, as also for removall of Taxes, & other pu[b]l[i]q[ue] grievances'.[38]

In Ian Gentles' study of the second ranks of the Leveller movement, Samuel Chidley emerges as an ideal 'symbol of protestantism allied to the spirit of capitalism', who 'neatly embodies the Weber-Tawney thesis'.[39] He was also another of the Levellers who entered public service in a minor way at the start of the republican period. He operated from Worcester House, which handled the sale of crown estates, and became first a debentures' broker and then an agent for the sale of land.[40] Chidley was probably already known to Marten – especially in his work at Worcester House, which was furnishing Marten with estates in Herefordshire and Derbyshire – but Chidley may have addressed his petition on a 'glorious and flourishing Commonwealth' to Marten because the latter was chair of a committee appointed to look into the satisfaction of the state's creditors. The committee eventually proposed that debts be discharged from the stock of escheated Irish lands, a decision by Marten that was possibly to have more serious repercussions than any seemingly more profound. The policy of satisfying individual investors in republican government before the army was a primary reason for the Rump's eventual demise.[41]

There were a number of other connections with radical figures whose political interests were more conventional. Captain George Bishop, a vocal Leveller at Putney, who published numerous pro-parliamentary tracts during the 1640s, worked for the Council of State from its formation. He was named as one of the commissioners to report on the state of the royal forest of Dean. Marten had an interest in the boundaries of the forest as a populist political issue and in Dean itself, where Wildman had investments. Marten could contribute timber from his nearby lands. In his capacity as commissioner, Bishop wrote a depressed letter to Marten in October 1649, complaining of the intransigence of vested interests, 'h[ow] ever Justice is an hon[ble] grave for the best to be interd with'.[42] Marten subsequently encountered entrenched west country traditionalism when the republican *arriviste* met his royalist fellow gentry in Herefordshire.

Marten's links with William Wetton extended his contacts to Wetton's cousins, William and Lucy Cockayne, with whom he did estate business in Derbyshire. William was the author of *The Foundations of Freedome Vindicated*, a reply to William Ashurst MP, who had criticised the *Agreement of the People*. Echoing the rallying cry of Marten's regiment with clumsier syntax, Cockayne called himself 'a wel-wisher to Englands freedomes; but an Opposer of Tyranny and Oppression in any whomsoever'.[43] He defended the demise of kingly government and attacked the Lords as a House full of the King's creatures. It may have been through Wetton that Cockayne offered his support for the second *Agreement*. According to Cockayne, the *Agreement* would protect against an arbitrary representative. He reiterated the commonplace that republican government was one in which sovereignty lay with the people, and in the case of the Rump, this had been secured by the second *Agreement*, by imposing biennial elections and tests for the membership of the Commons. By 'making parties by subscribers and non-subscribers', he concluded '*no power is intended to be above this Representative*'.[44]

Marten's popularity and power in Berkshire obtained the election of several likeminded radicals. His own re-admission to the House in 1645 had paved the way for William Ball.[45] His election secured, Ball was quiet in the Commons, but published a retort to arch-conservative David Jenkins, with whom Marten had also sparred. With no sense of irony, on the day of Charles' execution, parliament saw fit to publish the posthumous reply of Marten's Abingdon ally in the House. The fact that Ball's political musings were published some time after his death gave them the qualities of prediction and vindication of the administration's actions. His approach was less extreme than Cockayne, but he reiterated the main points. The people were supreme and the King was subject to their laws. Ball agreed with Henry Parker that *salus populi, suprema lex*, and weighed the concept of *salus populi* against that of *majestas imperii*.[46] With Ball's death, Marten was instrumental in securing the seat for Henry Nevile.

Coming to the end of a series of moves to change the constitutional aspects of English politics from a monarchy to a republic, Marten's attentions switched from England to France. Aubrey had noted that Marten's grand tour had crossed the Channel but had not travelled as far as Italy; one fact which may have contributed to his distinctive politics. Unlike Milton, Sidney or Harrington, Marten showed little interest in the Italian Renaissance, but continued his links with France. During the war, his brother sailed to and fro across the Channel. In the 1650s the English republic needed information on the state of the Stuart court in France. It was also keen to aid French protestants and rebels, as much to destabilise a powerful neighbour as to show religious solidarity.[47] The state re-employed Marten's links with France, and his early career organising spying rings. Letters of intelligence were sent; some anonymous, some in code, some under aliases. G. de Perenaut wrote to Marten during May 1650,[48] sending wine, Bayonne ham and asking for employment, and there was also intelligence from a C. Besse.

Marten's connections with France were at first defensive and then offensive. In 1649 and 1650 the English government was more concerned with its own security, pre-empting the plotting of its royalist opponents. An Orleans' correspondent, '886.461', who may well have known Marten intimately enough to have been acquainted with Mary Ward, wrote of consignments of pistols and that 'ces diables de 197 sont enrager cont[re] vostre republicque'.[49] Another, who was on good terms with both Marten and Ward – who wrote to Marten as Joseph Batailby, and signed himself Daniel Batailby – gave news of the French king's troop movements.[50] Another, who wrote in English and whose alias consisted of two, slanted parallel lines, was Marten's correspondent in Rouen. From here, he or she reported on the activities of the Stuarts and their followers, confirming Marten's distrust of the Scots, now plotting abroad, 'for they never laye downe the feud'.[51] This correspondent appears to have been a paid agent of the state, though considered Marten a personal friend. Others sent newsletters that passed on information about the Irish lords, Inchiquin and Ormond, and the fortunes of the royal fleet.

More formal connections with France were made in the autumn of 1651, when the English state, in the form of a secret Council of State committee for French affairs, decided to maintain closer links with the radicals around the Gironde. A five-man mission, led by the Leveller Edward Sexby, was dispatched to Bordeaux. One of the others was called Thomas Arundel, posing as a merchant in the town.[52] There had been active rioting against the government for over fifty years around the Gironde, though the degree to which the area caused a serious threat to the regime in Paris varied. Events in England gave them new hope. Republicanism was openly preached from the pulpits, and popular songs proclaimed brotherhood with the republicans in England and with *Les Niveleurs* (Levellers).[53] A letter of Condé's secretary, Pierre Lenet, to his English agent, Barrière, described Sexby and Arundel having been a long time in Bordeaux and La Rochelle, where they 'veuloient imiter l'Angleterre dans sa nouvelle façon de gouverner'.[54]

Although Sexby was sent to France by dint of a committee decision, it was to Marten – 'Honest Harry' – that he corresponded, using the name Stephen Edwards. Marten's pseudonym was Stephen Benfield. Letters would reach him via another merchant, Jeremiah Potter.[55] There were other links. Sexby also corresponded regularly with Thomas Scot and Henry Nevile.[56] One of the key organisers of the Bordeaux project was John Wildman[57] and one of the other three with whom Sexby and Arundel acted may have been Richard Overton. We know little of Overton's activities between 1649 and 1654, but a letter from Sir Marmaduke Langdale cited Sexby as the source of his information that Overton was employed by Cromwell among the Huguenots 'and brought a paper under thousands of their hands to Cromwell to invite him to send some forces into France to join with them to assert their privileges'.[58]

The French struggle paralleled that in England. The activists of the Fronde were finding it hard to reconcile the aristocratic and autocratic leadership of the duc de Condé with the republican radicalism of the *Ormée*, which drew its support mainly from Bordeaux' artisan and apprentice communities. Under the slogan *Vox populi, vox dei*, their first aim was to gain control of the *jurade*, the municipal government of Bordeaux, intending to widen the franchise in the town. When, during 1652, Condé's third campaign in the Fronde seemed to be going badly and he fled to the north, the *Ormée* gained control of the city. From June 1652, for a period of thirteen months, the ruling body of the *Ormée*, *la Chambre de l'Ormée*, constituted the city government.

The Commonwealth of England was prepared to assist the rebels, first with a supply of soldiers, released from fighting in Ireland by virtue of the Act of Settlement. Subsequently, there were plans to supply 12,000 English troops. Sexby lobbied the English government for political as well as military aid, and it was with this in mind that he addressed a plea to 'Honest Harry . . . truths solicitor [and] Libertys champyon'. Despite the flattery of his entreaty, there was poison in the tail. Sexby berated the leaders of the Commonwealth for having squandered the chances for liberty offered at the end of the 1640s. Here was their opportunity to make amends in France: 'tis to be Lamented his many pyrsses [purses] have ben put into your hands, [and] wt hath not been weakely manadged hath ben Covetously manopolised: not becomeing the worthys of a Comonwealth: now you have another ball throwne you'.[59] Sexby counselled them that the interest of the people was the only thing that could be trusted, and now the people of Bordeaux gave the English another opportunity to advance the cause, with the shout 'oh England Come [and] helpe: your lawes shall be ours'.[60]

Sexby had already penned a 'method', an 'agreement', which he had few doubts would elicit signatures and which he had sent to Henry Nevile. Marten's response was to compose *Les Maximes de bien gouvener pour maintenie la LIBERTIE dans l'obeissance*. This tract on liberty and government was specifically designed for the administration in Bordeaux, on the lines of the *Agreement of the People*, but written in the form of a letter from an Englishman to a friend in the French town.[61] Uncharacteristically, perhaps, in view of his parochial concerns for England's liberties during the 1640s, Marten's piece reiterated the belief that the events in France would signal the same debate throughout the world. It hinted at a sense of internationalist revolution, but, like many of Marten's projects, the allusion survives only as the draft of a title page.[62] A fuller form of an agreement of the people, *L'Accord du Peuple*, was accompanied by a *Manifesto* and presented to the people of Bordeaux by Condé, his brother, Conti, and the officers and dignitaries of the *Ormée*. It called for religious toleration, an end to arbitrary taxation, a regularly elected parliament, and the sovereignty of the people under a full franchise of all men over twenty-one, provided that their will was not under the control of another.[63]

Marten's political network during the 1650s was of a similar structure to that which had been his support during the previous decade. He was at the centre of a political grouping inside the House, which, whilst it concerned itself with legal and social reforms, kept the support of extraparliamentary radicals. Marten remained a close ally of Thomas Chaloner and his brother, James. He used Thomas Scot as a spymaster in a similar, but much more effective way as he had filled the role himself in the early 1640s. He secured the election of Henry Nevile and retained the friendship of pious, Scripturally-inspired republicans such as Edmund Ludlow and Grey of Groby. Blair

Worden suggests that Henry Smyth, Cornelius Holland, Augustine Garland and Luke Robinson were also part of this group.[64]

There were tensions too. Grey and Algernon Sidney clashed acrimoniously and Sidney was convinced that Grey would oppose him at every turn, though he associated him, too closely, with the military junto led by Cromwell and Ireton.[65] There were politicians, whose membership of the Rump and later careers have led to them being branded republicans, with whom Marten was clearly at odds. He regarded Sir Henry Vane as a political opponent and a somewhat risible figure.[66] Sir Arthur Haselrig was a frequent thorn in the side of the constitutional radicals, always slowing the speed of change by trying to keep moderates on board. He was particularly keen to block moves to decentralise the legal system.[67] Jonathan Scott has refined the political allegiances of the early 1650s by drawing out the tensions between Marten and Sidney and Vane, which he characterised as a clash between 'Vane's religious radicalism and social conservativism, and Marten's irreligious social radicalism'.[68]

Not only did different interpretations of republicanism develop, but it undermined the Rump itself, which had long been about survival. Marten initiated measures that would screen those who sought to act for the Commonwealth because the defeat of royalism had only silenced their enemies 'for the present' and survival depended on 'true-hearted Englishmen' coming together to defeat those who would oust the Commonwealth.[69] The reallocation of royal, Church and delinquents' estates to those who had served the Commonwealth was a means to defend the revolutionary settlement.[70] Levellers and minor officials, who had expressed their support for politicians such as Marten during the 1640s, were rewarded with employment in the 1650s. They were friends, they shared a political vision, but they could also be trusted not to betray the revolution. However, the more pragmatic the moves became to expand the membership of the House, and the more conservative the MPs as a whole, the more the process of change was hampered.

The chance to move forward came in 1652. The Commonwealth was militarily victorious. The royalists in England had been scattered at Worcester. Scotland, then Ireland was defeated. The Commonwealth launched a naval war against the Dutch mercantilists, although this was not a policy favoured by the republicans in the House such as Marten, who preferred political alliance with supposedly kindred spirits.[71] But with military success came a dilemma for Rump radicals. Triumph encouraged men like Algernon Sidney to return to government, having been reluctant to endorse the purge, trial and execution.[72] It also encouraged some to see the destiny of the Rump fulfilled by its military commander, Oliver Cromwell, consistently seen by radicals such as Marten, Sexby and Wildman as a man harbouring ambitions beyond his status. Cromwell would turn state-server into state's saviour. To Edmund Ludlow, 'General Cromwel had long been suspected by wise and good men', but having moulded the army to his own whims and been dismissive of the militia, '[h]is pernicious intentions did not discover themselves openly till after the battel at Worcester, which in one of his letters to the Parliament he called The Crowning Victory'.[73] In a triple blow to the Commonwealth, the end of the fighting within the British isles released large numbers of soldiers for more active political lobbying. They found that whilst they had been sent away to defend the government, the government-men had been dividing the spoils amongst themselves.[74] The economics of the military were thrust to the fore in a way they had not been since 1647. In particular, there was considerable debate over the soldiers' share of the franchise and its material counterpart, their share of arrears paid in Irish land. In the latter instance, it was enough to bring the government down. The axis of Marten-Chaloner-Grey-Ludlow was being replaced by Vane-Sidney-Haselrig. Beneath the shifts in power in Westminster, the grandees applied the pressure of the army. This political shift can be mapped in the changing nature of the editorials that Marchamont Nedham penned for *Mercurius Politicus*.[75] Nedham had articulated the interests of the Marten-led group in the first three years of the government. After 1652, the emphasis shifted to foreign affairs, the successes of the army and England's healthy balance of trade.

Repaying Debts

The career of the Rump Parliament was exquisitely reflected in Marten's personal fortunes. Marten had promoted the end of MPs' immunity from prosecution for debt, but his own financial position was perilous. Over a period between the outbreak of war and 1 August 1647, Marten had borrowed about £20,000 in order to finance his political career. £1,000 was payable to George Savage, whose suit was the cause of notice from Marten's 'loving ffrend', Henry Rolle, Chief Justice of the Upper Bench, of a suit for its recovery.[76] In Bow, on 1 April 1652, Marten was forced to recognise a debt of £2,000 to Simon Musgrave. A list of minor creditors, many of whom could be found in Bow Lane, pressed him for the repayment of monies lent during the war. Marten was forced to seek succour in a new piece of Commonwealth legislation; the appointment during this year of seven new indemnity commissioners.[77] The excuse for non-payment made on his behalf was that 'Mr Marten have lately married a daughter or two and that must not bee expected to bee don but wth large somes of monie; that and other things have disabled him at present to hellp his frends though he be never so willing tell hee have somewhat recovered monie into his custody again'.[78] Marten's eldest daughter, Mary, was married to William Parker, Lord Morley and Mounteagle, Baron Rye, whose status was in keeping with that of a worthy of the Commonwealth, although a Catholic, but whose dissolute lifestyle was as costly to maintain as Marten's own. He had been committed to the Upper Bench prison for debts of £7,000 in November 1649.[79]

Marten may have been conscious that his grip on power was slipping. In December 1651 John Wildman began negotiations with Anthony Wither. Wither, of Bedford Street, was one of the governors of the new parish of Covent Garden,[80] although described as of 'noe valluable estate'. Wildman acted for Marten in the purchase of 'y[r] house in Cannon Roe'. This was Derby House itself. The property had been built by William Stanley, Earl of Derby, between 1598 and 1618, was surrendered to parliament during the war, and was the place where John Pym had died in 1643.[81] Under the Commonwealth, it was used for various committee meetings. The proprietors in 1651 were difficult to determine, though Michael Oldsworth was listed, and it was to him that Wildman directed his attentions.[82] Whoever the proprietors were, they were Commonwealth loyalists and could not be ejected under cover of delinquency. They were also reluctant to sell. Wither had 'struggled harde to gett my name into y[e] certifficate frō gouldsmiths Hall. y[e] Comission[rs] p[ro]testing before my face it went ag[t] their consciences to sett their names to it when a name was in it'.[83] Nevertheless, Wither managed to free the encumbrances by February of the following year and, by March 1652, Marten received all correspondence at Derby House.[84] Although Marten could no longer get elected to the Council of State, it had to rent its meeting rooms, and here they were guests of Marten and Mary Ward, dressed in scarlet satin.

On 20 April 1653 Cromwell marched a detachment of troops into the Commons' chamber and forcibly dissolved its sitting. The army claimed it had a desire to perpetuate itself and, 'through the corruption of some, the jealousy of others, the non-attendance and negligence of many', would never call fresh elections and institute a parliament that was representative and active.[85] Moreover, Cromwell levelled a charge of unparliamentary behaviour: 'some of them were whoremasters, looking towards Henry Martin and Sir Peter Wentworth'.[86] In fact, as Blair Worden and Austin Woolrych have demonstrated, it was the fact that they were on the point of calling elections, with provisions that would minimise the army's influence, which precipitated the coup.[87] There was also a measure of truth in the General's claims. By April 1653 the committees and commissions responsible for reapportioning the land of kings, clerics, malignants and rebels had been in session for up to four years. Many civilians loyal to the government had benefited from land sales; debentures and fee farm rents were creating a flourishing market in stocks and futures' speculation. Marten had been compensated in land and money for his expenditure during the war. He had helped his friends and supporters to pensionable employment. John Wildman was notorious for his inside knowledge of land speculation and had accumulated great personal wealth as a result. Marten had suggested that land confiscated in Ireland be used to compensate state servants. In all these changes, there seemed little sign of the payment of the army's arrears.[88]

Marten had opposed the calling of fresh elections in a speech in 1650. The government was like an infant, he counselled, 'like Moses'. Pharaoh's daughter had searched for a nurse for the infant but returned to its own mother. Thus, 'they themselves were the true mother to this fair child the young Commonwealth'.[89] The Commons had been actively debating a bill for a new representative for over a year by the time Marten made this remark in February, but there were seventy-two consecutive adjournments of the committee. It took until November 1651 before it was decided that 'the Time for the Continuance of this Parliament, beyond which they resolve not to sit, shall be the Third Day of November, One thousand, Six hundred Fifty-and-four'.[90]

The dissolution of the Rump caused irreparable damage to relations between Cromwell and many leading republicans, who complained that no body could dissolve parliament but themselves.[91] It marked the nadir of relations between Marten and Cromwell. The dissolution of the Rump was a bitter personal dilemma as well as the end of the republican experiment. It was not quite the end of his political career, but it was the end of his political power, which had always hinged on the influence that he could exert in the Commons. The dissolution laid him open to the attacks of his opponents, who found a fallen idol an easy target.

Marten continued to occupy Derby House, renting rooms to the committees of the Nominated Assembly and the Protectorate. He even continued as a churchwarden of the MPs' church, St Margaret's in Westminster.[92] During the summer of 1653 the army officers gathered men 'fearing God, and of approved fidelity and honesty' to form a new assembly.[93] Among Marten's papers is a draft of a pamphlet, in the form of an open letter replying to a clearly bogus invitation from Cromwell to join the saints at Westminster. This is one of the few drafts that does not seem to be in Marten's otherwise unmistakable hand. Nevertheless, the style, a mixture of caustic jokes and damning vitriol against the Lord General, is his. It could be a scribe's clean copy, ready to be sent to the press. If so, Marten thought better of it.[94] The author feigned astonishment at an invitation to join the men of integrity, employing the traditional language of false modesty: 'I cannot apprehend my selfe either call'd or qualified sufficiently for such a Trust'. Gracefully declining the summons presented the opportunity for corrosive prose in outlining his reasons.

The tone went beyond the ironic jokiness with which he usually deflated opponents. Marten accused the General of using the sword to usurp the distribution of power. Having defended Pride's Purge at its inception, he now claimed it was an augury of the way in which the army would abuse parliamentary power. The difference between 1648 and this use of force was that the former had been to restore to the people the power to make law, whereas this example of military might denied parliaments altogether: 'the same thing which the last King and his Father did so long designe, and attempt, your Ex^cy hath brought about in the morning'. Marten denied any knowledge of corruption but, had there been, the parliamentarians' inexperience was the cause. The consequence of their naïvety was wasting their time in appeasing the soldiers:

> For their neglect of duty and insensiblenesse of what was incumbent upon them, I must confesse it was not excusable in any kinde, excepting p[er]haps in this that their whole tyme was scarsly sufficient to p[ro]vide for the pres[en]t emergencyes of their affaires, and for supplying the Armyes with money, and p[ro]visions, and if there was the least remnant of tyme which was not taken up in this, it was not more subject to bee spent in particular peticons by any then by you Ex^cy, all of [wh]ich were not constantly for the most just things neither.[95]

There were few days on which parliamentary business was not interrupted by army business, making the Rump look sluggish and 'odious' in the eyes of the people. Quartering the army necessitated the high taxes, though the soldiers roamed among the people, complaining at their lack of pay and accusing the parliamentarians of having pocketed the assessments.[96] '[N]othing is more frequent in the mouthes even of the meaner sort of People', Marten concluded, 'then ye ingratitude of the Army towards those who not only raised them, but have beene besides so eminent benefactors to them that the Kings lands heare, and most of the delinquents estates in England, Scotland, and Ireland, have hardly been able to furnish enough for their liberallity towards them'. The mistakes the parliament had made could be summarised: it had allowed power in all three nations to settle on the head of Oliver Cromwell.

John Wildman worked with Colonels Okey, Saunders and Alured in an officers' petition against the return of single person government. Vice-Admiral John Lawson took over Thomas Rainsborough's mantle as republican agitator in the navy, protesting at Cromwell's 'usurpation'. Robert Overton let Wildman know that there was a party in the army in Scotland that 'would stand right for a commonwealth' and Wildman was joined by former Levellers, Sexby and Bishop. Grey of Groby was also involved.[97] The alliance that had taken power in 1649 conspiratorily reformed.[98] It did so without Marten. He was undoubtedly sympathetic to the old cause and remained in contact with Wildman during this period. However, the power that he could exercise was limited by his loss of office and by the volume of law-suits against him. The two were not unconnected. Marten's creditors had filed against him whilst he was still in the Rump, but once he was no longer a parliamentarian, the protection that power offered was no longer to hand. One of those from whom Marten had borrowed money during the war was Thomas Hampson: another was George Savage, who had already issued his suit. As a result, Marten was outlawed in 1654. In the words of Oliver

St John to the sheriff of Berkshire, 'the said Henry so outlawed doth hide and runne from place to place in yor County in Contempt of us [Cromwell] and priudice of the publicque peace'.[99]

Returning to parliament would restore Marten's power to agitate for republicanism, testing the nature of the Protectorate regime, and relieve the pressure of his creditors, restoring the parliamentary buffer that kept them cowed. At the end of June 1654 a correspondent from Lambourn advised Marten that 'hear is newes of an elechone for knites of this sher'. The Grand Jury was already in session.[100] Marten put aside his contempt for the Cromwellian regime to stand for Berkshire. The election took place during July. On 12 July he wrote to Mary Ward that he was resting at the Holy Lamb in Abingdon, awaiting the results.[101] He was one of many unsuccessful republicans: those returned were soon excluded by a clause that called on them to approve government by a single person and parliament.[102]

As an outlaw, Marten should have been debarred from standing for election. Commentators, however, made more of the fact that he was in debt than that he had been prosecuted for it. His correspondent in Lambourn had written to an address known as the 'Thatched House' in the Rules of Southwark, that is, in the area around the prison where, on payment of a fee, prisoners were allowed to live on parole.[103] The marshal of the prison, to whom Marten made regular payments throughout the 1650s, was Sir John Lenthall, brother of the Speaker for whom Marten had so little respect. Marten and Mary lived in the Rules for the rest of the decade, often lodging with Mary's sister, Frances. He had thus gone straight from the heights of Derby House in Westminster to the rather squalid area of south London that had spawned so many of his Leveller supporters.

When Cromwell was pushed into summoning a 'supplementary' parliament in July 1656, he called on electors to certify that those chosen had already agreed to abide by a government of single person and parliament. Nevertheless, the republican coalition was again in action, forming a disparate opposition of Levellers, sectarians, Fifth Monarchists, republicans and some royalists.[104] The possibility that Marten would stand was canvassed. Marten wrote to his Leominster agent, Thomas Deane, to solicit support for his election for Herefordshire. Deane went to see Patshall, the man he thought most likely to be chosen, but at the previous assizes Patshall had denied he would stand, 'for his sight was so dime that hee knowe not the next man unto him'.[105] Deane put the case for his 'friend'; Patshall counselled him to 'forbear':

ffirst; at the generall meeting at the assizes last, it was in question who should bee the men, and hee being spoken unto first did refuse and naming some other they were not well thought on nor accepted of, in refference that allthough they had very considerable estats yet not shewing themsellves but as straingers in this

County, were not accepted of and, sayes hee, it may doubtlesse prove this gentlemans casse.

secondly, a man in durance will cause to arise many doubts.

thirdly, it was partly concluded on at the assizes and that this very day the gentry of this County were met at hereford to determine who to stand for and therefore this motion would come to late for the voyces would this day bee engaged.[106]

Unconvinced that debt and lateness were a hindrance, the following day Deane went to see the governor of Hereford, Wroth Rogers, who thought Marten at fault for having so lately declared, but agreed that he would use his best efforts to secure the votes of Leominster foreign. The vote for Leominster borough had been missed and Colonel John Birch, recruiter member for the borough, was re-elected. But there were many 'who much mutter that my frend will bee in question'.[107] Marten's Berkshire estates were being managed by the Tuckwell brothers, who wrote on 12 August because their 'neibores In the Cuntrey will fors mee to Right unto ye to know weither ye will bee pleased to shewe ye self for knight of the shire or noe and that ye will to send ye mind downe that I may shew it our neibores of abingdon and other places'.[108] Marten's electibility had taken a severe dent; he was politically out of fashion, an absentee and a debtor. He was not returned for either shire. Wroth Rogers was elected for Herefordshire, as he had been in previous parliaments, and was to be again in 1659. He was also created sheriff in 1656. Marten's neighbour, Samuel Dunch, who like Rogers had a continuous record of shire government throughout the 1650s and who, unlike Marten, had been visible around the county, was elected for Berkshire, along with the little known Fifth Monarchist, Vincent Goddard.[109]

Once excluded from the centre of power, the republicans sought a forum to express their politics. Sexby, Wildman and Grey were reclusive during the mid-1650s because of their sojourns in exile or in prison. Once Wildman was free, he purchased a tavern in Bow Street, Covent Garden, an area 'large and open, with good houses, well inhabited and resorted unto by gentry for lodgings'.[110] The vendor was probably a Dr Whitacker. Wildman's trusted servant, William Parker, who had shared some of his employer's captivity, was installed as proprietor. They called the tavern Nonsuch, which may have been a piece of republican witticism. The only year in which Parker was rated on this property was 1658, when he paid a poor rate of £6 6s. 6d., though Parker was present several years before this. These 'clubs' provided talking shops and convivial company for like-minded politicians.[111] Marten used the club, but could not take as active a part as he might once have done. After the Restoration, however, Will Parker's brews were still brought to his prison.[112]

Oliver Cromwell died on his providential day, 3 September 1658. The incomplete nature of Cromwellian reform and the inability of Oliver's son, Richard, to sustain it, provided new opportunities for the republicans. The champions of Rump republicanism were lobbying for the return of the 'Good Old Cause', which referred to the heady feelings of expectation engendered by the activism and victory of 1647/8. The electorate were presented with the return of the straight choice, 'eyther to submit our selves, and posterity perpetuall Slaves to the uncontrollable dictates of one mans will, or by our strengths united to breake his bands a sunder'.[113]

Depite the rhetorical vigour behind the Good Old Cause, it could not be matched by unity. The difficulties of the Commonwealth years had bred a variety of ideas of government and the intervening years between the dismissal and recall of the Long Parliament had made for muddled thinking. A supporter of Sir Arthur Haselrig put forward twelve points for consideration that would lead to *A Commonwealth or nothing*. But the author managed to combine Norman Yoke theory, in which kings were a product of William I's conquest, with a call to Brutus, the ancient British hero, who would return to eject kings. Nimrod, the biblical kingly tyrant, was invoked to contrast with the good republican examples set by Venice, Holland and ancient Sparta. Although good practice came from abroad, there was a call to 'publick spirited Patriot[s]'. The need to exclude those who had supported single person rule was combined with a Harringtonian desire for rotating parliaments, a council of state fulfilling the function of separating the legislative and executive elements.[114]

Another twelve 'healing questions' were propounded by the author of *The Dispersed United*, who called for fellowship between parliament and army.[115] This was also the aim of a composite piece, *The Armies Dutie*, written in April 1659 and published in the form of two letters to Lieutenant General Fleetwood. It was claimed that the impetus to publish had been Fleetwood's failure to listen to the same advice in private; public exposure to the arguments may 'quicken up' the army's leader. Like the other contributions, the composite creation of *The Armies Dutie* reflected different traditions of thought. Of the authors, Henry Marten and John Wildman represented 1640s' republicanism; Henry Nevile was part of the brand of republicanism that harkened to ancient precedents and which became fashionable after 1652; John Jones and Samuel Moyer were two who had flirted with republicanism at points along the way. The final name was 'I.L.', possibly John Lambert.[116] They did, however, start with one of the phrases that identified 1640s' republicanism: they aimed to 'procure a settlement of that common freedome, which hath cost so much bloud and treasure'.[117]

The group opened with a rehearsal of the blood-guilt rhetoric of the late 1640s, no doubt designed to spark recognition in the rank and file of the army, which had fostered it ten years before. The phrases were carefully chosen from the canons of the foundation of the Commonwealth. '[Y]ou [Fleetwood] caused the exercise of the chief Magistrate in *England* by a single person to be abolish'd, because it was dangerous . . .

as well as uselesse and burdensome'. The King's power was 'begotten by the blasphemous arrogance of Tyrants upon their servile parasites'. These were lines lifted, first, from the act abolishing kingship and, secondly, from the petition of the army from St Albans in November 1648.[118] The tone changed on page nine. Marten inserted a piece in which he was as witheringly sarcastic about Fleetwood's pretensions to power as he had been six years before about his father-in-law, Cromwell. Single person rule could not be stabilised without the support of a mercenary army and 'their interest will change as often as they get estates that are of more value then their pay', an allusion to the New Model and its campaigns for payment in land during the Commonwealth. The implication, not well hidden, was that the New Model had turned into the mercenary army that Marten's allies in the junior ranks had claimed it not to be. Finally, there was a touch of Harringtonianism, Nevile pointing out that the balance of landownership in England had changed and that the people's interest was now too strong to reimpose single person rule. England was now 'unnatural soyl for a Monarch'.[119]

Marten continued to live in the Rules during the latter half of the decade, but when Richard resigned and the Rump was reinstated in August 1659, he was recalled. However, for Marten, the republican reprieve came too late. In August he was called back to the Rump in order to complete a quorum and he had to be fetched from debtors' prison, which rather undermined his effectiveness in the House. There were a couple of small victories. He was in a position to stop the sale of Somerset House chapel, arguing that it was used by French protestants. Although he himself showed little interest in religion, he was still anxious to accommodate the religious views of others. He then nominated Edmund Ludlow as commander of the army in Ireland as a means to oust the Cromwellian officers still in control.[120]

A Remote Exile

Marten's career during the 1650s consisted of disappointed goals. He had motivated people in the previous decade, uniting the seemingly disparate interests of army, parliament and civilian radicals behind rallying cries and slogans. He had built a republican expectation on phrases such as *salus populi, suprema lex*, and 'the people's freedom, against all tyrants', and had pronounced the overthrown monarchy 'unnecessary, burdensome and dangerous'. But in the situation that he faced after 1649 there was insufficient time to stabilise the government or to introduce radical change. There were too many interest groups to satisfy. The slogans began to appear empty rhetoric. In a parallel process, Marten became the personification of hopes dashed by experience. Of all the telling phrases of revolution that he coined and never made flesh, perhaps the most apt was the 'cost [of] so much blood and treasure'. As he was plunged into the bankruptcy courts, Marten was unable to bring political power to bear, or to act as a symbol of unity for philosophically close but socially diverse groups of activists. The effort of achieving the republic had been so great, both politically and financially, that there was insufficient momentum to maintain it.

After the final self-dissolution of the Long Parliament, the royalists were convinced that Henry Marten had joined the exodus of republicans fleeing to the continent. It was assumed that he had gone to Amsterdam.[121] But, at the same time as the politicians talked of free elections to ease the return of monarchy, there was confusing news about whether Marten would stand and for which seat. Three people were put up for the county of Berkshire, Sir Robert Pye, Mr Powell and Mr Sorby: 'Harry Martin is chosen always for a town in his own in Wales, an estate given him out of the Duke of Buckingham's'.[122] There was a hamlet called Wales in the parish of Hinton, in which Marten had some small remaining interest, but Wales was half a dozen riverside cottages, not a parliamentary stronghold. The reference to land given him from Buckingham's estates seems to mean Herefordshire, which might conceivably be described as the Welsh borderlands. However, Marten never stood for the marches seat.

Marten was excepted from pardon. Nevertheless, he did not flee the possibility of royalist reprisals, nor stand again for election. Instead he surrendered according to the Caroline declaration of 6 June 1660. He was tried and taken to the Tower. The cavalier parliament reopened the fate of the regicides who had surrendered, and again it seemed possible that he would be hanged. Mary Ward was dispatched to listen to the sermons before King Charles, in the hope that this would divulge some sense of the mood.[123] In general, the messages were optimistic. His brother-in-law, Sir George Stonehouse, passed on the news that only a single voice could be found to promote a debate on the regicides' execution within the House of Commons, and there seemed to be little in the speeches of the King or the chancellor which intimated danger.[124] Marten's estates having been seized, though encumbered with debts of over £30,000, he was paid an allowance of £2 a week, originally through the Stauntons, but subsequently from his sister, Elizabeth.

State prisoners who provided the greatest threat or the greatest blot on the face of the restored regime were transferred to prisons as far away from the political action as possible. John Wildman and his son went to Guernsey Castle, and Marten to the other end of the country, either to Berwick-upon-Tweed or Holy Island.[125] The warrant for his removal from the Tower was received by its governor, Sir John Robinson, on 25 July 1662, ordering James Lambert to transport him aboard the *Anne*. At Berwick he was in the keeping of William, Baron Widdrington, but it was from Holy Island that Marten was ordered to be transferred to Windsor Castle on 19 May 1665.[126] The sight of him walking the walls at Windsor was said to have upset Charles II and, on 7 December 1668, Marten was ordered to the distant outpost of Chepstow.

This was one of the few garrisons that, ironically, had not been allowed to run down or decay during the interregnum. At the Restoration, it was immediately returned to the next generation of its traditional commanders, the Herbert Marquises of Worcester. It was thought that Marten's confinement was at first rigorous, the castle having been extensively strengthened and repaired, first in the early 1650s and again in 1660. He was guarded by half a company – reduced the previous year – consisting of two serjeants, three corporals, a gunner, a drummer and sixty soldiers.[127] The area was thought to be a focus for possible anti-royalist risings during the early 1660s, though nothing came of it. The only real scare occurred in 1678, when Titus Oates was convinced by local man William Bedloe that the Marquis of Worcester was part of a Jesuit plot, embracing all the Catholic powers of western Europe, to assassinate Charles II at Newmarket races and burn down London.[128]

With the passing years and his increasing age, Marten's stay at Chepstow became a relatively pleasant one. Within the eastern tower, formerly known as Bigod's Tower,[129] were fifteenth-century quarters, on two storeys, which were modestly comfortable. According to an eighteenth-century antiquarian, '[t]he chamber in which he usually lived is not less than thirty-six feet in length, twenty-three in breadth, and of proportionable height; it was provided with two fire-places, and three windows, two of which appear to be the original aperture, and a third was probably enlarged for his convenience'.[130] There were servants' rooms,[131] above those that are always described as inhabited by his wife and family, although the party that joined Marten in Welsh seclusion was, in fact, Mary Ward and their three girls.[132] Not only were Marten's lodgings more than adequate for a state prisoner, he was allowed visits and leave to call on the local gentry. He became something of a celebrity, albeit a notorious one, discovering that emasculation now rendered his extremism unthreatening. He was a curiosity and an entertainment. This, combined with his wit, made him excellent company at dinner. He even paid visits to Mr Lewis of St Pierre, a local royalist who had seized the castle for Charles I during the second civil war. Lewis, however, asking him whether he would change his life if he had it to live over again, was shocked to find that Marten still maintained his republican principles, to the point that he would repeat his signature on Charles' death warrant. At which moment, Marten ceased to be eccentric amusement and was reconstituted a violent revolutionary. Lewis barred him from returning to his table.[133]

A strange quirk may have resulted in Marten's confinement in Chepstow, his lenient treatment, or possibility the connivance, seemingly without offence or scandal, at the presence of Mary Ward and their children. Law records from the first few years of the seventeenth century note among the Chepstow cases, as both defendant and plaintiff, one Bartholomew Pettingall. Pettingall seems to have owned land in Chepstow in 1607/8[134] and the name seems too unusual not to question whether this man was in some way related to the Pettingalls with whom Marten had business dealings and who were rivals for the affections of Mary Ward.[135]

Marten died in September 1680, 'by a stroke of apoplexy which seized him while he was at dinner'.[136] Anthony Wood did not hear of his death until December: 'in the beginning of this month I was told that Harry Marten died last summer, suddenly, with meat in his mouth, at Chepstow in Monmouthshire'. He was sufficiently sanguin about Marten's posthumous reputation to add his name almost immediately to a list of 'writers' that he sent to Thankfull Owen.[137] Marten was buried in the Anglican churchyard on the ninth of the month and his notoriety was not sufficient to deter the congregation from siting a gravestone within the church, engraved with an elegant and telling acrostic verse.

He died with much the same reputation as he had lived, as both a 'violent republican' (Coxe) and a 'kind master', in whose employ servants were able to put money aside. His long-suffering wife died only months before him. His son, Henry, was, at the time of his father's death, a man of forty-one, and had married a woman called Mary, with whom he had eight children. However, what remained of the Marten estate that had not been sold or mortgaged was confiscated and vested in James, Duke of York, eventually to return to creditors. With sparse exceptions, therefore, the Marten family that had risen so quickly to prominence in times of crisis, returned as quickly to obscurity in the more stable conditions of the late seventeenth century.

III
Between Hobbes and Machiavel

Colin Davis has pointed to the absurdity of labelling anyone 'before their time'.[1] Henry Marten represented a political tradition, even if it was a minority taste. He was not a philosopher, in the manner of Hobbes, nor a populariser like Nedham or Milton. However, many writers have identified two certainties about the mid-seventeenth century: that Henry Marten was 'the only exception', an 'avowed republican',[2] and that republicanism was shaped by Harrington, Sidney and Vane. We need to find the common ground between these two factors to gague Marten's contribution to republicanism. In part, Marten dug his own premature philosophical grave. He was a political activist in perpetual motion, whilst at the same time being lazy and feckless. An idea would seize his brain, obsess it briefly and fly, before it had been subjected to any rigour or committed to paper. Many of Marten's statements remain in manuscript; drafts of the title pages to *magna opera* that he would have completed, if only the world had not been so full of enemies, friends and beer.

Marten was not such an isolated figure. During the 1640s he had a range of contacts with fellow parliamentarians, Levellers in London and agents in the army, and in the following decade he was at the centre of the government, forging links with like-minded people on the continent. The purpose of this overview of Marten's political philosophy is to piece together the manuscript fragments that remain unpublished, the revealed remarks of his published writings, his actions, and the writings, speeches and activities of his political allies, to reveal the position on the ideological spectrum held by Marten and his select band of political extremists. It identifies and defines a series of political terms, such as natural and common law, conquest, liberty, ancient constitutionalism and balance. In order to describe Marten's place among these, it is necessary to add some more: parochialism, patriotism, dualism, representation and accountability. These were the concerns of Marten's republicanism.

Historians have debated the roots of Marten's political theory. Williams believed that his 'very great Fortune' produced a gentleman, unable and unwilling to shake off the ideological baggage that 'betrayed the interests of his class'.[3] John Pocock and Blair Worden noted Marten's friendship with Thomas Chaloner as a link to the 'classical republicans', alluding to their admiration for and emulation of the anti-imperialists of ancient Greece and Rome. Marten's contribution to a political philosophy, sufficient to 'sober men', suffered because the libertinistic pair were rarely that. Marten's friend and Berkshire colleague, the equally witty and Baccanalian Henry Nevile, however, earned greater status through his connection with James Harrington.[4] Jonathan Scott, in his study of the classical republican Algernon Sidney, also identifies Marten as a gentleman whose politics were 'anti-aristocratic' and 'irreligious' social radicalism, but concludes that his republicanism was at odds with that avowed by Sidney.[5] Most recently, Richard Tuck has tantalisingly referred to Marten in the context of Monataignian stoicism, with the opinion that 'Marten's general republicanism may not have been as unusual even in 1643 as has often been thought'.[6]

Rights and Precedents

Marten was considered to have been on poor personal terms with and at some political distance from his father, who employed his learning in the civil law in loyal service to the crown and was commended by James I for his resourcefulness in designing arguments to strengthen the prerogative. Sir Henry Marten could be 'extremely moderate'.[7] In fact, there were several points of common political principle between father and son. Marten showed little interest in arguments from common law, or their manifestation in the principle known as ancient constitutionalism. The fact that a precedent could be cited in its favour did not imply the rightness of any principle. Sir Henry Marten had been the only civil lawyer to defend the 1628 Petition of Right. Henry Marten the younger frequently cited the Petition as a starting point for the struggles of the next generation. It was his talisman, unlike other Leveller-inspired politicians who cited *Magna Charta*. His respect for the Petition of Right was also the only reference that Marten made to past attempts to curtail the exercise of prerogative.[8] Marten did not cite precedent, for his philosophy dictated that he tried to institute the unprecedented, substituting higher notions of good and right. Finally, Marten could have taken his mode of argument from his father, who used logical form to express the clarity and simplicity of points of political philosophy and to deflate the pretensions of rival arguments. Sir Henry Marten's arguments in favour of the Petition used the same logical construction and illustration with homespun example that was to be his son's rhetorical trademark. An example comes from Sir Henry Marten's speech on 23 May 1628, in which he sought to persuade the Lord Keeper, John Finch, with 'better methode and order' that the Petition was the product of rationality: '[t]he old way (I have heard) is to remove grievances. We must not tie and bind ourselves by all that is done before. I have gone over the Thames in former times on foot, when it was all on ice, but that is no argument to persuade by, to do the like now because I did so once'.[9]

The ancient constitution provided a justification for the immemorial rights of English people. According to Pocock, 'what occurred was that belief in the antiquity of the common law encouraged belief in the existence of an ancient constitution, reference to which was constantly made, precedents, maxims and principles from which were constantly alleged, and which was constantly asserted to be in some way immune from the king's prerogative action'.[10] The weakness of the theory was exposed by the invasion of William of Normandy, because it posited a debate over whether William's authority rested on conquest, or had been subsequently ratified by the people. Ancient constitutionalism was 'antithetically related' to the theory of the Norman Yoke – that 1066 had instituted a systematic replacement of native, representative institutions with arbitrary foreign impositions, of which kingship may have been one.[11]

In the debates of the 1640s, notions of conquest, inherited oppression and pre-existent rights became confused and contradictory. The search for a settlement after the first civil war was, among other things, an attempt to reconcile them. At the turn of the year 1646/7, George Thomason secured a copy of a pamphlet entitled *Regall Tyrannie discovered*. He ascribed its authorship to John Lilburne and in terms of style there is little reason to question it.[12] *Regall Tyrannie discovered* took the commonplace (used during the debate on the Petition of Right), that 'power (in the hands of whomsoever) ought alwayes to be exercised for the good, benefit, and welfare of the Trusters', and added the logical step that it was 'against the light of Nature and Reason, and the end whereof God endowed Man with understanding, for any sort or generation of men to give so much power into the hands of any man or men whatsoever, as to enable them to destroy them'. The first, potentially republican import of this natural law discourse is followed by a second, more specifically aimed to show the 'Tyrannie of the Kings of *England*, from the dayes of *William* the Invader and Robber, and Tyrant, *alias* the *Conqueror*, to this present King *Charles*, Who is plainly proved to be worse, and more tyrannicall then any of his Predecessors'. In support of the first of his propositions, Lilburne claimed that it was the sin of Adam to seek magistracy over other things without their free consent; that all government should be by free consent (prerogative was a violation of this principle); and that the King was a 'meer man'. In defence of the second proposition, Lilburne narrated a history of England from 1066 to his own time, designed to prove that magistracy was the result of voluntary accord. Charles was meant to rule by a mutual agreement and contract, which he had consistently broken.

Lilburne articulated a number of shifts in opinion that were part of a radical response to the anger, bitterness and frustration felt at the end of the first war. There was certainly scepticism about the nature of monarchy and disillusionment with Charles Stuart in particular. There was a belief in the general post-lapsarian 'tyranny' of the nature of mankind; in the collective tyranny of kings because they sought to rule by prerogative will and not by consent; and in a native history of tyranny by English kings because of their descent from William the Conqueror. There was also an anti-Stuart trend, fuelled by the thinking time granted by the end of the fighting, the continued support that Charles seemed able to claim, and the discovery after Naseby of his letters to Henrietta Maria, which revealed foreign plots and invasions.

The key political issue at the end of 1646 was the peace negotiations over the Propositions of Newcastle. It was at this point that radicals within the Commons – in particular Marten and Thomas Chaloner – could start to formulate an agenda. Although it has received little attention from scholars in their overview of the period,[13] it seems clear that Marten believed that the central point at issue in 1646/7 was the disposal of the person of the King and the role in this that might be played by the Commissioners from the parliament of Scotland. In October 1646 Thomas Chaloner rose to make a speech with two central, radical, and ultimately revolutionary points. He argued that there was no role for the King in the peace negotiations. He also challenged the continuing presence of the Scots. They demanded a say in the proposals, even as they affected England, bound by its adherence to the Solemn League and Covenant to support the personal dignity of the king. Chaloner's contribution became known as the 'Speech without Doors', the implications of which were so extreme that all manner of minor scribblers were encouraged outside the portals of Westminster to make vitriolic comments about their King. There are eleven extant printed pieces on Chaloner's contribution alone. From the period of just over a year, between Thomas Chaloner's 'Speech without Doors' and the Vote of No Further Addresses to Charles, seven separate contributions written by Marten and dealing with the same theme survive: four in print – two of which he claimed publicly – and three more in manuscript.[14]

The main printed contribution, *A Corrector of the Answerer to the Speech out of Doores . . .*, published at the end of 1646, consists primarily of a rhetorical, caustic and bitter attack on the presumption of the Scottish Commissioners to demand a say in the future of England. It ranked Chaloner with the brave men of 1628.[15] It also drew attention to points made in *Regall Tyrannie*. If the Scots were allowed a role in determining the future of Charles, the conclusion that both kingdoms ought to draw was that Charles was a tyrant but should himself be punished as a mere man. There was no difference of degree between a king and a commoner before the law, so if the punishment for a commoner was death and disinheritance, so should it be for a king. Previous treaties, either among themselves or between England and Scotland, that sought to protect the King's person were nullified by the realisation that to protect a tyrant was in itself 'evill and sinfull'.[16] The inclusion in the peace proposals of the King's 'negative voice' – the prerogative veto over legislation – if pressed by the Scots, would render the peace untenable: 'it will render the Parliament more incapable of preserving the Kingdome now then ever, and while you pretend to avoid perjury, you would enforce the Parliament upon an inevitable slavery'.[17] Within a syllogistic structure, Marten sought first to show that the Scotch Papers could be reduced to a simple logical statement and, subsequently, that that statement was based on false premises and internally inconsistent.[18] The strength and (to opponents) the weakness of this approach was positing an unquestionable starting point, based on a notion of justice that was assumed to be held by all. A just argument was presupposed, and an aspect which did not fit that mould had to be ruthlessly disregarded or suppressed.

These themes underpinned Marten's concerns for the next two years. By the early months of 1648, addresses to Charles for peace were being sent to Carisbrooke Castle on the Isle of Wight. The Scottish Commissioners still pressed for a personal treaty and the inclusion of the King's negative voice. Marten made another two pamphlet contributions to the discussion, *The Independency of England endeavoured to be maintained* and *The Parliaments proceedings justified in declining a personall treaty with the king*.[19] He reiterated the argument against persisting with the practices of the past, especially the obligation to continue oaths and treaties that had outlived their usefulness: 'what should the Covenant do, but like an Almanack of the last yeer shew us rather what we have already done, then what we be now to do'.[20] Marten, ever fond of every-day allegorical parallels, had turned up one that in rhetorical form and content was very similar to his father's counsel not to repeat a walk on the icy Thames, though with more revolutionary impact.

The Politics of Balance

The second idea to emerge from the debates of the later 1640s is best illustrated by a pair of balance-scales. There are only two pans to such scales and any reference to balance in the constitution should not therefore be confused with notions of checks and balances. This dualist form replaced traditional, Aristotelian notions of a tripartite governmental structure with a more bleak, straightforward and revolutionary distinction. Martenesque balance-scales introduced the judgement of value.[21] An institution, person or idea could be weighed against another, though the reasons why one thing should be light or heavy in the balance varied. Thus, for instance, if the determinant of the debate between the English parliament and the Scottish Commissioners about the future of Charles Stuart was justice, so strong was the 'stream' of justice on Marten's side of the argument that he 'dare oppose the Reasons of my single barque, against all the advantages of Number, Abilities, and Countenance that you can meet with'.[22] There could never be an equal treaty in which Charles Stuart took a personal role, because the parliament was negotiating for the whole nation, the King for himself and perhaps his family.[23] If the English parliament were to be weighed against its opponents, even the King was more tolerable than the Scottish nation:

A King is but one Master, and therefore likely to sit lighter upon our shoulders then a whole Kingdom, and if he should grow so heavy as cannot wel be born, he may be sooner gotten off then they. You shal see a Mounsiours horse go very proudly under a single man, but to be *Charge en crouppe*, is that which nature made a mule for, if nature made a mule at all.[24]

The same point was made once the republican government had been set up. The merit of a proposal should be questioned according to 'what weight of arguments for it, not what number of hands unto it'.[25]

Such stark contrasts had a number of disputational advantages. In terms of juxtaposing good against bad they had a simplicity that appealed to those untrained in philosophical or politic niceties, unwilling to see shades of grey, and more ready to make a choice, irrespective of the force of its consequences. It was a rhetorical device which allowed Marten to present ideas in a form that other interests would recognise. Thus for those of a religious inclination, choices represented the ultimate dilemma, that between good and evil:

either an absolute tyrant over us, or no King; . . . either we must not be safe at all, or else we must be content with that shadow of safety that [Charles] is to determine . . . with his breath in stead of all other things which the Parliament can propose for the present Peace . . . some of his friends . . . will by way of discourse ask me what a Devil We would have besides the strength of the kingdom by Sea and Land? let him have that but for a month, and he shall ask nothing else, I answer them almost in their kinde: the prince of the aire . . . seemes more reasonable in his demands then our heavenly Father, for where God requires the whole heart, he will accept a little peece where he craves in effect no lesse then all.

The same structure also allowed for the wit of inversion:

The power of the Sword is to a Monarch of absolute necessity for the maintenance of his tyrannicall government, and that power had need to be alwayes actuated; the same in the hands of a Parliament . . . is not so much the power of the Sword as of the Buckler, and will not be exercised at all, but in cases of Rebellion or Invasion; if all the quarrell betwixt the Parliament and the King were (as it is preached in some Pamphlets and libelled in some Sermons) which of them should domineer over the people, the forenamed offer might perhaps serve their turne.[26]

The inversion allowed for wit – secularists preach and clerics libel – but it also allowed for a more dynamic and important shift in rhetoric and ideas. Things that had once been absolute were made relative and a new set of absolutes was interposed in order to decide between the new relative categories.

Monarchist absolutists had tended to regard conquest as a legitimate way to instigate rule. Resistance theorists had regarded armed resistance as justifiable if the ruler had broken the pact between people and government. Civil war constitutionalists explained conquest in terms of subsequent ratification by the people.[27] Marten interposed a higher absolute that made conquest a relative category. Justice was the ultimate arbitrator. He believed that the Levellers were mistaking the point in ascribing Charles' lack of authority to the Norman conquest. The question was not how long we had been 'ridden' but how justly.[28] Conquest could be an arbitrator when Charles and kingship were weighed in the balances because it was a certain judge. In religious terms, this was an argument from Providence – the cause was just because God gave the army victory. Marten generally preferred a secular form, which demonstrated the unfairness of a fight between all of the people and a sectional interest of the elite. This may have been an extension of the Grotian argument that the 'law of arms' justified the overthrow of tyranny.[29] Grotius' essentially anti-Aristotelian natural law theories argued that human society was derived from nature but that civil society was a human creation.[30]

Similarly, it was not the existence of a parliament that conferred legitimacy on government. Even parliament was not an absolute. It was not the people's representatives in parliament who were sovereign, but the people themselves. Hence, the absolute of the 'common good' was sufficient to override the power of the House of Commons, if the Commons was not considered to be acting in the interests of all of the people. The definition of the 'people' who constituted the Commonwealth and those who were considered fit to arbitrate on the nature of absolutes did, of course, make the whole theory problematic. In December 1648 Marten considered the army a suitable judge, and justified Pride's Purge to William Prynne:

Besides, the Parliament was then [1641] honest, fit to reform, which it was not now [1648], at the time when the Army came to *London*. If it be a sin in a particular person to neglect an opportunity of doing good it is much more a sin in this Army, whom God hath owned so wonderfully in all their Actions, and whom . . . he hath raised, to do this work. It is (therefore) ignorance or malice on them that publikely write and pate in Pulpits, and at other meetings, That it is a great Breach of Parliament priviledg, to stop the Members going into the House to discharge their duty. Had it been to discharge their duty to the Countreys and Towns, for which they were elected, they had not been stopt. But Mr. *Prynne*, and the rest of his imprisoned friends came with no such intention; they came to serve the common enemy . . . They indeed may live gallantly, and enjoy every thing but a good conscience, and dying, shall leave their children a rich inheritance of slavery and thraldom.[31]

Experience had taught the parliamentarians that Charles Stuart was the embodiment of untrustworthy monarchy. Indeed, it could be argued that radical republicans were most likely to be those who identified in the early 1640s that Charles was the sole source of governmental chaos.[32] Sections of the political nation had been misled into supporting Charles, because their reverence for monarchy or willingness to be led astray by malignants dictated that they continue to accept that monarchy had been corrupted by evil counsellors. Now the evidence had made the issue clear, and the radicals were able to reimpose absolute measurements. Experience had generated more reliable judgement and this necessitated, presupposed, and justified the conquest of the malignants by those who acted in the interests of the people (or godly people): 'there is a more naturall way to peace and to the ending of a warre then by agreement, namely by conquest'.[33]

Marten's approach parallelled the Leveller language of the fundamental liberties of the English people. Both attacked the constitutional role of the House of Lords and did so in a way in which baronial power was tied to kingly prerogative, necessitating the fall of both together. Whereas the Leveller's starting point was frequently Norman Yoke theory, predetermining rights that were enjoyed by Anglo-Saxon Englishmen and usurped by the conquerors, Marten was distrustful of historical precedent. Instead, his notion of the alien nature of kings was dictated by his belief in a naturally self-contained and circular model of the ideal constitution, in which every element was linked to every other, in a giant chain of which each link was inherent and necessary. Therefore every link was accountable to every other and each link represented some necessary element of every other. The King was a foreign imposition. He was alien because William the Conqueror was French. He was alien because he had conquered England and imposed his rule. Vitally, however, he was alien in the sense that his role was outside and antithetical to that in which a representative and accountable system was necessarily self-contained. Any outside influence broke the perfect relationship between the governed and the government. The question of England's liberties was not to discover the point at which they had been usurped or to look abroad for parallels, for what mattered was 'not whether wee have any fellowes in other countryes but whether wee should not bee all fellowes here at home'.[34]

Marten was a patriot. Being partial on behalf of his fellow English was integral to his public persona. He was unashamedly partisan because he was 'trusted for his fellow commoners' and addressed anyone, 'supposing them an Englishman', as if it were the greatest honour to be 'thy countryman'.[35] England was a 'Noun Substantive', an absolute, against which all other issues must be measured.[36] The coarse language against the Scots was an immediate reaction to their constant interference in the peace negotiations, but it reflected a wider concern, in which peace and a constitutional settlement could only be effected in England by the English people. Patriotism was a measure of loyalty and conflicting measures of loyalty was one of the key questions facing the radicals during the latter years of the 1640s. The interference of an outside body – something which did not represent the English people; King, Lords, or Scots, for example – would break the hermetic seal between represented and representatives and would introduce something that blocked the flow of representativeness around the body politic and destroyed the system. Such circularity justified both patriotic, insular zeal and, first, the sidelining and subsequently the refusal to readmit the King or the House of Lords to a place within the circle, for all Englishman must be subject to English laws 'otherwise the one part shall make hewers of wood and drawers of water of the other five'.[37] When Thomas Chaloner made a similar point, he was accused of 'homespun slovenly malice'.[38]

Whilst the parliamentarians were debating the degree to which the Covenant and other treaties bound them to the Scots or to protect the King's person, Marten's allies in the army and civilian pressure groups were conducting a parallel argument at Putney. Of those who participated at Putney, John Wildman, and Thomas Rainsborough – whom Richard Gleissner would see as articulators of a secular natural law theory – Edward Sexby, and Maximilian Petty had direct links with Marten.[39] There is ample evidence of the co-operation of several of these figures – as well as others who were part of this group, such as William Walwyn and William Wetton[40] – in drawing up the *Agreement of the People*, which was the radicals' contribution to the Putney debates and, in effect, a codification of the complaints in *The Case of the Armie Truly Stated*, which had been their starting point at Putney.[41]

Sexby made the first radical interjection, mirroring the sense which Marten had offered that the balance of the state should be dualistic, as well as the belief that trust had been placed in a weak vessel. The soldiers had placed their trust in a man who sought deliberately to break the circular flow of mutual inter-relationships that constituted the common weal: 'We sought to satisfy all men, and it was well; but in going [about] to do it we have dissatisfied all men. We have laboured to please a king, and I think, except we go about to cut all our throats, we shall not please him'. The King and the people were out of balance, both because they were weighing the interests of one man against those of all of the English people and because such a man had proved an untrustworthy repository of their trust.[42] Trained in the law, Wildman at Putney and Marten in *The Indepedency of England* argued that an oath or a contract made in good faith ceased to be binding were it subsequently proven to be unjust.[43]

Both Wildman and Marten were also prepared to extend their belief in the representativeness of government and the absolute nature of the people's sovereignty to the legislature itself. Wildman continued his theme of the morality of keeping engagements. If a proper parliament was created, he asked, and it proposed legislation that committed an injustice on the people, were the people to be expected to sit still and suffer? The radicals at the Putney debates were not prepared to accept the grandees' point that tinkering with the geographical and numerical extent of the franchise was sufficient security for the liberty of the individual.[44] Only a full franchise could constitute part of a just system. As Gleissner put it, '[o]nly through enfranchisement would consent of the governed become a reality, instead of a constitutional fiction, and the original agreement of people to establish government become self-renewing.'[45] The preamble to the first *Agreement*[46] established the procedure and principle that, in order for the people to be justly, equally and adequately represented, the rights of the parliament must be settled before a role for the King was reinserted into the constitution. The degree to which those responsible for drawing up the *Agreement* had already made the decision not to allow Charles back to power is a moot point, though the vitriolic statements about his untrustworthiness, tyranny and crimes against the people made throughout the 'Speech without Doors' controversy and the army campaigns of 1646/7 would seem to indicate that Charles, at least, was unwelcome.

The Political Circle: Representation and Accountability

War had created the conditions in which concepts that others had taken for granted could be forcibly challenged. Here, Marten's simple and direct use of logical reasoning could expose what had previously been thought certain and demonstrate its inappropriateness and absurdity. Since for Marten, custom could make law,[47] but did not necessarily make right, 'if any one thing could bee made to appear to have bene constantly practised through all ways without interruption (which I beleeve will bee very hard to be beleeved) I shall notwithstanding for my part esteem it iust or uniust so farr as it shall in my understanding bee consistent with or opposite to right reason'.[48] 'Logic' was used in both of its separable but interlinked forms. Marten constructed arguments in syllogistic form. Each stage of an argument had to follow from the first and, as such, constituted a circular self-justification: 'if a, then b; if b, then c; if c, then d; if d, then a'. This construction gave the argument its strength and irrefutability. Every step was directly derived from the former, even to the point at which the argument invariably returned to its starting point. Any 'alien' idea, individual or institution, which attempted to join or distort this circle, had to be ruthlessly excluded. Logically speaking, it also said something about the nature of truth: that the predicate was always included in the subject. In Marten's republican philosophy, the individual was always predicated on the nature of the state and the state always predicated on the nature of the individual.

'Right reason' was the absolute that underpinned Marten's attack on the negative voice, the personal treaty, and the role of the Scottish Commissioners. The people could place their trust in it. Right reason would be the measure employed by the people because it encompassed representativeness and its sister, accountability. John Lilburne had cited George Wither's *Vox Pacifica* as early as 1645 to establish that it was representation that made authority:

> Let not your King and Parliament in one,
> Much less apart, mistake themselves for that
> Which is most worthy to be thought upon:
> Or think they are, essentially, the state;
> Let them not fancy th'authority
> And privileges upon them bestown,
> Conferred, to set up a majesty,
> A power, or a glory, of their own.
> But let them know 'twas for another thing,
> Which they but *represent* . . .[49]

Marten claimed for himself the essence of representativeness; he was an individual, but also one of the people of Berkshire; he was a member of the House that was representative of the people of England, which was best able to speak for, negotiate for and decide on behalf of those whom it represented. He rebuked the pro-Presbyterian and pro-treaty petitioners of Suffolk who were mistaken in directing their grievances to the 'Kings peeres' when there was 'a house hard by consisting of your peeres & chosen by their peeres on purpose to hear their complaints and provide remedyes'.[50] His rhetoric of representativeness manifested itself in xenophobia, parochialism and insularity, at least as far as settling the peace. It was not simply that his primary concern was with the English people: the English people were his sole concern.

Marten was a believer in fundamental rights, of the kind enshrined in an *Agreement of the People*, because that was a declaration of 'what ought to have bene done' rather than 'what had bene done'.[51] None of Marten's efforts were committed to the printers, but for two years, from 1646, he had five separate attempts at drafting them in manuscript. The fundamental liberties of England were vested in the House of Commons, although, in the circumstances of the war, the army constituted their 'bulwark'.[52] When John Selden defended the House of Lords, Marten accused him of denying his own House, and of speaking for the King's prerogative. This point had been made by Lilburne in *Regall Tyrannie discovered*, though the Leveller's relentless campaign to prove himself against courts made up from the Lords injected his pen with greater bile.[53] Marten felt the need to reiterate the point so forcibly to William Prynne, replying to him around the year 1647, that he put it in capitals: 'NEITHER THE KING NOR THE HOUSE OF PEERS IOYNTLY OR SEVERALLY HATH ANY IUST RIGHT TO AN EQUALL SHARE IN THE LAW-MAKING POWER WITH THE REST OF THE NATION: NOR TO ANY POWER OF THEMSELVES TO IUDGE A COMMONER OF ENGLAND'.[54] Prynne the lawyer should be 'ashamed at this time of day to wear C.R.' on his sleeve, though the King constituted the lawyer's 'Arch-clyent'.

Parliament was the highest authority in England, but was nevertheless man-made, 'derived' or 'mediated' as a result of the collective deputation of the people. The act of deputation conferred on parliament a 'Commission to advance or to conserve at least, not to infringe ye interest of those whom they are deputed'.[55] Hence, in the balance, a body that had commission to act on behalf of all of the people would invariably take precedence over one that represented a small body of people chosen by rank, or a single individual chosen by lineage. If there were other elements, such as King or Lords, then the 'subject's liberty' to choose who might represent him in parliament was something granted by a third party. It was therefore not a natural right – a birthright – but a privilege, bestowed by others. Something bestowed could be be taken away, reducing the subject to 'slavery'. The traditional tripartite system, in which King, Lords and Commons were together meant to act in the interests of the people, was a logical nonsense. It would never be in the interests of a king or lords to act on behalf of the commons. The history of England since the failure of the Petition of Right had established regal and baronial prerogatives to take away this sole privilege, denying the House of Commons any genuine representativeness. The only proper balance for the constitution weighed the people against their representatives. It would never become top-heavy and thus deprive the people of their liberties, because no delegated body could create one greater than itself. The people chose 500 delegates to parliament, said Marten, but should the people find themselves compromised, they could choose to elect 1,500.[56]

Thus, 'the English nation is a free people, undeniably possessed of liberty in their persons, & of property in their goods, as it is declaratorily expressed in divers acts of Parl^t & particularly in the Petition of Right'. From this it followed that the English people must live under laws of their own making. Because the post-war settlement was the foundation for a new constitution, Marten resisted any interference by the Scottish Commissioners. The people also had the right to refuse to obey any law that they believed would do them harm. The consent of the people's representatives in the Commons was the only thing that made binding law. Whether and when the Commons sat, and the nature of their discussion, was only to be determined by the people, according to what was 'conduceing to yᵉ glory of God, to yᵉ safety, wealth and honour of yᵉ Nation'.[57] These were the principles enshrined in Marten's declaration of 4 January 1649:

> That the People, are, under God, the original of all just Power. That the Commons of England, in Parliament assembled, being chosen by, and representing, the People, have the supreme Power in this Nation. That whatsoever is enacted, or declared for Law, by the Commons, in Parliament assembled, hath the force of Law; and all the people of this Nation are concluded thereby, although the consent and concurrence of King, or House of Peers, be not had thereunto.[58]

The statement derives its rhetorical force from its logical construction. Authority is derived from the people. The Commons derives its position from the people; authority makes law and therefore the people are governed and protected by that law. It was necessarily circular, because that was the people's guarantee that all issues would return to the foundation point, which was that sovereignty lay with the people. '[I]ndeed', said Marten, this was 'the very Foundation of all the rest'.[59]

What constituted 'the people' was among the most controversial topics of the peace debates. For the radicals, it was the fundamental point of principle: 'that which is the engagement of all, which is the right and freedoms of the people'.[60] What appeared from the *Agreement of the People* to be a commitment that all men should be included within the new constitution, echoed by Marten in his statement that we should all be fellows, was watered down by a process of attrition. At Putney, Rainsborough betrayed the original statement that by natural law all men deserved the right to put themselves under a law that would both bind and serve them, in trying to counter Ireton by arguing that the soldiers had proved themselves worthy of the privilege of the franchise, by fighting for the settlement.[61] Others were forced to agree that those who were bound by constraints of personal service or beggary were not in a position to exercise the free will to place themselves under the law. When Marten became part of government, the Rump was forced to deny representation to all of those whose intention was to destroy the 1649 settlement, and thus the experience of war removed royalists, delinquents and malignants from the franchise.[62] The needs of security outweighed the intention to be inclusive.[63]

The settlement of 1649 did not end the vigilance that was required against malignants in all three kingdoms. The day-to-day management of affairs proved difficult within a unicameral structure, even one with only fifty active members. The former Derby House committee was reconstituted as an executive Council of State, but it was apt to block the direct flow of representativeness between people and parliament.[64] A universal oath of loyalty would lessen the possibility of snide comments about the Council's unrepresentativeness. It would be required first of members of the Council, then of all MPs and later, on a descending scale of subscriptions, of all people over eighteen. It was initially designed to be inclusive of those who were loyal. The drafters also took care that this Engagement was entirely secular, and contained no religious element that might in future compromise people's consciences and be as divisive as the experience of the Solemn League and Covenant or the obligations entered into by the army.[65] John Lilburne, otherwise hostile to the idea of a Council, took the Engagement, '[b]ecause the Members of the 3. said Counsells take it as well as any others, and therefore it is not abstract to themselves that they take the Engagement to be true to; for it is incongruous in reason, for a man to be true to himself, because it is inherent in him'.[66] Despite his condemnation of the Council of State, therefore, the Engagement had, in Lilburne's opinion, revived the notion that a delegated power could never be greater than those who delegate.

Classical Republicanism

Marten hardly put pen to paper between 1649 and 1653. The sole exception to this dearth is a draft of a justification for a declaration of war on the Scots.[67] This is a testimony to how busy he was with the practice of politics, but also to his overall satisfaction with the structure and philosophy of the Rump, which he regarded as 'the best frame of lawes yett extant in yᵉ World'.[68] The problem for historians trying to piece together the philosophy behind the Rump was how little participants commented on the creative process in which they were engaged. As such, it could be argued that the republican government was an *ad hoc* edifice, not constructed to any pre-arranged philosophy but gradually built up piecemeal, in response to issues as they arose.

It has been claimed that Marten fell into a category of thinkers that congregated around Marchamont Nedham's and John Hall's editorship of the government newsletter, *Mercurius Politicus*, during the early 1650s. There may have been some connection while Nedham was writing *The Excellency of a Free State*, though the degree to which Nedham constituted an innovative thinker rather than a servant of the state can be overplayed.[69] There were certainly statements by Nedham in the early years of the Commonwealth with which Marten could have agreed. Both were sceptics, though Marten's scepticism most often addressed religious dogmatism.[70] Hall and Nedham utilised a language that Marten would have recognised. The Hall metaphor, that monarchy represented a private interest that upset the natural harmony of a commonwealth, and Nedham's view, that the will and pleasure of a monarch was antithetical to the interests of the state, may have been more advanced statements of the self-containedness of the Commonwealth representative system.[71] Marten could have joined this pair in praising the pluralistic way in which a harmonious republic incorporated the diversity of human nature.

However, the way in which the republic began to be described after about 1652 and the statements of Marten in the late 1640s showed up some real differences of approach. During 1652 Nedham justified the republican government by drawing a distinction between 'natural' and 'political' government. The former was that granted to the pre-lapsarian family, paternalism being a natural state. Even the original, natural government was temporary, having been subverted when Nimrod founded the first tyranny. Politic government was that in which the origin of power lay with the people's consent and compact; demonstrated by the often-told biblical account of the people's choice of Saul. This form of government retained the right of the people to change it: Marten had argued that the people could create 1,500 representatives in order to outweigh a parliament of 500. However, Nedham and Hall, along with Milton, Sidney and Harrington, stressed the fluidity that should be present in a republican system. This undermined Marten's self-contained republic.[72] According to Nedham, providence 'pulls down one kingdom or government and sets up another', having changed Europe from principalities to republics and back to kingdoms, often using the power of the sword, afterwards ratified by the people's consent.[73]

Nedham popularised the form of republican thinking that has been termed 'classical'.[74] It is perhaps better understood as a resource than as a definition, describing a pool of source material from which diverse thinkers and polemists could drew inspiration and justification for the republican state of which they were part. It utilised the writings of the ancients, particularly Aristotle's division of the branches of authority, Cicero's latinising of the same as the union of the forms, and Polybius' notion of (counter)balance between them.[75] These were wrapped in an admiration for the successes of republican regimes in Renaissance Italy and contemporary Venice and the United Provinces. The adoption of classical republicanism is generally regarded as a retrospective philosophy, pushed into the centre of an *ad hoc* framework of statute, to form the core justification of the Commonwealth. 'On the edge of an axe', claims Scott, the Commonwealthsmen created a practical state, and, in the leisure provided by victory, two or so years into their existence, they crystallised an ideology.[76]

Oliver Cromwell, Lord General of the army of the Commonwealth, was both the mailed fist of classical republicanism and its loosest cannon. As the General was to remind the Commonwealth when he ousted it in April 1653, the Rump owed the peace it had enjoyed to military vigilence and valour. Cromwell and his forces were the blessed instruments of God, the bulwark of the people's liberties, and the mighty conquerors who had demonstrated how England's interests could be fostered by non-monarchical government. Conquest of Scotland and Ireland and victory over the English royalists at Worcester was, in 1653, followed by a naval challenge to Dutch trading wealth.[77] The gladiatorial, classical Roman hero was a mould that well fitted the Lord General, but one which divided the republicans. Milton, Marvell and Nedham wrote in his favour, either as a heroic or Mosaic character. Sidney and Nevile went into opposition. Harrington retained a fascination with Cromwell as a puissant figure who inspired both fear and admiration, a characteristic which Machiavelli had recognised in his Prince, but about which he had been wary in his republic.[78]

Classical republicanism revived the debate about the culture of political power. What type of person was fit to hold office? In 1649 the group that took power had come from different backgrounds but had held a common commitment to the revolution and the resultant form of government. Grey of Groby and Edmund Ludlow feared God and saw political forms as a stage towards the millennium.[79] On the other hand, there was a clear, but as yet little understood connection between the republicanism of men like Marten, Chaloner, Sir Peter Wentworth and Thomas May, and a culture of secularism and libertinism.[80] Cromwell's speech to the Rump and his subsequent justification of the army's role in its dissolution may have been full of obfuscation, but he was clear that Marten and Wentworth were contemptible because their personal behaviour brought the practice of politics into disrepute.[81] The men of a classically-inspired republic had to live up to the Roman heroic image. Men were singled out to hold power because they possessed virtues on which the people could rely for wise and just stewardship. In the culture of the 1650s, pious Christian virtue was also a prerequisite. Hence one classical republican, Algernon Sidney, was able to describe another, Henry Vane, as a man of 'Valor and wisdom and that Glory of unblemish'd life' who even though he was a man of peace, rather than martial prowess, had 'industry and prudence [which] did not less contribute to the obtaining of Victories than the Valour of the Generals'.[82] Marten was no military hero and conspicuously lacked all the virtues deemed necessary for leadership. He would not make a senator in a republic led by a 'natural' elite. His frailties marked him out as a common man – quite literally a representative.

The Cromwellian coup was a defining moment for a number of republican politicians.[83] In Marten's case this was so in several ways. The expulsion of the Rump ended the only form of government that he believed had been a satisfactory safeguard of both the liberty and the security of the people, unjustly overturned by the 'turns of affairs' or by the sword of the army. There followed a period of enforced exile from politics, courtesy of Cromwell's attack on his moral and political rectitude, his increasingly private life, and his indebtedness. This seclusion, however, provoked a second flurry of writing. There were fewer contributions in the press, in part because a combination of the reasons for his fall made him a less saleable commodity. The extant material, however, does bear witness to how tragic an event he believed the fall of the Rump to have been.

Marten possessed an education in classical literature and language common to men of his social status. He had penned a juvenile and gauche Latin memorial to his mother in 1618.[84] Classical allusions took their place in his political expression, along with references to the Scriptures and homely examples of his own.[85] Generally, however, they were employed as secondary and anecdotal illustrations. He was not immune to or unaware of the revival of classicism in the mid-1650s. Between the spring of 1653 and the early months of the following year, Marten began two pieces he thought better of sending to the press: they carried extreme implications and a bitter and sarcastic tone that he seemed unable to moderate. He reworked a lyric poem by Catullus, lamenting the death of his mistress' sparrow. Marten's version made full use of the Alexandrean influences, combining both learned side-glances and apostrophic encomium to his subject.[86] His subject was Cromwell's assumption of power. Marten placed a mirror to Cromwell's supporters, who believed that they had witnessed the General's heroic conquest and would benefit from the strength of his protection. Marten's version can be translated as '[t]his mighty Cromwell, long the worthy hope of north and south, a man to be lauded from where the Sun rises to where it sets'.[87] Marten reflected Cromwell's portrayal as the archetypal Machiavellian prince, whose personal courage, will and fortitude could override fickle fortune. He was the hero whom 'the Fates of the English' decreed should now overshadow 'all the heroes . . . that the land of Greece brought forth . . . and that land which rivalled Greece and which belonged to the descendants of Romulus'.

Marten's intent, however, was inversion. He was building up his subject so high in order to bring it crashing down. In keeping with his logical style, he intended to make his subject's pretensions look ridiculous. 'This mighty Cromwell' was about to 'fill the throne'. There was a reference to the suspicion that a Lord Protector aspired to kingship. However, the Latin word for 'throne' translated equally well as 'tub' or 'coffin'. The poem was a tyrannicidal prophecy. Cromwell, who had overridden fate, had placed himself in diametrical opposition to Marten's notions of republican sovereignty: 'not for him the canvassing of the fickle people for the right to rule'. He 'knows the arts of force to hold the people down'. As the people 'sing a hymn of Joy' they should ask the Alexandrean questions: 'Is it right? Where is he from? What a man? Where is he going? Where does he stop?'

It was a literary, potentially tyrannicidal, and prudently unpublished reworking of ideas that Marten had expressed in length in a satirical letter to the Lord General, declining an invitation to be a member of the saints' assembly.[88] He was also to repeat these concerns, in an anglicised version which included many of the same allusions, in a pamphlet that purported to continue Clement Walker's *History of Independency*, whilst, in fact, subverting Walker's message.[89] When Cromwell had forcibly suppressed the will of the people, he had returned English politics to unjustified conquest:

I shall not at all speake of conquest nor am I soe weake as to imagine that any cann rationally make scruple, to govern what they have subdued; neither is it my intenc̄on or the businesse of a l[etter] to decide the controversy between Mr. Hobbs and Machiavell conc'ning tiranny and liberty or to weigh in an equall balance the inconveniencies which arise from op̄ression in the one, and factions in the other; it is sufficient to cleare my Judgmᵗ in this poynt, that your Exᶜʸ hath not at any tyme declared for Conquest, nor indeed can it bee sayd that the Army hath subdued this nation and people from whose authority they received their Swords, from whose purses their pay and from whose councells their direc̄cons; So that your Excellency not having assumed the Supreame power in the Nation your selfe, or p'tended any title unto it, I shall hope to seeme pardonable to you if I doe scruple how I can bee authorized to receive my share of it from you.⁹⁰

The charge is heavy with sarcasm but, within it, Marten was combining questions about the use of force and the heroic Cromwellian image, the role of conquest, the people's right to exercise the franchise, the impossibility that a delegative authority could create something with greater power than itself, and the two giants of political philosophy on whom the English political nation relied for example and exemplar.

If Marten was placed on a continuum that balanced Hobbes against Machiavelli, he would edge towards the latter, for the gravest error committed by the Long Parliament had been eventually to settle sovereignty over three nations into one pair of hands, by which they 'manifested to the World that they understood nothing of a Com̄onwealth but the name'.⁹¹ However, he was not unaware of the difficulties inherent in Machiavellianism and the problems associated with maintaining the security of the people whilst protecting their liberties. It was a problem that had always been implicit in the maxim *Salus populi, suprema lex*. His French version of an agreement of the people for the Bordeaux Frondeurs acknowledged the predicament. The maxim of good government was to maintain 'la libertie dans l'obeissance'.⁹²

A government founded on the twin pillars of force and unrepresentativeness, being unaccountable to the people, would never produce the stability that would safeguard the people's liberty. The founder of Marten's state was neither Hobbes' nor Machiavelli's. Hobbes' *Leviathan* described a polity founded on the principle that a free people in the state of nature chose to abandon their freedom in exchange for leadership and protection. Once contracted, the authority could not be reassumed. This was the antithesis of Marten's state. Here, the freedom of the people was guaranteed because it was perpetual: they could never create a ruling body more powerful than themselves. This was not the Machiavellian notion of constant rotation or fluidity, however, which logically, was syllogistic nonsense. For Marten, the people's security was guaranteed by the indefinite perpetuation of their sovereignty through frequent and regular meetings of their representatives in parliament and their continual recourse to the franchise. In contradistinction to Machiavelli, the perpetual movement in the system was provided only by recourse to election and by regular changes of personnel within the representative. It was not the result of fatalistic cycles of the natural rise and fall of governments, nor of the princely exercise of the virtues, which by demonstrating leadership qualities could rescue a decaying body politic. Cromwell was neither Leviathan nor Borgia, not even Savonarola, but an undisguised usurper, who would have to suppress the will of the people by the might of the sword:

> every new change introduces a necessity of force to support it, and much more eminently in this Case then in any other for in all other differences the quarrell is between faccons and partyes, so that if yᵉ conquering power bee but furnished with a strength to keep under the adverse party it is sufficient, But those whom these men are to keep under, whose right and place they must unjustly deteyne from them, are yᵉ whole people of Engˡ; they are not Cavalliers or Presbiterians who are to bee looked upon as their antagonists, but mankind, agᵗ whom they must naturally have the same hate and jealousy as an Usurper hath towards a lawfull Prince.[93]

The Rump had made a start on a 'prudent constitucon', by which Marten meant a form of agreement of the people. This would replace inadequate foundations based on statute and custom, both of which were the product of *ad hoc* constructs dictated by circumstances. Marten disapproved of the post-coup rationalisation of a philosophy, provided by the classical republicans, and demonstrated why with a homely illustration. A constitution that was built 'by necessity rather then wisdome [justice] [with] the subtilty of mens minds dayly inventing new crimes and evasions' would be a house of ill-fitting, poorly matching stones, with as many different masons as there were interest groups. Even the wisdom of Solon and Lycurgus[94] had found that the 'humour of the people' would seek to alter any 'frame of lawes cast in a mould'.[95] Marten's vision of republic was inclusive and universalist, because man was not a hierarchical creature. On the contrary, everyone 'by nature [was] . . . equally holy, & high-minded'.[96] Marten's ideals, however, could not meet the practicalities of the 1650s, and he encountered the same difficulties that his model, Solon, had found in ancient Athens. There was a real difficulty in balancing the liberty of the people, especially within an inclusive republican framework, because security required that while some individuals lacked a sense of commitment to the new absolute values of government, they had to be excluded. The governmental ethos came to destroy itself. It could not be inclusive because so many refused to be included.

Marten's writings at this time are reminiscent of the most famous tyrannicidal tract, *Killing noe Murder*. There has been considerable debate about its authorship, but it is believed to have been written by Marten's friend, Edward Sexby. Marten's concerns and style can be found in the preface, an art in which Marten excelled. The author expressed bitterness at his enforced leisure. There was false concern for 'His Highness's' welfare and mocking tone at the nature of Roman triumph:

> How I have spent some hours of the leisure your Highness has been pleased to give me, this following paper will give your Highness an account. How you will please to interpret it I cannot tell; but I can with confidence say my intention in it is to procure your Highness that justice nobody yet does you, . . . To your Highness justly belongs the honour of dying for the people; and it cannot but be unspeakable consolation to you in the last moments of your life to consider with how much benefit to the world you are like to leave it.[97]

In the main body of the piece, the definitions of a tyrant – either one who had no right to govern or one who governed by oppression – were provided by the civil law.[98] Justifiable paternalistic rule appeared, sanctioned by the laws of Solon, a hero to Marten because he tried to frame just laws of government, but was always doomed because it was ultimately a counterproductive exercise. The notion of delegatable power was repeated: several families form a commonwealth, each family unit being equal and autonomous, and 'nothing can introduce amongst them a disparity of rule and subjection but some power that is over them; which power none can pretend to have but God and themselves'.[99] *Killing noe Murder* outlined list of questions that the people should demand of their new leader. It was reminiscent of Marten's bitter mock eulogy for Cromwell: 'Who made thee a prince and a judge over us? If God made thee, make it manifest to us. If the people, where did we meet to do it? Who took our subscriptions? To whom deputed we our authority? And when and where did those deputies make the choice?'[100] *Killing noe Murder* praised the native desire for freedom exhibited by English people and lauded the attempt on Cromwell's life by the quarter-master, Miles Sindercombe. Sindercombe was sponsored by Wildman and Sexby. Despite Marten's period of enforced leisure, he may well have had a hand in a huge document drawn up by two of his longest-standing friends and allies.[101] *Killing noe Murder* was undoubtedly a composite effort. It included a broad sweep of justifying sources: Plato and Aristotle, Augustine, Solon, the Bible, Machiavelli and natural law.

Marten's semi-confinement in the Rules of Southwark during 1655–7 depressed him. He was an 'idle person', although he kept abreast of political developments. He began two contributions to the debate on sovereignty, which display him at his most maddening. James Harrington had completed his maxims of republicanism, *Oceana*. Marten got no further than a draft of the opening page of a response to one of Harrington's critics. He managed little more of a reply to Thomas White's *Grounds of Obedience and*

Government, published in 1655.[102] He did, however, make a statement that made more explicit his belief in unicameral government and the dualistic balance between represented and representatives. He combined this with a Grotian interpretation of the relationship between the atomistic, autonomous possessor of rights and the state which emerges organically from individuals' collective delegation of power. Marten believed that White had missed the point. The point was that government meant the legislature, 'made up of these 2 Correlatives ye persons governing & Governed'. The people must be an integral part of the state, not a body of atoms controlled by a state superstructure, for otherwise one must always oppress the other: 'though o[u]r Author (White) see it onely for ye Domineering part thereof, & therefore treats of its correspondent Obedience (which might perhaps have bene called Subiection or Subdition)'.[103]

Marten started a response to White's 'first discourse touching Perfection of Governm[en]t' and, in doing so, touched on issues that might indicate where his opinions differed from Harrington. He admitted himself on the same side of an argument as Harrington, though his voice no longer carried any weight. Marten's 'doctrine may be erroneous, [but] cannot be dangerous, 'tis so unlikely to be followed'. 'A commonwealth' according to *Oceana*, 'is but a civil society of men'. Harrington's commonwealth, however, possessed an elitist interpretation of authority. Harrington's belief that the wisest rose to authority through natural selection because there was a basic inequality among the individuals within civil society did not sit so easily with Marten's ideas of an equality of rights.

> Twenty men [Harrington alleged] . . . can never come so together, but there will be such difference in them that about a third will be wiser . . . than all the rest. These . . . will be Discovered and (as stags that have the largest heads) lead the herd; for while the six, discoursing and arguing one with another, show the eminence of their parts, the fourteen discover things that they never thought on, or are cleared of divers truths which had formerly perplexed them; wherefore in matter of common concernment, difficulty or danger, they hang upon their lips as children upon their fathers . . . Wherefore this can be no other than a natural aristocracy diffused by God throughout the whole body of mankind . . .[104]

Marten was not convinced that this was human nature. In his eyes, every person was equally confused. He was aware that in times of crisis, people had a tendency to look to a leader without stopping to question how they might be sacrificing their own freedoms.[105] Anything that admitted a hierarchy among people, either natural or conceit, was to inculcate, by stealth and soft words, the domination of one over another. Thus, both Harrington's and White's model insinuated kingship by the back door, resorting to the 'K[ing] of hearts' rather than the 'K[ing] of clubbs'.

The Roman Poet [he continued] that fetched ye world from its cradle like Moses & (as some think) by reading Moses, could observe that man was a holyer creature, & capable of a high[er] thought then ye rest & therefore fitt dominari in caterva not in seiunctim over his own kinde, every one of whom is by nature (if un-interrupted) equally holy, & high-minded.

For all that I must crave leave to think, that ye most understanding among beasts & birds are most materable by man when they find their concernm^t wrapped up in it. & so are men by each other pro suo.

My Author [White] beginnes w^t ye honestest piece that belongs King-craft. wishing every governour to take up his advice upon ye Heads of his subiects. & grounds this advice upon ye sure foot of Nature.[106]

If one's premise posited a hierarchy of mankind in nature, one was providing hostages to fortune for those who sought to recreate a 'natural' hierachy in the state. Marten's approach – that all people were equally wise or foolish, holy or sinful – was a secularised version of the sectarian notion of the equality of the spirit before God. Such individuals could not say anything of illumination about God, for all people were equally perplexed as to God's nature. Neither could any individual or cabal lay claim to impose a government for the common good, if those who made up the commons were not at its core, for it was not in the nature of rulers to be any wiser than those they ruled. In God's service there was 'perfect freedome'.[107]

IV
Opinions on God

Henry Marten was accused of atheism, a charge that was easily sprayed across seventeenth-century Europe. Although cheapened by the frequency with which it was used to discredit thinkers and polemicists, the jibe could also induce fear. Scholars have had difficulty identifying atheism because it was invariably defined by believers. Nigel Smith has attempted to add to our definitions of radicalism by trying to disentangle the confusions and obfuscations that writings on religious doubt often deliberately retained. David Berman seeks to circumvent the problem that atheism was defined by the pious by drawing a distinction between the repression and suppression of (counter) beliefs.[1] Concerned with attempts to counter atheism, on the grounds that it must have existed for authority to want to stamp it out, Berman concentrates on the period after the 1697 act 'for the effectual suppressing of blasphemy and profaneness'. However, there had been earlier attempts, mentioning atheism, to define what constituted acceptable belief.[2]

Was Marten an Atheist?

In the light of critical reassessments of unbelief in the seventeenth century, where should Henry Marten's clearest, and many would say only, statement about God be placed?

> Of God
>   With good reason do I give it y[e] first place in my opinions because what ever hath bene said by any yet conceiving him, is but of opinion.[3]

Ancient moral philosophy consisted of a dualistic epistemology; belief was either knowledge or opinion, the latter having a transient and imperfect quality. Philosophers of the seventeenth century struggled to escape this two-fold categorisation, to replace it with something more subtle and responsive, but whatever categorisations were devised, the notion of opinion was hard to shift. Opinion described the most problematic and vague form of knowledge. The most concrete form of truth – absolute truth – was the knowledge possessed by God, followed by types of man-centred scientific knowledge in descending degrees of certainty. Usually, religious belief was within the category of least certain but was, nevertheless, higher than opinion. Even base opinion could possess a number of degrees. As Barbara Shapiro points out, the juxtaposition of opinion with belief, a kind of real knowledge, would have momentous consequences for philosophy, particularly the philosophy of science. For if opinion about empirical matters rested on an evidentiary base, just as did belief in God, it became difficult to relegate empirical truths to the realm of 'mere opinion' in which one man's views were as good as another's, without relegating religion to the same realm.[4]

This was Marten's contribution to religious thinking; one person's religious notions were no better nor worse than any other.[5]

Marten's statement about opinion occurs in a curious and infuriating piece, not least because this was the only substantive sentence completed in *Opinions offerd by H.M.* Even then, Marten thought better of it and scored out his epigram on God. The piece was to have been dedicated to Sir Francis Pile, baronet, lord of the manor of Compton Beauchamp, friend and neighbour of Marten, and his fellow shire MP in the Long Parliament. Not well known, Pile hardly merits the fawning dedicatory epistle that precedes this aphorism. This is all the more curious since it was written in 1648, when Marten was at the height of his power and Pile was close to death. Marten was conscious of the controversy his words would arouse. A dedicatory epistle, he declared, was like the porch of a house that sheltered beggars. Thus, in literary terms, it was where an author sought patronage and thus protection. Marten laid great store by the loyalty of his circle and in writing his opinions was giving himself 'ye happines of thinking to you'. He was in need of the shelter provided by his friends because of the 'declination of my fortunes & ye questionablenes of this discourse'. Marten intended to display his interest in questions of religion and morality, venturing an opinion in an epigrammatic style, on, in this order: god, religion, love, fear, hope, grief, anger, jealousy, honour, death, sin, stage plays and opinion itself. Opinion, he opined, was the only judgement and measure of all things; a statement of the profound scepticism of Marten's epistemology.[6]

If we pursue a modernistic and absolute definition of an atheist, as 'someone who denies God in any of the senses that current uses of the term allow', Marten was not one.[7] He did not deny the existence of a deity, but questioned whether human beings had the ability to construct its definition. This sentence identifies Marten as a profound sceptic. This, however, merely takes us back to the point at which scholars attempt to distinguish what contemporaries called atheism from what was, in fact, deism, mortalism, corporealism or any number of ways, many obscurantist, in which questioning people sought to make sense of their world. In the context of what little of the pamphlet he finished drafting, Marten's statement might appear mundane, but it was central to the way in which thinking about religion influenced political thought and action during the interregnum. If opinion was the only judge of matters religious, ethical and spiritual, then Marten's contrary thinking – 'because what I say, is not said by every body' – was only permissible 'with liberty in yᵉ year 1648'.[8] It justified the libertinism of his own life and a statement of toleration towards the beliefs and lifestyles of others. Toleration was a catchphrase of political Independency in the 1640s but it usually implied freedom of worship hedged in by political expediency. Marten preached it in its fullest form and practised it comprehensively.[9]

Aubrey believed Marten was 'as far from a Puritane as light from darknesse'.[10] Marten's anti-puritanism was obviously manifest in his inability to live life according to a strict moral code: his lifestyle was hedonistic, more Bacchus than Bastwick. Aubrey used a similar phrase about Thomas Chaloner, who was 'as far from a Puritan as the East from the West. He was of the Naturall Religion, and of Harry Martyn's Gang, and one who loved to enjoy the pleasures of this life.' Tom May, also one of the gang, '[w]ould, when *inter pocula*, speake slightingly of the Trinity'.[11] This was a group of close friends and political allies who shared a common scepticism, most clearly manifest when it spoke from the bottom of a glass.

To these, we can add the views expressed by John Wildman during the debates on the role of the magistrate in matters of conscience, which took place at Whitehall in December 1648. Wildman reflected Marten's utter scepticism about the nature of individual religious practice: 'God hath not given a command to all Magistrates to destroy idolatry, for in consequence itt would destroy the world'.[12] A magistrate could not be trusted to make any decisions touching the conscience, given the confusion about the nature of religion and of God, and disagreements about the interpretation to be given to the word of God in Scripture. Wildman's scepticism was similar to Marten's *Opinions*. It was beyond the capacity of the human mind to conceive a form for God. It was therefore outside the capacities of man to formulate a moral code based on God's existence:

itt is nott easily determinable by the light of nature what is sin; and if the Gentleman [puritan divine, Philip Nye] speake of thinges betweene man and man, of thinges that tend to [destroy] humane society, hee is besides the Question; if concerning matters of the worshippe of God, itt is an hard thinge to determine. Itt is nott easy by the light of nature to determine there is a God. The Sunne may bee that God. The Moone may bee that God. To frame a right conception or notion of the first being, wherein all other thinges had their being, is nott by the light of nature. Indeed if a man consider there is a will of the Supreame cause, itt is an hard thinge for [him by] the light of nature to conceive how there can bee any sin committed.[13]

Hobbes was another with similar views. In the eleventh chapter of *Human Nature*, Hobbes addressed the difficulty encountered by human beings in talking about God:

And forasmuch as God Almighty is *incomprehensible*, it followeth, that we can have *no* conception or *image* of the *Deity*, and consequently, all *his attributes* signify our *inability* and defect of power to *conceive* anything concerning his nature, and not any conception of the same, excepting only this, that *there is a God*: for the effects we acknowledge naturally, do include a power of their producing, before they were produced; and that power presupposeth something existent that hath such power.[14]

Restoration bishops called for Hobbes to be burnt as a heretic, but Aubrey was convinced that he was a Christian.[15] In the context of Hobbes' modern reception as a genuine atheist, the scepticism behind Wildman's statement is striking. We still do not have sufficient evidence to call Marten and his circle atheists. However, John Gaskin provides a useful distinction between atheism and unbelief. He defines the latter in three ways. An unbeliever denies the existence of supernatural agents. As a consequence, he or she also denies the existence of divine revelation through such events as miracles. Thirdly, an unbeliever may not have a conception of personal survival after death. It is possible for an unbeliever to accept A and B but not C, or vice versa.[16] This may make their personal philosophies more shallow, in that they were only concerned with religion's impact and not its core. However, it was a telling set of beliefs in seventeenth-century England, because whilst the central issue remained reconciling authority and individual conscience, Marten and his friends had an overarching philosophy designed to ensure that the two did not meet. They made no reference to an existence after death; they were concerned only with the practical applications of ethics, morality and religion to those on earth.

Seventeenth-century theologians produced huge tomes, in comparison with which the statements by Marten and his circle do not amount to much. They are nevertheless important. They were empiricists, asking what the human mind could know, starting from the perception of the senses. In this sense, they were believers in the light of natural reason. This may have been what Aubrey referred to as 'natural religion', as opposed to religion by revelation. It must be distinguished from the more common use of natural religion to mean those who, during the latter half of the seventeenth century, searched for a rational religion based on the evidence of nature.[17] The reasoning of Marten *et al* does not presuppose the existence of God and therefore His manifestation in the natural world, but assumes the existence of the natural world and asks what can then be said, if anything, about the nature of belief. It does not necessarily deny the existence of God or a god, but the deity's form, nature or purpose are not or cannot be disclosed to man. People could not know the nature of God.

The Place for Religion

Marten held that with the nature of God so obscured and the possible interpretations of God so numerous, one should not attempt to formulate a moral code, based on the nature of that god. If everyone had a different conception of His (its?) nature, and there could be no firm foundation on which to base an ethical code, no one could know how he or she might be trangressing it. To have force, this reasoning relies on a concept of universal fallibility. All mankind trespasses and even if there were some objective concept of sin, the levelling effect of human error could make investing a minority with the task of imposing an ethical code both nonsensical and dangerous. Here again, therefore, is Marten's motif: false belief, political or religious, is illogical and therefore destructive. What is left is a supremely individualistic concept of morality and a practical, utilitarian notion of a moral society. Individualism, extreme doubt, and an awareness of one's own and others' fallibility bred tolerance towards the views of others and libertinism for oneself. No one had the right to interfere in another's pursuit of his or her moral code.

Marten agreed with Wildman that civil magistrates had no place legislating in matters of conscience. In 1646 he drafted a reply to John Lilburne's *Rash Oaths Unwarrantable*; a piece that he intended to call *Rash Censures Uncharitable*.[18] In setting up captious oaths to compromise the conscience, Lilburne accused the Commons – and in particular Marten, who chaired the committee examining the Leveller leader – of adding to the law that had been given by Christ to the visible Church. Furthermore, he asked '[w]hether there can be greater treason committed on earth, by men against Jesus Christ, then to disclaime and renounce him and his absolut Kingship? by swearing that either the Pope, or any King, Parliament, or Potentats, are the head . . . in all Speritual [*sic*] or Ecclesiasticall things'.[19]

Marten's response relied on an absolute and unbridgeable distinction between spiritual and temporal matters. It was not given to man to understand that knowledge which 'Hee' had reserved for 'a farther time' – the absolute form of knowledge, the knowledge of God, that was beyond human comprehension. Attempting to establish an issue of conscience on earth was to construct 'a castle in the aire'. Marten argued that the ways in which Lilburne believed he had been denied earthly liberties would affect his future salvation. Lilburne had maintained that a mundane, visible Church had been established by the Gospel. Marten countered him. In order to be of spiritual importance it could remain visible only to God. If it became visible in a worldly sense, it would instantly come under the jurisdiction of the earthly law:

The spirituall House, citty, or Church of Christ on earth needes not demurre to ye iurisdiction of all ye Kings, Parlts, & magistrates in ye world. for it is out of their reach. Neither do I remember that ever I read or heard of any civill magistrate that troubled himself w^t making lawes for ye soule spirit or inward man, . . . when your church grows visible once, it is tangible too, & comes within ye purliewes of ye secular conusance.

Marten denied that the Commons sought to add or subtract anything from Christ's law to the visible Church. Marten denied the Church's visibility but could also claim to expound better scripture than Lilburne. Christ himself had assumed human form 'rather to fulfill & expound ye old Law then to make a new'.[20]

The sort of toleration and religious independence offered by Marten was a long way from the more mainstream Independency to which Cromwell and Ireton adhered, as the exchanges between Wildman and the grandees at Whitehall hinted. Ireton's functionalist belief in toleration disguised a profound desire for the civil authorities to lay down strict rules about religious and moral conduct, in order to restrain sin and foster godliness. Marten's position – that of profound scepticism about the nature of religion and spirituality itself – freed individuals to find their own path, unfettered and untroubled by the law. Marten's views were in the minority, but represent an important other strand of thought about religion: his views on man and nature had implications for both political and religious thinking. Others could dispute theology, but they were only erecting dogmatic castles in the air. It is therefore more important to an understanding of Marten that one studies the practical implication of his religious views – toleration. It is better documented than his musings on the nature of God, sin or eternity because that was what was important to him.

Henry Marten's father, Sir Henry, was a member of the Court of High Commission, and attacked as one who had implemented the policy of Laudian orthodoxy.[21] His judgements against schismatics and those who abused their canonical office were among the harshest of any of the Commission, including Sir John Lambe and William Laud himself.[22] Sir Henry Marten was concerned with the unity and status of the Anglican communion in law. Nevertheless, his interpretation of the Church was coloured with a broad brush-stroke. He defended the right of the majority of the congregation of St Gregory's, London, to define appropriate worship. In 1633 he clashed with Archbishop Laud over the Privy Council ruling on the position of the communion table.[23] When Laud gained control of the diocese on the death of Archbishop Abbot, Marten was removed from his position as Dean of the Court of Arches and replaced by Sir John Lambe, who had always been in competition with Sir Henry. On the latter's death, Lambe wrote to Laud asking to succeed to Marten's other offices, where he could continue 'the conformity of the Church'.[24]

Sir Henry Marten's son was therefore raised in a household in which individual religious self-determination was important: his father had come into conflict with the establishment for maintaining the principle. Sir Henry Marten was, however, relatively orthodox. There was little evidence in 1640 that his son's views on religion would be so different. During 1641 Henry Marten was chosen to sit on the committee to examine Montague, the Bishop of Norwich. It proposed that clergymen should be disabled from holding secular office; a move that was rejected. He was a member of the committee on the 'popish hierarchy', and a group that examined the punishment of members of the convocations of Canterbury and York. These responsibilities were a small proportion of the numerous committees that he attended, unrelated to ecclesiastical matters. He was added to the committee that examined the reduction in the number of committees.[25] In 1643 he supported statements made by the divine, John Saltmarsh; first in a sermon, and in two subsequent pamphlets. In *A Peace but no Pacification*, Saltmarsh opposed the terms of the Oxford peace treaty, but it was Saltmarsh's statements about monarchy that earned Marten's backing, not his religious views.[26] Marten was expelled from the House, and developed his enmity towards the Presbyterians, but his statements were always directed against their politics.

When Marten returned to parliament, early in 1646, he resumed his concern for religious toleration. In fighting for a free conscience, he was prepared to be unremitting and unbending in his hostility towards those who stood in its way. During 1646 English parliamentarians were increasingly exercised by the presence of the Scots' army in England and the Scottish Commissioners' insistence on taking part in peace negotiations. Scottish politics was dominated by Calvinists, which frightened some who had previously supported Scottish involvement in English affairs. Thomas Chaloner's speech without doors spoke out against the Scottish presence in England, not least because calvinisation was a key part of the presence on the Scots in the northern counties.[27] In what amounted to a defence of sectarianism and an attack on Presbyterianism, Marten directed his wit towards the Scottish Commissioners:

> You are justly attended with the common unhappinesse of hypocrits, which is to over act . . . you sing this song to the tune of the old Letany, *from the plots both of sectaries and malignants good Lord deliver us.*
>
> But Sir, are you sure you are no Sectary? It is much to be feared you are, ther is risen up of late a sect called the *Scotch paper sect* . . . it is not supposed you are zealously of any other sect or Religion what ever you professe, . . . for most of those that are called sectaries, are true lovers of Englands interest, and have a care to admit none but honest men into their fellowships.[28]

By 1648 Marten was more explicit, and no longer writing anonymously. The zeal of the Scots 'needs carry their care [of religion] so far from home', but English people's 'ears are by this time . . . habituated to the Doctrines you frequently sow among them;

those Doctrines so improved by your Seminaries'. He chided that the English had unfortunately not enquired into orthodox Covenant Presbyterianism before they had sworn to uphold it. The Presbyterians were entitled only to the 'quiet' profession of their religion – an important distinction between the passive spiritual pursuit and proselytising – for enquiries about the philosophical truth of a doctrine might possibly be the role of a university theology department, but were certainly not a duty of government.[29]

Marten's policy of radical non-intervention, which led to such caustic views about Scots' activity, also applied to English involvement in Ireland. Religious orthodoxy could not be beaten into a conquered people, Ireland could not be converted to Protestantism and besides, the struggle between England and Ireland was about nations, not religions.[30] There was a link between nationalism and religious toleration. Marten was careful to avoid the word 'papist', thinking better of both it and 'priest-ridden' in his reply to Lilburne. He substituted 'Prelaticall or classical'.[31] Though he was wary about ecclesiastical categorisation, however, he was capable of resorting to the traditional language of abuse when it served his turn. He had likened the Scottish calvinists to those trained in a seminary and accused Lilburne of the sort of queries 'a Romish Bigot would do to his ghostly father when hee is upon ye stroke of going to ye Eucharist or to Purgatory'.[32] Anti-catholicism was utilitarian when it mocked religious ritual. Nevertheless, in 1648 he spoke in favour of toleration for Catholics. He was cowed from pressing it to a vote by the sheer weight of opinion against him.[33]

Religion: the Local Background

Marten carried his policy of radical non-intervention in religion into his daily life. On the estates that he controlled, he practised what he preached. On 20 February 1645 the new minister to arrive at Inglesham was orthodox Presbyterian Robert Babb.[34] During 1648 Babb was a signatory of the *Concurrent Testimony*, in which the Presbyterian ministers of Wiltshire bore witness to their brand of Protestantism. They followed the London brethren, who had testified in support of the Westminster Assembly. He was still the minister at Inglesham in 1654, despite holding religious views that Marten had argued were politically dangerous.[35] In 1648 the Anglican parish church of St Andrew at Shrivenham boasted an orthodox minister, Hugh Pugh, whose patron remained Charles I.

The minister at Buckland in 1651 was Benjamin Way, who seems to have steered clear of controversy.[36] The same could not be said of Samuel Fell, inducted into the parish of Longworth in 1620.[37] Longworth was a considerable living. A terrier of 1634 recorded a parsonage, two sizable barns, stables, pigeon house, glebe pasture, the land at Harrowdown Hill (70 acres), a tithe of corn and hay, and another of corn. There was a further barn at Charney. The terrier was witnessed by the Longworth churchwardens, John Couldrey and William Harbard, and those of Charney, John Moulden and Richard

Cox. The former of each pair were unable to sign their names.[38] Samuel Fell was not as famous as his son, John, born in Longworth in 1625, later to be immortalised in verse by Tom Brown, the Dean of Christ Church. Samuel, however, had journeyed from Calvinism to unswerving support for Laud. Sequestred for delinquency, he was given a choice of which living he would wish to keep. John Donne of Hartfield in Sussex counselled Fell that Marten offered some protection.[39] Mary Ward having been recently safely delivered of a child, it was considered a good time to press Donne's case, before the possible abolition of tithes deprived him of anything to lose.[40] Fell was both a political as well as theological enemy of Marten. He was an active royalist and the vice-chancellor of Oxford University, imprisoned by the parliamentarians in 1647 for his refusal to appear before their visitation. He was said to have died two days after Charles Stuart, shocked by the news of the King's execution. The living seems to have remained empty during the 1650s: Peter Ingram was presented to it in 1662.[41]

At the same time as Fell was nominally in charge of Longworth, the village also boasted a baptist cell.[42] A certain amount of academic endeavour has been expended in trying to assess the degree of independence of the Longworth church in the 1640s and 1650s. Stanley has concluded that it was more important that it separated without animosity from its mother church in Abingdon and retained friendly links.[43] John Moulden travelled in the counter-direction to Samuel Fell. He was a churchwarden in 1620, but was ejected from the congregation of Baptists in Longworth in 1658 for neglecting the church.[44]

The centre of Marten's parliamentary power, Abingdon, was known for radical sectarianism. As a centre of the Medieval wool trade, it had a reputation for Lollardy. At the Restoration, when officials surveyed the state of national Church, Abingdon was described as possessing 'sundry meetings' at which were 'Parliamentary Army men' and 'old Rump rebells'. It was here that Marten was declared elected for both the Short and Long Parliaments and in 1641 a crowd of 2,000 townspeople gathered at the Market Cross to sing Psalm 106 on hearing the news that Charles had yielded to the demands of the Scots.[45] Once Abingdon was firmly under parliamentary control in 1644, repulsing the attempts of Prince Rupert to take it for the royalists the following year, the town became a refuge for those whose religious views or political standpoint put them out of favour with the establishment. This was where John Lilburne surrendered his lieutenant-colonelcy and the centre of the army mutiny of 1647.[46]

When Colonel Thomas Rainsborough arrived in Abingdon, trying to gain control of his mutinying soldiers, he managed to keep order and they stayed at the garrison. Since 1643 the church of St Helen, Abingdon, had been under the control of its lecturer, the Oxford-educated Cornishman, John Pendarves. Pendarves became chaplain to Rainsborough's regiment.[47] He held the winter lectureship in Abingdon; the summer lectureship he held at Marcham. In 1648 the will of Richard Wrigglesworth, citizen fishmonger and native of Marcham, secured his position for the next eight years, until his death in 1656. The Abingdon baptists, including Pendarves himself, were predestinarian; the only general baptist congregation in the area was at Newbury.[48]

There is scant evidence for the religious views of Pendarves during the 1640s. He became more famous in the following decade, so much so that John Cox had printed one of his last sermons before his death and dedicated to the congregants at Abingdon, who would be so bereft without his guiding spirit. The sermon, published as *The fear of God: what it is and exhorted to*, was hardly likely to endear Pendarves to Marten. Pendarves counselled his flock – at this date Longworth was still joined with Abingdon – that they could recognise the Beast from the qualities it lacked. The godly were recognisable by their great light, purity, and acknowledgement of Christ as the king of saints. The ungodly were 'of a loose and wanton conversation'.[49] It may have been the death of Pendarves that finally caused the full separation of the baptist congregations at Abingdon and Longworth. 'Att a meeting of the Churches of Longworth', it was noted, 'with several messengers from the Churches at Abingdon, Wantage and Oxford at Barcourt [Barcot on the Marten estate] the 27th day of ye 9th month, 1657, it was agreed unanimously . . . that those Members in and neare Faringdon doe stand upp as a distinct Church'.[50]

The dedicatory epistle to Pendarves' funeral sermon was written by William Hughes, the minister of Hinton Waldrist, the neighbouring village to Longworth. Hughes preached the assize sermon at Abingdon at midsummer 1651. We do not know whether his patron, Marten, was present to hear it and, when it was printed, Hughes may have inserted fresh material of which Marten might have disapproved. Hughes dedicated his pamphlet to Cromwell, then approaching the zenith of his military reputation and, for Hughes, an embodiment of godliness and nobility. Hughes believed in a godly, moral magistracy, whilst his patron, Marten, made an absolute division of the civil and spiritual spheres. Hughes' language was Martenesque. Alarmed that the injustice of the pre-war period had given way to disobedience under the Commonwealth, he declared 'I'de gladly be a Leveller to make them equal'.[51] There were references to the old arguments against monarchy, for the 'court paracites' had not learnt the lesson of I Samuel 8. It was the Israelites' rejection of God that provoked Him to bestow on them a king. Further, 'if *Monarchie* must be mens darling, or their *Idol* . . . I would beseech them . . . to consider its founder, *Nimrod* . . . the event doth almost prove it natural, for *Monarchy* to degenerate into *Tyranny*'. People insisted on kings, he believed, because they had never tasted the sweet fruit of freedom.[52] There was also a reference to the oppression of the Scots in 1648, who sought to impose the strict formality of their rules on the English.

Hughes also made an absolute division between civil and religious affairs. At the assizes, the jurors would deal with civil affairs, whereas the 'pastor' would look after the soul.[53] It was the role of the magistrate to protect virtue and punish vice, the magistrate would also protect 'the Gospel, and professors of it; that under them we may lead a quiet and peaceable life, in all godlinesse and honesty'.[54] The flock must revere magistrates, and not disrespect them because they were of socially inferior birth. Cromwell was to be admired for his nobility of bearing, not his breeding. Marten was keen to see magistrates' financial commitment to the war rewarded and Hughes warned that the civil magistrate was due respect for 'the work they do . . . It is meet they should *expend* their time, *exhaust* their *estates*, and *expose* their *persons* for our Common interest.'[55]

Magistrates should be esteemed because they had cut down monarchy. They may then have followed some strange paths, but they were not necessarily the wrong ones. Although 'there was some *transgression* in attaining; wilt thou *transgresse* too in resisting?' Nevertheless, governments, ordained by God, could be changed if the circumstances were just. Hughes was a *de factoist*, mixing, rather uneasily, republican rhetoric within the guise of Christian duty, loyalty to the de facto powers and the possibility of change. He was preaching an assize sermon to men who would execute the terrestrial law, and he exhorted people to obey the government of which Marten was a part, whilst maintaining in his preface, 'Reader, three of the famous *Monarchies of the world* are down, the misallary[?] *fourth*, sure, is setting: marke way, the *fifth*, the *last*, the *everlasting* one, may *rise* upon us'. Hughes advocated a more inclusive brand of religious toleration than Pendarves. There must be toleration for those who exercised God's worship as it was prescribed by God, but no constraints on the others. Although a godly ministry should be supported, there should be no censure on those who could not walk down the same road.[56]

Hughes was sufficiently conformist to be appointed to a Berkshire Commission in 1654 and was outraged two years later when a rising against Cromwell was planned in Abingdon. From his rectory at Hinton he penned *Munster and Abingdon, or the Open Rebellion there*.[57] The rebels were spurred on by a speech by Longworth mercer John Jones, 'an ancient grave Christian'. In fact, there was little evidence of an anti-Cromwellian republican/royalist plot, either in Abingdon or on the downs at Wantage, despite the arrest of Lady Mary Howard, daughter of the Earl of Berkshire.[58] Hughes lost his Hinton living at the Restoration and retired to Abingdon. He later licensed himself as a teacher in Clapham and was to conform to the established Church, earning the chaplaincy of St Thomas's hospital in Southwark in 1677.[59]

There is insufficient evidence to cement the link between Marten and radical sectarianism in the Abingdon area.[60] The numbers of religiously motivated radicals may have been a bulwark of his political support. The existence of sectaries in large numbers may have pushed him into a more radical stance. Marten at the height of his political power could hold out to the heterodox a degree of protection greater than the level of toleration offered by the Commonwealth. To a lesser extent, the same was true under the Protectorate, although his power was on the wane. Certainly, after the Restoration, the speed with which the government acted to restore religious orthodoxy, deprive the Martens of their landed power and imprison their patriarch, was impressive. When repairs to the parish church at Longworth, about to be taken over by the Anglican Peter Ingram, were planned, the list of parishioners liable for a tax was comprehensive and took no account of religious affiliation. Henry's unmarried daughter, Anne, was taxed on one and a quarter yard lands. Also named was John Moulden, John Jones, the ancient grave Christian who had incited rebellion, and a member of the Baptists of the Longworth congregation, yeoman Nicolas Mayon. In 1662 Mayon took his turn as churchwarden.[61]

Marten was neither pushed into a political stance on religious issues by the presence of so many religious radicals in Berkshire, nor was he the magnet that drew them to the area. Nevertheless, the numbers of sectarians probably helped him, providing a localised power-base more robust than Westminster. Marten attached the same criteria to the practice of religion by sectaries such as Pendarves and Hughes as he did to more orthodox ministers such as Fell and Babb – religion and civil politics were two entirely separate realms and he would not interfere with theirs if they did not interfere with his. However, as his experience as lord of the manor in other parts of the country was to demonstrate, membership of the gathered churches did not necessarily guarantee sympathetic congregations.[62] Neither did Marten exhibit any support for the theological views of the gathered churches. The views of Pendarves were alien to him, though he had liberty to preach and several of Marten's tenants were uplifted by his words. Hughes was in favour of the more widespread toleration advocated by Marten, but not for the same reasons, and his support of the 'establishment', irrespective of its colour, did not sit easily with Marten's unshakable principles, especially when Hughes so openly praised the Protectorate. There is no evidence that Marten supported the coups planned against Cromwell, but it is likely that he did so. Many of his associates, such as John Wildman, were involved, and Berkshire was considered a centre of anti-Cromwellian activity.[63]

Practically, it was not always possible for Marten to retain a strict separation of the spiritual and civil spheres. He came into conflict with the sectaries over tithes. Terriers made in 1634 showed the Martens were entitled to the tithes of Shrivenham, Bourton, Watchfield, Longcot and Fernham, as well as other tithes and tenths payable in corn, wool and lamb, and all the tithes of Longworth. There is no evidence that either the minister of the established Church or Marten ceased to receive these tithes during the civil wars and interregnum.[64] There is no extant statement of his opposition to tithes. Nevertheless, many of his supporters within the Leveller movement and the gathered churches believed that he opposed a nationally financed ministry and had high expectations that he would petition against the 'publick faith mony' in parliament. Joanna Savile wrote in July 1652, to remind Marten of Samuel Chidley's campaigns against tithes. She chided that now only Marten stood in the way of progress.[65]

Marten had to walk a tightrope in order to exercise some form of localised control on his estates and to maximise his tenants' opportunity to choose their own kind of religious guidance. He ran into problems at Shefford, north of the Thames and the home village of his Derbyshire agent, Richard Peters. Marten had exercised some influence over the ministers preaching at Shefford and, judging from the responses of his tenants, had made some poor choices. Joseph Nixon had persuaded Marten and Alexander Popham to invite a Mr Pecke to the living, but Pecke had subsequently proven dishonest. He had been ejected from a previous living – he was an 'outed man' – though he had combined with powerful parishoners to keep his position there regardless.[66] The following year, 1652, one parishoner wrote to Marten to express his approbation for the current minister, Mr Milat, who was local, single, '[a]nd on that hath gained the Love and Good will of Every one in the parrish'.[67] Milat, helped by Nixon, was supported financially by Goodman Cox, paying £35 in the first year, taking over Mr Milat's bargain. In the following years, he would pay £50 a year in lieu of fifths. Nixon, who 'Nither desyer truth nor peace', disputed the arrangement. In September an application was made by another potential minister, Henry Hull, who could muster many testimonials on his behalf, including 'Dr Barnard preacher at Grayes Inne one that is knowne to [and] favoured by my Lord General his Excellency'. He had been approved by 'a good part of the parish' but was not receiving much income from tithes and asked for Marten's financial support.[68]

In 1650 John Goldsmith of Highworth applied, with some insistence, to be the minister at Fernham, 5 miles to the east. A letter to Goldsmith, by a 'loving friend', insisted on the strict separation of political and religious affiliation. Goldsmith's loyalty to Marten's political cause would not help him to a living if his prospective parishoners did not approve. Reminding Goldsmith that the key of the church was rightfully in the churchwardens' hands and not his, the letter continued,

I have applied my selfe to Mr Martin in the busines And he is far from in forcing a minister upon us wthout the Maior pte of or concents wch you are soe far from gayninge that you cañot I beelieve have the approbation of any one man of worth or honesty eyther in ffernham or longcott [the neighbouring parish which formed part of the same congregation] yet you have promised it and it is expected from you; for yr affection to ye parliamt none shall doubte it And for such rumours as I have heard of you I take little notice of them; Only I must lett you know I would not willingly ([and] the whole p[ar]ish is of the same minde) loose that liberty the parliamt hath gieven us in chusinge or owne Minister.[69]

Goldsmith was advised to content himself with his current post or to look elsewhere.

Not all of the sectaries had such a liberal approach to toleration as Marten. Pendarves openly opposed the Quakers in print.[70] Quakers were hostile to the Ranters. Marten drafted a reply to one attack made on the Quakers, which he called *Justice Would-bee*. Quakers, he said, were 'harmles people'. Marten was one 'who knows as litle of them' as the so-called Ranter who felt so free to vilify them.[71] The 'Ranter' claimed to have been present at a Quaker gathering in the Bull and Mouth tavern in Aldersgate, well known as a meeting place, 'but yor manner of talk . . . makes an ordinary reader very iealous that either you never saw Aldersgate in your life, or els you were there when no body els was'. It is not clear to which pamphlet Marten was responding. It may have been *The Quaking Mountebanck, or the Jesuite turn'd Quaker*, by Daniel Lupton, published in 1655. More likely was William Prynne's *A new discovery of some Romish Emissaries, Quakers*. Marten's continued reference to ranting make it probable that whilst he may have engaged with the fervent disagreements within the sectarians' ranks, his old adversary, Prynne, ranted as much as any.[72]

Toleration

Justice Would-bee is not much concerned with the doctrines of the Quakers; more with attacking someone intent on castigating people for faults that were part of the universal and generally fallible state of humankind. Always alive to the necessity to accumulate evidence from the senses, Marten charged the author with inventing groundless theories about the Quakers. He dismissed as plainly ludicrous the charge that the Quakers were like Jesuits. This allowed him to play and pun on the word throughout: it was the ranting author who was jesuitical.[73] According to Marten, the Quakers were a long way from earning censure because they 'embrace[d] poverty, humility . . . mean habit, short & cource fare, hard lodgeing, which makes them refrain from acquaintance, quitt their neades & decline all things of profitt or pleasure which ye rest of ye world runnes after'.[74] They claimed to value both light and liberty, but 'neither do I know any man that hath an ey in his head & a heart in his body but in a Quaker, if his prizeing those 2 things make him one'. Accusing the Quakers of uncleanliness, presumption, dissimulation, envy, uncharitableness, ignorance and gestures was a disguise, because these vices were more conspicuous in the Ranter.

Marten's pamphlet did not go to the press but, unlike most of his other attempts, *Justice Would-bee* is a full draft, not abandoned when more pressing business emerged or when the putative author became bored with his latest project. It was probably not the finished draft: it is covered in changes, insertions and corrections, and is, in essence, a slight piece. Two things worthy of record slipped from his pen. He was about to discourse on the supposed profanity of Quakers' relations between man and man. His theme was to have been respect – described as honouring parents, the sabbath, the sacraments, and marriage. He then thought better of taking part in the debate between adult and paedobaptism. Another line indicates that he not only fought shy of theological debate, but held it risible: 'As for clayming immediately from God', as the author of the attack had suggested, 'doth not every priest of every religion, & every prince of every reign do yᵉ same? Why [it is][75] commonly done now that it ceaseth to be policy, it cousins nobody.' This was a blow against the divine right of kings, episcopacy, all forms of spiritual prophesying, ministry, and on any civil power that claimed its authority by offering an interpretation of the will of God.

Marten tolerated total religious freedom of expression because he believed that religion, a relationship with God and the notion of spirit, were entirely personal. A discussion of his own morality is therefore valid. Royalist journalists, pamphleteers and gossip-mongers created a lasting image of a drunken, lascivious and promiscuous buffoon. They believed he was totally amoral, that he lacked any sense of a private morality because he had no faith, conscience or belief in damnation. Marten had undoubtedly broken the eternal moral law, encapsulated in the Ten Commandments, particularly the third injunction of the second table; Marten's adultery with Mary Ward was shameless, publicly displayed at the centre of the Commonwealth government.

Among the Marten manuscripts are copies of the last two folios of a tract on polygamy, written towards the end of the 1650s. This appears to be a copy of the 1657(8) translation of Ochino's *Seven Dialogues*.[76] It is part of what was originally a thirty-four page pamphlet, in the form of a dialogue between the traditionalist voice of reason, O, and a potential supporter of multiple marriage, T. The author sometimes gets confused and transposes the letters. The O-figure described himself as 'regenerate [and] spirituall' and a 'Gospeller'.[77] He was, however, aware of the frailties of the human condition, and when presented with T, who found the single or constant life difficult to sustain, he counselled prayer to strengthen his resolve.

The putative Marten figure, T, made several points of potential scandal. He posited that there was a characteristic within man that was outside and beyond that which God could influence through the conscience. Humankind possessed a 'natural' core, known only to him or herself, and there was no basic common characteristic by which this inner person was manifest. Hence some men were naturally drawn to a celibate life, whilst others were drawn to the constancy of one partner. Others were 'by nature' not suited for either the single or the constant life. T returned to and then adapted the classical, stoical definition of the law of nature.[78] Within this framework, prayer was rendered useless: '[i]f any one were called by God to marriage, [and] had not the gift of living a single life, he should in vain pray to God . . . he would never obtain it.' T then denied the force of conventional morality and its link with God, since God may stir men up to do things that were against the law. T asked the reader to invert the argument, so that God called men to take 'sundry wives' and polygamy was not unlawful. The reader would then have no difficulty in believing that the fundamental nature of a person overrode normal morality. If God appealed to the fundamental, and marriage was an institution to be applauded, it was pharisaical to deny mankind the right to practise this glorious institution as many times as the conscience called: 'And what is more foolish then under a spurious pretence of holinesse to shun holy marriage as a profane thing, although both God hath instituted it, [and] nature doth dictate it, [and] reasō[n] perswade it, [and] Christ confirm it, [and] the sacred [and] profane nations approve it, [and] the examples of good men invite us to it?'[79] T was fundamentally redefining the nature of marriage. '[W]hat is more barbarous [and] inhumane', asked T,

> then to abhorre marriage nature inbred in us? what is more ungratefull then not to procreate children as we were procreated by o[u]r parents? Truly they seem to me to kill so many men, as would have sprung frō them, if they had bin unmarryed, unlesse they be invited to a single life by God. It hath some similitude [and] appearance of murder not only to procure abortiō & barrennesse with medicines, but also without just cause to eschew marriage.

If God had ordained marriage to celebrate a union between men and women, the more moral position would be to legitimise all children and bring them up in a virtuous environment. Current morés relegated inconstancy towards one's wife to private, underhand liaisons, producing the more immoral outcome of unrecognised or terminated pregnancies. The pamphlet ended tamely, frightened by the direction of its own logic, and T was left to pray his hardest that God saw fit to bestow the gift of constancy. In reality, this was not to happen for Marten, and he was left to justify an adulterous relationship, which to him was a second marriage, to an appalled and scandalised public.

With regard to other traditional Christian values, Marten was more orthodox. In particular, he was a practitioner of the virtue of charity, in accordance with the family tradition. Sir Henry Marten had been the patron of St Giles' church in Oxford, providing the congregation with sermons.[80] As a High Commissioner he was an executor to oversee some provision for other London clergy. The curate at St Mary Somerset Brokenwharf was left with 'but small allowance though greate Chardge of wife and Children' by the death of the rector, Thomas Burton.[81] He also provided for the poor of St Botolph's parish, in Aldersgate, London, where he had his city residence. A donation of 44s. provided 12d. for each of forty-one householders.[82] The poor of Longworth benefitted by £3 6s. in 1622 and father and son acted together in providing for almshouses and church repairs at Shrivenham.[83]

Marten's uncle, William, was also a considerable benefactor of charitable projects. His will of 1632 described him as 'late of the Universitie of Oxon', leaving £20 to the town council for the 'house of correction', recently built at Northgate.[84] Three years later Sir Henry was still administering his brother's will, sending £100 to the mayor and burgesses of Reading to place orphans into apprenticeships. He advanced an installment of £100 to the corporation of Newbury, which William had contributed to paving the market place.[85] William's only bequest to an individual was a gift of £99 to the children of a clerk, Robert Boynton.[86] Although it could be argued that a will is the obvious place to express charitable desires and that William Marten was clearly a wealthy man, the use that was made of the money suggests an interest in good works and community projects.

Henry Marten inherited this community spirit, although he also applied his philanthropy towards individuals. The primary institution to benefit from Marten's wealth was a local school.[87] During the 1650s Marten redirected £5 a year from his rents in Longworth, towards the 'encouragement' of the school there, providing for a schoolmaster by the name of Henry Griffin.[88] Marten's son, also Henry, probably attended the local school.[89] There is no evidence that he was sent to the traditional family school, Winchester, nor to Westminster, where Marten was named a governor in 1649.[90] He chose not to educate his own son in the system but had him privately educated, after which he did not attend university. During 1657 the youngest Henry Marten reminded his father of his promise to send the schoolmaster's five-year-old son a coat – 'Pray lett is bee laysed, or else it will not bee healfe so pleasing'. More importantly, Marten's name would attract pupils:

I doe suppose you may healpe my Master to some Schollars by yor commendation, which will much pleasure him: for hee heath nothing but what hee doeth gitt by his teaching, except twenty pound a yeare, and that hee heath nolonger then his wife liveth, and you may give him a geaft [gift? great?] commendation, boath as fare as I know, which doe give him many thankes for his care, and panes.[91]

Individuals solicited Marten because he had earned a reputation for charity towards the poor. In the later 1650s, when his political credibility was at its lowest and his finances in a perilous condition, a tradition of concern for those lowest in society followed him into debtors' prison. Robert Vesey or Versy wrote to him from Chimney, a parish on the north bank of the Thames, to recommend John Symes to a tenancy because he was 'a sadd object of pittie' who was 'bereft of all worldly comfort'. Symes was spurred on 'by the many presidents of your goodnesse and charitie to others'. He had spent what money he had nursing his sick wife, but would be able to find some little for the tenancy, 'besydes you will by this worke of charitie, gaine immortal honour . . . [a]s it hath bine alwayes your desier to doe workes of charitie and mercy'.[92] Petitioners could tug at familiar strings, as did William Gregory, when he wrote for help in keeping together his family of seven. He had 'borowed for [his] nesecitis so long with use: that I can borow no longer'.[93] When Gregory referred to Marten 'whome here to fore hath bin the raiser of families' he was not making light of Marten's extended family of legitimate and illegitimate offspring. He plucked from obscurity poor, local people, such as his Herefordshire agent Thomas Deane, and paid for their education and social elevation. Despite his individualism, Marten was conscious of his role as mentor and patron. From the Upper Bench prison, he took issue with Cromwell over the allocation of £27,400, borrowed from the treasurers at Weavers' Hall. Poor petitioners complained that the money was to be given not to them but distributed to the soldiers to satisfy war arrears. Cromwell was thus altering a previous decision of parliament, whilst depriving handicraft men, poor widows and servants of money to 'refresh' them. Furthermore, 'the 27400^l allocated for the said poore is altogether under 10^l a peece Wh[e]reas the same 27400^l if it be disposed to Rich men who have lent great [and] large summes, as is desired, it will be swallowed upp and never p[er]ceived'.[94]

There are occasional clues in his father's library which may point to the origin of Marten's unconventional views. At Oxford he read a traditional humanist curriculum. Sir Henry's collection contained the standard texts of the well-read classical scholar: Polybius, Lucian, Homer, a volume of the Greek orators and Aristotle's *Politics* and *Ethics*. He showed an interest in history and had works highly regarded by the humanists, such as Plutarch, and more modern humanist scholarship, including Erasmus. On religion, Sir Henry read Hooker on ecclesiastical polity, Foxe's 'Book of Martyrs' and a Greek edition of the Bible.[95] Sir Henry's learning was dominated by Aristotelianism and in particular by its logical forms. His son retained his love of the language of syllogistic logic but, when analysing religious thought or concepts of God and mankind, he chose to reject it as a means to enlightenment. In abandoning Aristotelian syllogistic logic, Marten was reflecting the intellectual trends of the times. Peter Ramus in the later sixteenth century and Pierre Gassendi in the seventeenth had arrived at a logical terminology for the new age by mounting a full-scale attack on Aristotelian notions, whilst at the same time acknowledging their debt to the ancient master.[96] Marten analysed the religious thinking of others by retaining the language of logic whilst at the same time demonstrating logic's inability to find answers to the problems of moral philosophy. He reversed the form that divines used to 'prove' their case. In responding to Lilburne's attacks in *Rash Oaths Unwarrantable*, he aimed to prove Lilburne's work internally illogical; in using the Ramesian term, he would seek to 'reduce [your particular charges] into as much method as they will well endure'.[97]

'Method' was the predominant term of Marten's analysis of others' views of human nature. Lilburne's disquiet at the conscientious difficulties posed by parliament's imposition of oaths could be reduced to a number of 'if p then q' illogicalities:

> And what do wee impose on any body? ye nationall covenant, & ye negative oath. ye covenant (no darling of mine by ye way) I am more ready to defend, then you are to accuse it, for except a regiment of Cavaliering words which you putt upon it, as damnable, hellish, Divellish &c. you have no particular exception against it. I say none, because I count it as good as none, when you finde fault that it opposeth ye same oathes which you oppose your self. That is much like this, first you tell us wee make oathes which cannot be kept, & then you are angry wth us for not keeping them. Notwithstanding all which I am of opinion 1. that ye oathes wee found may [well] enough bee taken for any thing that is in them to ye contrary, 2. or for any thing done to them by the oathes wee have made, & 3. that all of them are well enough kept for ought you have said to ye contrary, & 4. that if none of them were kept, there would follow no periury for ought that you can say.[98]

Lilburne's work lacked 'order'. It had no sound logical base on which to hang examples from the Scriptures. Parables and stories should illustrate, not define:

> your obiections against swearing in generall are privative & positive. [P]rivatively, where you tell us wee have no rule in all ye new testament to ground this point upon suppose wee should tell you wee fetch it out of ye old, I hope it would serve your turn, for it is ye testament from whence you have picked out all ye posies you use . . . for ye trimming this very discourse of yours about in ye forhead.

Marten criticised the Ranter's 'method' of attacking the Quakers, employing the same analytical and rhetorical device: any assertion the author made was undermined because it lacked the experiential evidence to back it up. If the Ranter had been present in the Bull and Mouth in Aldersgate, and had experienced faults that the author claimed were obvious, why did he need an 'intelligencer' to find them out? The Ranter asserted without evidence and posited arguments without demonstrating them: '[s]o you make as if you concluded, when you did nothing els all along, leaving ye premisses to be admitted which should enforce your conclusions.'[99] Having begun like a 'predicant with a regiment of texts', it was the Ranter, rather than the Quakers, who emerged as a Jesuit, for using religion to obscure the inadequacy of his reasoning. The fault was an Aristotelian one: first defining one's terms and then asserting them as premises. No person could have a clear enough perception about religion to be able to assert its premises as truths.[100]

Everything mankind knew about itself, God, and the arguments that men employed to discuss such issues, should be founded, according to Marten, on empirical evidence. He did not look to sensory evidence as a sign of God's existence – a better description of natural religion. Neither did he assert that the dubiousness of sense-perception argued for scepticism. Rather, Marten's mistrust of sense-perception was that the variety of sensory experience made certain deductions impossible. As Wildman had observed, if God was present in nature, how was anyone to distinguish the nature of God? Evidence of an interest in the scientific method, both old and new, was present in Sir Henry's library.[101] Although Aristotle was there in works of science such as *Parva Naturalia* and the *Organon*, there was also Galen, Mercator, and the logician Zabarella.[102] The elder Marten had shown some interest in the activities of the Hartlib circle and was a patron of John Dury.[103]

Dury mentioned Epicurus in a letter to Marten's father. For Dury, Epicurus was merely an aphorism, but the Greek philosopher may hold some clue as to the ways in which the learning of the younger Marten had moved away from that of the previous generation. Marten toured the continent in his thirties, but had gone to France and not to Italy.[104] He was skilled in the French language and retained close contacts and affiliations with the country.[105] It is possible that he came into contact with the new wave of French intellectualism that produced Montaigne, Ramus, and Gassendi, revealing a preference for this school rather than the distinctive and distinguishable reinterpretation of the ancients favoured by Italian humanists.

The most apt description of Marten's thinking about the nature of man is Epicurean. He was even more pure in its profession that its populariser, Gassendi, who was unashamedly Epicurean but hoped to Christianise it, albeit in an unorthodox way. As happened to the thought of Epicurus himself, an Epicurean was accused of having a philosophy no deeper that a hedonistic revelry in good living, so Marten was remembered for his seeming amorality and his lack of concern with judgement or damnation. Seventeenth-century commentators were keen to draw attention to what they saw as the links between the morés of the coffee-house wits and a belief in atheistic Epicurean atomism.[106] However, Marten's Epicureanism was more profound. The importance that Epicurus placed on the bonds of friendship was evident in the way in which Marten organised his life. His circle of friends was paramount. His unorthodox views made him a focus of opposition, for which friends were both a buttress and a solace. They also provided an intellectual and political circle of allies bound together by a common thread of sociability. The ale-house and coffee-house society of republican discourse, established in Covent Garden by Marten and Wildman, pre-dated Harrington's Rota by five years. This was the porch in which political outcasts could shelter. The network of activists went beyond kinship and interest, and when Marten was frequently at odds with establishment opinion, it provided him with loyalty. This was a security that he could not expect from his parliamentary colleagues.[107]

Gassendi had argued that natural philosophy ought to give way to moral philosophy, except when the former could free mankind from errors that disturbed the tranquillity of the mind.[108] Withdrawal from the debate about religion was 'a temporary refuge from dogmatism'.[109] Richard Tuck draws attention to Marten's connection with another French thinker of the modernist tradition, Michel de Montaigne. The common features were the combination of Epicuean scepticism and stoicism.[110] Tuck cites Marten's letters from the Tower of London to Mary Ward. It was in prison that Marten was finally, if forcibly, freed from the burdens of an active life and could embrace contemplation. It is hardly surprising that these more reflective elements of Marten's thinking did not emerge until the last years of his life, when he sought inner tranquillity. An R. Bridwakes wrote to Marten 'late, very late' to enquire politely why Marten had failed to meet him as arranged in the Golden Lion, but nevertheless to recommend, in person and in writing, the work of a Mr Stowet, who '[w]hen you have leisure to breake up his seales, you will find him an honourer of yor litle great philosopher Epictetus (the Stoic) [and] you'.[111]

Marten's moral philosophy was derived from a combination of scepticism about the nature, and epistemological value, of sensory perception and a belief that sensory perception was the only measure of reality possessed by man. It was atomistic in the sense that there was a limit to the subdivisibility of matter that could be known by the human mind. He was probably materialistic, that is that natural forces could be reduced to the existence of matter.[112] His epitaph was full of irony. It revealed his religious unbelief, belief in the universality of matter and a scepticism bordering on disbelief in the afterlife and the existence of the soul. It was the piece that he had the most leisure to compose. In acrostic verse, he wondered what would be left to fly away from his mortal frame after the carrion had taken his earthly remains:

> Here or elsewhere, all's one to you, or me,
> Earth, air, or water grips my ghostless dust,
> None knows how soon to be by fire set free.
> Reader, if you an oft tried rule will trust,
> You'll gladly do and suffer what you must.
> My life was spent with serving you and you,
> And death's my pay, it seems, and welcome, too;
> Revenge destroying but itself, while I
> To birds of prey leave my old cage and fly.
> Examples preach to the eye; care then (mine says)
> Not how you end but how you spend your days.

V

The Lord of the Manor

Henry Marten inherited a huge landed empire, built up by his father to demonstrate the social position of his family. He invested in land, endowed charitable bequests and made marriages for his children: he was founding a dynasty. The Martens did not join the feudal elite, and the downward spiral of the family's affairs can be charted using the huge surviving corpus of estate literature. The responsibility for plunging the family back into obscurity lies with Henry Marten, but the sheer weight of extant material dealing with the minutiae of estate management must make us question his traditional portrait: the drunken and lazy wastrel.

Founding a Dynasty

Marten family history beyond Sir Henry is obscure; so much so that the family tree is a stunted specimen, with Sir Henry at the stock and his four children forming the only branches. Local historians have attempted to grub through the roots but they are engaging in some inspired guess-work, founded on the coincidence of surnames.[1] We know that Sir Henry's wife was called Elizabeth, the daughter of a common lawyer. We do not know which one. Sir Henry Marten amassed considerable wealth through his practice of the civil law, with which, like all those who aspired to invest England with a sense of their family's permanent legacy in order to compensate for its lack of ancestry, he acquired a sizable landed estate. On 16 February 1618 Sir Henry Marten paid £5,800 for the purchase of the home farm of the manor of Beckett, in Berkshire, from Sir William Owen of Shrewsbury and his wife, Ellen.[2] Over the following years, Sir Henry expanded his holdings in the parish of Shrivenham, of which Beckett was a hamlet. Shrivenham lay on the river Cole, close to point at which it met the Thames, thus giving the Martens a stake in some of the finest arable country in England, on a strip of greensand in the Vale of the White Horse. The home farm boasted a fine Elizabethan manor house, Beckett House, into which Sir Henry moved his family in 1620, equipping it with the furniture and brewing equipment that had been in the Owen's 'chief dwelling house'.[3]

This first purchase was relatively modest. A year later, however, Sir Henry augmented his holdings by purchasing a more profitable estate – nearby Longworth, at a cost of £9,500 – from John Fisher, a member of a prominent local family.[4] Unlike the Owens, who left Berkshire on the sale of their estate, the Fishers remained in the area. The purchase was contested by Thomas Leake, and the proximity of the Fisher family prolonged the sale of Longworth.[5] In view of Leake's prior claim, Sir Henry withheld £1,500 of the purchase price, for which Francis and Katherine Fisher were still suing in June 1624.[6]

Prior to purchase, Sir Henry engaged a surveyor. The parish of Longworth ran for 3 miles along the upper Thames: prime, though unimproved grassland.[7] The estate measured over 1,000 acres of land, of which 178 acres were arable and 727 'good pasture if it be lett lye'. Some 137 acres of the grassland was meadow, and there were small areas of coppice wood and osier beds. The surveyor listed the values that could be achieved with improvement; the best soil was in the Breach coppice, 11 acres of land 'well worth 4 nob[les per] ac[re] if the wood were of';[8] over 100 acres were mead, worth £1 12s. an acre,[9] and a further 66 acres were marshland, available for development by draining or diverting the river.[10] There was a resident fisherman and a mill, where the river had already been diverted to provide power for grinding corn and 200 acres of race.[11]

However, Longworth was sold as a place of leisure. Its attraction lay not only in the land available or in the type or degree of cultivation: the surveyor itemised a stone-built paradise for the leisured classes. Longworth was a country retreat for a gentleman of means with the opportunity to enjoy its rewards. The estate included 'a great pigeon howse, a warren of conies, fishes [and] fowles, partridge [and] hares plenty . . . It lyeth in a very pleasant country for health . . . p[ro]spect [and] pleasantnes, [and] is sittuated in the Vale of white horse . . . [and] is very pleasant for hawking, fishing [and] fowleing'.[12] There was a view that panned for 20 miles to both north and south, but no vista was quite as important as that from Harrowdown Hill, a knoll to the north of the village:

[t]here is a hie hill or mount of xii acres of ground standing in a valey wch hill hath a p[ro]spect over divers countryes. ye may uncouple your hounds into covert of furseys beneath the hill [and] a hare will come up to the top of this hill [and] roundabout this hill [and] Gent[lemen and] gentlewomen or Ladyes may walke upon the top of this hil [and] see the hare [and] the hounde in ther sight hunted. . .

So likewise ye may spring Partridge in the pastures beneath the hill [and] stand uppe the hill [and] see your hawkes fly/

You may round aboute the howse find hares [and] hunt them [and] that they will come in messages through the walle into the orchard [and] ye may walke in the walkes in the orchard [and] see the hares hunted and parteridge hawked/

There is wthin a mile of the howse 2 miles 3 miles or 4 miles divers hawking rivers [and] plenty of fowle in them in the winter time [and] very faire feilde to hawke parteridge in the summer time.

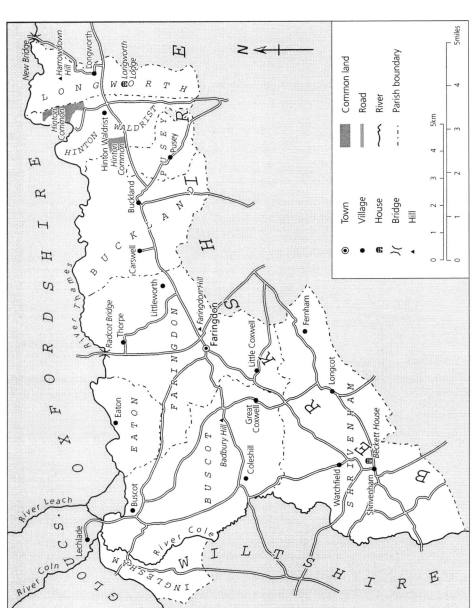

Parishes within the Berkshire extent of the Marten estates.

In his more reflective moments, Sir Henry could stroll through the ash trees that ringed the orchard, and watch the hares and partridges produce the next generation of creatures for sport. 'In the desert in the orchard at the spring time', the surveyor concluded, 'you shall have the nightingale [and] many other kind of bird bread ther [and] sing ther very pleasantly.'

The land was free of encumbrances; it had never been mortgaged and was held *in capite*. The manor came with the gift of the parsonage, at £250 a year – though later in the survey it was adjudged to be worth only £200, to be sold at five years' purchase – together with the first fruits, worth £28. The right to name the encumbent was confirmed in July 1619, when James Kidder, minister of the parish of Shipton on Cherwell, some 16 miles north-west of Longworth, renounced his interest in the rectory.[13] Longworth boasted proximity to parkland and forest – seemingly 8 miles in any direction – and race meetings a mere 5 miles away at the newly established track at Wantage, while it was close to others at Lambourn, Burford, Brackley and Ilsley. It was within easy distance of markets at Abingdon, Faringdon, Wantage, Witney, Oxford, Bampton, Woodstock, Burford and Lyworth, and although 52 miles from London 'you may bring any carriage on the river of Thames from London to this Lordship'. The overland journey was 'a very faire way'.

Longworth Lodge was not as grand in scale or demesne as Beckett House, but whereas the latter was built in the old style, close to the church and cottages of the tenants, John Fisher had built in the modern style. The house was surrounded by 7 acres of ground and 2 acres of gardens and orchards, on the track out of the village towards the main London to Bristol road. It was well away from the village and any other tenants. The only people to live close by were the immediate servants of the household, in well-appointed cottages behind the lodge. This was to be the private playground of the private man.

Sir Henry consolidated his holdings. He paid the last instalment on Longworth in May 1622[14] and began to lease the land, usually over ninety-nine years. He engrossed his lands in Longworth, increasing the acreage in 1626 with purchases from local worthy, the yeoman Tristram Stone.[15] On the whole, however, Sir Henry was a cautious and traditional farmer, concerned for the patriarchal duties encumbent on a lord of the manor. He ensured that any improvement remained under his control. Stone was not allowed to turn or till any land that had not been put to the plough at the time the lease was signed, without paying an additional sum of 40s. per acre tilled, along with half of the resultant corn. Such clauses were popular in Sir Henry's leases, particularly in the later years of the 1620s: this example is one of the least punitive.[16] The lord would benefit, as landowner, from increases in the value of what was, ultimately, his land, but such restrictive measures could have the effect of discouraging tenants from improvement, since they were less likely to see the fruits of their labour.

In 1628 Sir Henry purchased the manor of Eaton Hastings, another Thames-side parish lying between Shrivenham and Longworth, largely consisting of mead and marsh. It cost £4,000, purchased by bond with Bridget, the widow of the Earl of Berkshire, and Sir Robert Hatton.[17] These transactions also saw the first venture into the property market for Sir Henry's elder son, who purchased first Home-ground, Park-close and Ram-lease, a total of 84 acres, and, subsequently, Furze-ground, Picked-mead and Further-ground in Eaton Hastings, engrossing his father's estate to the tune of 164½ acres. When Alderman Sir Nicholas Bainton of London was adjudged to be the prior purchaser of the latter, it was agreed with Marten that he should quietly enjoy the lands. However, the penalty of £5 per acre 'broken upp', which Marten imposed on Bainton, seems restrictive.[18] Marten also farmed the tithes in Eaton, earning a return of around £90 a year in 1628.[19]

In 1618 Sir Henry established the outer boundaries of the estates, and over the next fourteen or so years, his sons patchworked the fields between them. By the 1630s, when Sir Henry was in his seventies, most of the estate transactions were jointly administered by his two sons, Henry and George.[20] The elder had the final responsibility. In 1632 Marten further augmented the holdings at Eaton, purchasing another £600 worth of land from Jane Purefoy, Lady Glover. Piecemeal, he engrossed adjacent lands, creating an L-shaped interest that ran along the Cole from Shrivenham, and then along the south bank of the Thames to Longworth. In October 1632 Marten and his seneschal, Philip Yate, were holding a court baron[21] at Hinton Waldrist, the parish immediately to the west of Longworth, and, in May 1634, Marten and his brother-in-law, Sir George Stonehouse, purchased the mead manor of Inglesham. Inglesham was almost deserted but, nevertheless, there were some villagers remaining and a small church, the advowson of which was part of the manor.[22] Land at Inglesham was potentially fertile, since it lay on a finger of land, immediately south of Lechlade, at the point at which the Thames met not only the Cole but also the Coln, as it entered the Thames from the west. It was bounded by three counties – Berkshire, Wiltshire and Gloucestershire. Though the land sold at Inglesham was primarily pasture, with some meadow, there were 30 acres reserved for the production of beans, grown as fodder. As well as sheep, the land at Inglesham was considered good for foraging pigs.[23]

On 31 August 1634 Marten composed the first of what were to be frequent and regular lists of his holdings and the profits that accrued. The sums expended in building up such an estate were not being recouped in rents. In 1635 he owed several large sums to untraceable creditors, along with £1,583 to New College, Oxford. On the other hand, some were in debt to him for similarly large sums and he was owed £400 for cattle, corn and hay from Hinton, and £100 worth of wine and £80 of hay at Beckett. He decided to omit his silver, valued at £70, and added instead the rents due on Longworth, Eaton and Inglesham – another £1,109. On the reverse, Sir Henry checked his son's accounts. To counter debts amounting to £1,074, Sir Henry could raise £1,014. It was rumoured that Sir Henry was paying £1,000 a year to finance his son's high living. In a singular but nevertheless poignant hint that Sir Henry may have been exasperated by his son's expenditure, he headed his calculations with the simple phrase '[m]y sonne oweth'. There is no evidence that these were the wages of sin. Nevertheless, on the following sheet, Marten added further debts of £4,000, principally to Sir Thomas Morgan, and to the Earls of Hertford and Carnarvon.[24]

Running the Berkshire Estate

While Marten established himself as a politician in London, the management of his estates was placed in the hands of agents and stewards. When the death of his father in 1641 left him in charge of several potentially profitable manors along the Thames, and properties in Oxford and London, it was encumbent on him to pay the rents, make charitable donations and bear all his lordly duties towards his tenantry. During his first year as lord of the manor he wielded a new broom. A barn was constructed at Hinton, his newly inherited lodge house at Longworth was graced with freshly painted gates, and the trees that banged against the kitchen window were nailed up. The clerk, Henry Taylor, was paid 2s. 6d. for digging his father's grave and Richard Panton the same sum for shovelling the earth back. Marten also paid to fill in another grave that had been left uncovered.[25]

The deepening political crisis of 1641 transformed Marten's operations as a county gentleman. He had inherited sufficient landed wealth to provide him with disproportionate political power in Westminster. Politics would also drain it away. Small sums started to flow from the account to pay composition taxes on wheat. The sum of £4 15s. was paid to local man, William Dyer, the collector of the 'royall subsidie'. An extant bill of 5s. 3d., paid at Abingdon, was just one contribution towards equipment for the militia at Reading.[26]

This was additional to pre-existing encumbrances. The rents collected in the year to Michaelmas 1642 were insufficient to cover expenses, even before the full rigours of the war made a profitable estate difficult to maintain. In June 1642 Sir Nicholas Bainton and Eaton yeomen John and Edward Cox,[27] Henry Stephens, William Butler and George Iles purchased the Eaton estate. Marten maintained it was free of encumbrances, but the party found that they had taken over considerable liabilities. An original debt of £70 to Lady Glover had grown to £700. The land was mortgaged to Marten's brother-in-law, Sir George Stonehouse, on behalf of Marten's mother-in-law, Lady Lovelace, as well as to five other individuals who claimed a ninety-nine year lease. Statutes and judgements were owing to Sir Henry Pratt, Sir John Horton, Susan

Hadnett and Roger Norton, amounting to £13,000, and there was a recognizance to the King of £5,000. Marten claimed some of these debts were invented and, in a bizarre anticipation of his trial defence eighteen years later, a debt of £1,000 was said to be owed by 'another Henry Marten [and] nott the bond[e]r'.[28]

There was little chance to recover any of these debts, and military and political commitments exasperated his attempts to tighten the management of his estates. By October 1642 his agent, John Hedges, pleaded that 'I doe intend to call for ye rents of all ye tenants [at Beckett] as fast as possible. I can feare that sum of them will be slow in p[ay]ment.'[29] George Marten, master of the *Marten*, joined the summer watch and pursued intelligence, running up costs of thousands of pounds, and, by the end of the first war, was looking to sell his stake in Beckett, Carswell and Buckland to satisfy his creditors.[30] Whilst Marten was away from Berkshire during the spring of 1648, putting together schemes to defeat the resurgence of royalist activity, his sister complained that he had not been attending to the quarter sessions, and that his business was suffering as a result.[31] By the time he was at the eye of the republican hurricane, rebuilding the national economy was only the public face of a Commonwealthsman. Reconstruction by the republicans included rescuing their own estates from impending insolvency, including the very basic concern of paying arrears of rents. Marten had rents at Eynsham, Oxford, Longworth, Beckett, Eaton Hastings, Buckland, Ashbury and Buckland unpaid since 1647.[32]

The Berkshire estate was doubly damaged by the attention it received from other sections of the military. Marten's reputation as a fiery radical left his home prey to outraged and greedy soldiers. Beckett House was ransacked by detachments of royalists as they passed by. All the wisdom of Sir Henry, who had, in peacetime, invested in prime agricultural land, was worthless in war, when his son found himself in the strategically least advantageous position. His lands lay along the Thames, with, at either end, the crossing points of Radcot bridge to the west and New bridge to the east. Along the southern boundary was the main road from London to Bristol, a well-trodden path for troop movements. Marten's neighbour, Alexander Popham of Littlecote, sent his wife to safety in Bristol along this road, and Prince Rupert was to use it as a route-march for his forces. With the fall of Bristol to the royalists in the autumn of 1643, however, supplies could be sent to the royalist troops in Oxfordshire by crossing Marten's estates. The royalists had a headquarters at Abingdon, where Sir Lewis Dyves commanded the garrison and launched detachments into the surrounding countryside.[33] Rival armies jockeyed for position to the south of Oxford and, as the forces that happened to be in control of Marten's lands negotiated the banks, dancing strategically over the river, the lord was encumbered with taxes imposed by both. During September 1643 Marten was obliged to pay for the royalist forces under the command of William Raunce and Francis Carter.[34] As the parliamentarian troops regained control of the area, he was responsible for their welfare, and Cromwell's soldiers passed by on their way to lay siege to the royalist stronghold of Faringdon. The lord bore the burden of rehousing his tenants should their homes be destroyed by the soldiers. Marten was liable for the re-establishment of his own household, as well as those of others.[35]

The obligations of a landlord in post-war England provided a stark contrast to the easy existence of wealth and leisure to which Sir Henry had laid claim. Land that once yielded high rents was laid waste by soldiers who burnt fields in their wake, tramping over arable land or requisitioning grain for themselves and their horses. It was not only the defeated royalists who suffered financial deprivation in 1649. The anguished and insistent cry of the most radical and committed parliamentarians, that they had expended vast treasures during the wars in order to secure the desired outcome, was not a hollow one. The income that men like Marten had spent in winning the settlement of 1649 had to be recouped through the land.

In this respect, Marten had few options. It might have been possible to sell some of his land, but fields wasted by war did not fetch a high enough price and the post-war market was depressed. Marten could raise his rents, evicting those who could no longer pay, but this was a harsh and self-interested response to personal tragedy. Both the year of the second civil war and the first under the Commonwealth saw poor weather conditions. It rained so much during 1648 that John Evelyn saw fit to remark upon it and wheat prices soared to 85s. a quarter. Cattle were diseased. That winter the Thames at London froze and, despite a hot June, the ensuing scarcity of grain resulted in famine.[36] Making allowances for the misery of ordinary people, therefore, a third option for the republicans was to seek redress from parliament, calling for a redistribution of land from those malignants considered more culpable than the victors. Finally, impecunious landlords could seek to invest in their estates and, having provided improvements, could increase the rents to cover their costs. Marten employed the last two options, bringing his own actions into tension with his community-minded attitude to estate management.

Towards Didcot, about 8 miles to the south-east of Marten's estate at Longworth, Robert and John Loder ran a model farm at Harwell.[37] Loder's crops did not differ greatly from those on Marten's estates to the north. There was the standard range; wheat, barley, peas, beans and vetches and he produced some hay from his pastures.[38] Historians have debated whether Loder was ahead of his peers, or whether he was more remarkable for having left us such full records than for agricultural prescience. Nevertheless, there are records of improvements, such as manuring and water management, that do not appear in the Marten accounts. The Loders may have seemed modernist in comparison with the Martens because their respective landed estates fulfilled different functions. Robert Loder was conspicuous by his absence from county obligations and none of his relatives politicked in London.[39] Loder was a businessman, and the purpose of agriculture was to provide a living. It was, from the start, a profit-making enterprise. The Marten estates to the north-west emphasised ease and leisure: they were a social exercise and a retreat. It was up to others to make a living, profitable or otherwise – though preferably the former – from the Marten lands. All this changed in 1649. Farming was required to pay its way, and, if possible, to produce much-needed capital.

In August 1649 John Loder came to an agreement with several of his tenants to enclose the Ham, the name given to the common land in Harwell.[40] The following year, Marten began in earnest the reorganisation of his own estates, from which he hoped to recoup his extraordinary losses; both those that he had incurred as a direct result of the war, and those that encumbered his estate prior to 1642 and which he had been unable to tackle during war-time. In April 1650 he employed Francis Reade, of Farncombe near Lambourn, as bailiff on his estates in Berkshire, who hoped 'the Diligence [and] Fidelity I shall use in ye transaction of these affayres of yours, may soone produce some testimony of my readynes to serve yow, [and] make it appeare how great an obligacon is confessedly laid on me, by yr honouring me wth so great a trust'.[41] Reade was hard at work by May, paying off in timber part of the rent owing to Mr Pickering for Ashdown Park, the sequestered estate of Marten's kinsman, Lord Lovelace.[42] The wood commanded a high price, 'because the season of felling [and] Barking is now present'.[43] Timber was to prove one of the more lucrative products of the Marten estates, and every attempt was made to keep woodland within his control. Wood was also easy to steal, as John Cleveland, Marten's chapman at Ashdown Park, complained, though when he repaired to law he was unable to secure a warrant from the justices to arrest those who had stolen the hedges.[44] Also helping Reade in this respect was one Mr Petty – Maximilian Petty, the civilian Leveller, who had been so vocal at the Putney debates.

On 10 October Marten wrote to John Loder to ask how his estates might be improved, receiving a reply in just one week, which offered practical supervision through the offices of Francis Reade and Thomas Deane. Loder concentrated on the lands in Shrivenham. His advice was limited, and unlikely to yield the sorts of sums required. Loder suggested the sale of the Beckett and Salop farms at twenty years' purchase, which would realise £20,000. According to the valuation of the lands at Beckett, a total of £708[45] could be improved by up to £1 an acre by partial ploughing: 'iff it should seeme good unto you to plow up p[a]rt of those grounds ag[ains]t home leyes, piggion house Close [and] sum others, I beleive you might Improve 1^l at least upon every acre for 7 years and at the end of that terme continue it according to the above sayd rents'.[46] Unlike the Loders, Marten was not an encloser, and his leases continued to make provision for grazing beasts on the common. This was the case at Hinton, until Loder took it over, when he started to enclose.[47]

The war disrupted social as well as financial relations. When Francis Reade replaced Thomas Tuckwell as bailiff on the Shrivenham estate, the tenants gained an opportunity to press for changes in their leases. William Perryman wrote from Frilford near Abingdon that Tuckwell had promised him the full lease on a house that was destined for Reade, 'I haveing nothing now but the bare house desire to laye something unto it for the maynteynance of my ffamyle'.[48] Tuckwell had died, but more serious was the loss of the bailiff at Inglesham, David Dawes, due to his 'running away' in 1647. Inglesham had quartered a troop of royalist soldiers from Colonel Howard's regiment, officered by Lieutenant Cox, which had used some of the beans produced by the parish, besides those that were 'carryd unto Prince Rupert'. Nevertheless, money and produce had gone missing, beyond that which could be accounted for by a military presence, and Marten could not 'ptend yt it was lost by the souldiers'. Most of the goods from the estate had been sold very cheap to a Walter Matthewes. Matthewes had bought oxen, worth £13 6s., but purchased for £8, hay, a boar, Marten's horse called Nash, 140 wool fleeces, hedging, farm implements and household items, including a bed. None of the money had been received from Matthewes. Richard Ewer was appointed to oversee the collection of monies and rents on the estate and an inventory of the losses was drawn up by Henry Porter, who was 'hyred to keepe possession . . . in Mr Martins right'. He had little success, and Marten was still liable for the taxes on these lands even though he had received no income from them.[49] By 1653 Marten was still owed £140 and John Wildman £60 in Lady Day rents.

The Spoils of War

Royalists whose lands had been devastated by the war could expect no compensation for their loss of status. The winners, however, were in a position to find reward for their expenditure on behalf of the parliamentary cause. The state made a payment of £3,000 to cover Colonel Marten's outgoings, and a committee, set up to examine his losses during the war, decided to award lands to the value of £1,000 at Eynsham, to the west of Oxford, and another £1,000 out of the estate of the Duke of Buckingham, within the duchy of Lancaster.[50] He was made two awards: the manor of Hartington in the valley of the river Dove on the Derbyshire side of the Derbyshire/Staffordshire border; and Leominster Foreign, Herefordshire, with lands, 5 miles in radius, around the town.[51] With his lands along the Berkshire side of the Thames, Marten had, during the 1650s, huge estates in three different and distant parts of England, providing the historian with a means of comparing land management.

Leominster Foreign was the term given to the former lands of Leominster priory, amounting to nearly 10,000 acres. There were 269 tenants: 12 were leaseholders,

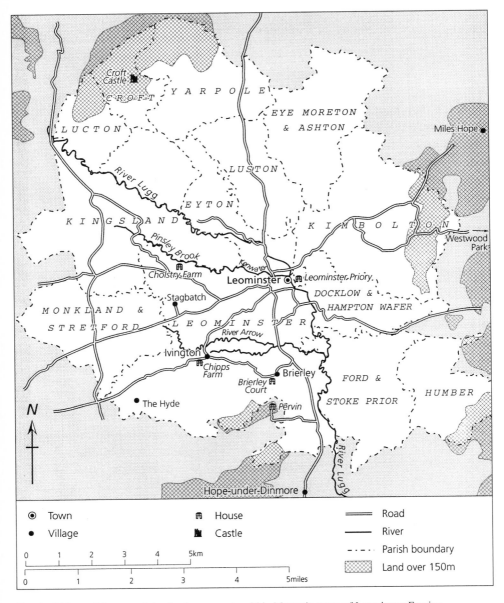

Herefordshire parishes containing land or property within Marten's estate of Leominster Foreign

127 freeholders and 130 copyholders.[52] The land was of average quality for Herefordshire, though poor in comparison with Berkshire. Waterlogged and hilly, it was fit primarily for grazing cattle. The town of Leominster had no real claims to economic fame. It was a trading centre for the locality. It was, however, a burgeoning centre of cider production.

Early in Hilary term, 1650, Marten was in London. He had purchased Derby House in Chancel Row, and it was here that messages arrived from Herefordshire, including details of his first manorial court in the presence of the Leveller, William Wetton.[53] The local people wished to re-negotiate their position with the new lord, anxious to know how Marten would establish himself, for 'many eyes in this Cuntry are upon you'.[54] This part of Herefordshire, butting the turbulent area of the marches, was a centre of religious radicalism, influenced by the proximity of the Welsh saints. One of the millenarians in the county was Miles Hill,[55] leading baptist and bailiff on the Leominster Foreign estate. He was also a former county treasurer and member of the county militia committee. In the spring of 1650 he petitioned for, among other things, strict laws against adultery.[56] Nevertheless, in what was partly a piece of feudal ingratiation, part assertiveness about the role of the saints, and part illustration of the strange alliance that had formed between radical saints and radical secularists, Hill outlined the state of the county.

He had called on Marten in London, had sent greetings by letter and now addressed another missive to his master. They had both, he excused himself, been busy with 'publique desires', which were 'more in our Eyes [and] harts at such a tyme as this then any thing of our owne & the Lord will by the hands of a few of his servants now in these Late dayes do great things'. Service to the greater lord had meant that Hill had not had chance to do his accounts. His economic lord was entitled to improved rents, even though most had not come in but, 'when you see him', Thomas Harrison would gladly give an overview of the 'Countyes money'. In return for the traditional obsequiousness of employee to employer, Hill hoped that he 'shall have yor good word in the howse when tyme serve', though probably not on the bill to punish adultery with death.[57]

Leominster Foreign was almost exclusively an agricultural manor and surrounded, but hardly impinged on, the town. At its centre was the old priory building, a long, three-storey barn-like construction next to the priory church, running alongside a fast-flowing stretch of the river Kenwater, close to its confluence with the Lugg (*see* plate 4a) Marten was therefore in control of 37 acres of prime site in the town,[58] a garden, two orchards producing cider apples, two fish ponds, several mills and the houses and fields of sub-tenants, most notably Edmund Stephens.

Stephens was one of several prosperous yeomen farmers who had benefited from the lack of regulation and supervision during the war: many had ceased to pay their rents. Stephens himself was in *de facto* control of a 9 acre meadow close to the priory, but 'hath never paid you [Marten] a penny for those Meadowes he howlds at Lempster'. Another yeoman with pretensions for self-improvement in the opportunistic climate of post-war chaos was John Norgrave the younger, whose father had died in the course of 1651, the last of three lives on the Norgraves' copy. Four heriots had become due to Marten. Hill was still establishing his position as the controller of the estate, engaging in parochial politicking with Norgrave, whom Hill had arrested. Norgrave tried to evade payment and Hill attempted to use his access to Marten's ear to diminish the reputation of one of his neighbours by recounting Norgrave's rudeness to the rent collector, James Munn:

> presently after I came to Lempster and gott awarrant from a Justice to app[re]hand him and his servant and Caused him to deliver yor heriotts s[e]ized upon the Baylife 3 of wch hee hath forborne for un till thay make thayr adresses unto you, soe that the said heriott is for Land at [C]holstry [and] proves absolutly to bee yor due, as well as the other three [and] I believe you will not give him away, yor sarvant Rceaving such an affront.

Hill was not above appealing to Marten's charity, claiming himself to be a better bailiff than those who had previously been in charge of the estate and not one who 'did get the poore tennants Catle in to thayr owne hands at a easie value to deseave the Lord', for 'I value yor Love more then the profitt of my office by farr'.[59]

Hill was not to see out the year as Marten's baliff at Leominster. By the start of 1652 he had been replaced by Thomas Deane. Deane was from Uffington in Berkshire, and a personal friend of Marten, who thus took the calculated risk that the problems associated with introducing a newcomer to such a tightly-knit community would be outweighed by having a trustworthy servant to oversee the affairs of a 'very solatary place'. Deane was likely to give Marten a more objective account of his new holdings. The soil was 'reasonable good' but the estate was depleted of stone, walls having been pulled down by local people who needed building materials, and timber sold for firewood or profit. In all, 'here is dayly willfull wast' and 'alltogether in a disorder'. Deane confirmed the impressionistic tenor of Hill's letters: Marten's tenants and employees were at each other's throats, currying favour – none too sincerely – from the lord. None could be trusted. Deane pleaded that his appointment be confirmed in writing as soon as possible:

> if you imploy mee in your bayliefes place delay it not but set som time a sid to put mee upon the imploym[ent]. your rent day is come and your tenants knowe not who to pay to and I cannot appear in it tell I have order, for as I would not

com short of duty so I will not presume, and no man can proceed here effectually unlesse hee have the rent roll and a coppy of the survey, w[t]hout w[c]h your bayleif shall bee baffelled and you never knowe what you have.[60]

Deane wanted the rationalisation of those employed by the estate: 'the imploying of many in this maks but a confusion in my esteeme for every on is striveing to find faults and tell you of them but non is amending or reforming of them but in such a way as that the cure is worse then the diseasse'. A Mr Power was added to the list of potentially disruptive elements at Leominster.[61] On 15 March 1652 the new steward gave Marten a depressing account of his future part in estate management:

I shall expect a commission from you under your hand or hand and seale to authorice mee in what you doe imploy mee in and to shew mee the limitation of my duty and what you will hand forth unto mee; in refference thereof, in a worde, to set mee in an absolut order w[t]h sufficient authority for you knowe I am here a meare strainger and I doe find here, though but a strainger, no smale disorder and will w[t]h no littel care bee reformed. here is much practiceing who shall act for you, pretending yo[r] good. I would it might prove so by som, but if care be taken and som put of[f] your imployments, you shall never knowe what is yours here at lemster oare. I knowe Mr hill is som hindrance to your inioying your right here and the Shreifes baylive doe abuse your liberty and right.[62]

Therefore, in early March 1652, Marten and Deane set about to reform the manor of Leominster Foreign with the same gusto with which they had taken over in Berkshire. Deane was instructed to abandon his interests in Uffington and commit himself wholly to Marten's administration. He let his Berkshire estates for four years and repeated his request for written confirmation of his appointment and an outline of the bounds of his authority, having 'unseated myselfe and betooke myselfe wholly to yo[r] imployments'. Marten was keen to build in Herefordshire, and Deane drew up plans for a new manorial house, a two-storey building with a single storey, open-roofed hall, parlour and kitchen, built of local stone and roofed with the indigenous slate, which was good but 'very wayty and the roofes are to be layed flat'. So much wood had been carried off around Leominster that Deane suggested using timber from Eynsham.

Deane hoped to move his family into the priory, which he was to rent from the elderly Robin Ewer. Ewer had also been a local administrator of the Leominster estate and was not pleased to be usurped by a newcomer. He vacillated over the rent of the priory, trying to raise it to the new 'improved' rate – £18 a year – using 'houshold words' towards the steward. In return, the prospective tenant was convinced that he had not acted in an 'unceemly or uncivill' way, professed a regard for Ewer, especially as he appeared to esteem their mutual master, and was apt to be tolerant of his ways because Ewer was an old man and 'his sonn Robert and I have professed great love and respect on[e] to another'.[63] A month later, however, it was clear that relations between Deane and old Mr Ewer were far from civil. Deane wrote to one of Marten's London household, Charles Whistler, at Derby House:

> I have the houseing of the priory and the grounds about it but old Mr Ewer does mee all the hindrance hee can. I hope his sonn Robert is not guilty of it for a man of reason must needs thincke that this is no playing matter to send mee so long upon duty and put of[f] my stock and dealeing and out mysellfe of a being and so to bee turned of[f]; but such is old Mr Ewer his intent, though I find our Master in a more stable minde for this man. Mr Ewer, if hee can gaine any of the letters sent to mee, hee breaks them up and if they licke him not hee burnes them. you knowe I am a great way remote and our master, if hee bee not called upon, is slowe in his proceedings.[64]

Although Ewer was refusing Deane a base from which to administer the estate, Deane was not above subterfuge. He told Ewer that he needed access to the priory because he was quartering soldiers in its grounds. It was not, therefore, only in national politics that the New Model Army was expediently used by the Rump to further its ends, whilst at all other times it was a threat and a nuisance. Although Deane had 'mad use of the souldiers names' he thought good to get agreement on the nature and extent of the army's role. He hoped the way in which the soldiers were thus quartered about the town 'shall not stand for a lawe. [T]hough generall harrasen [Harrison] bee a great man must wee crave leave of souldiers what grounds wee shall use.'[65] Deane moved himself and his family from Uffington to Leominster priory by August, but this was not without ejecting the widow of the previous tenant, to whom Ewer had given permission to remain.

Deane proved a conscientious, officious and bureaucratic administrator, from whom Marten sometimes tired of hearing, but his interminable letters convey, within the midst of numerous minor details of leases and bargains, several interesting points about Marten, estate management, local politics and the post-war chaos. Marten was on the gullible side of generous. Whilst he installed his trusted servant in the priory to administer his estate, he had not secured his position with written authorisation and he had left himself open to personal visits from his tenantry, circumventing their new steward, who remained in Herefordshire trying to tighten the local regime. Deane's position was

> unstable . . . and the disorder that your maner here is in; for if my iudgment doe not very much fayle mee I see such intruding upon your patience and such

intrenching upon your libertie and such feeding with flatteries that the whole ffabricke is sheaken, insomuch that it will cost you both paines and cost to put it in order againe.[66]

The steward did not presume to question Marten's charity, but his easy rates, personally negotiated with his tenants, forced his steward to complain that his 'power much is concealed'. He could not rely on the word of tenants here – 'if you yeeld unto p[ers]wasions you shall neither knowe what you have here nor inioy your owne' – and although he promised to operate with more honesty than the locals, Marten had installed a stranger, denied him written confirmation of the lord's authority, who therefore acted with little *de facto* power within an insular community.[67] In consequence, Marten's position was itself undermined, for the tenants complained that the journey from Herefordshire to London was unnecessary, time-consuming and expensive. Deane warned Marten of his position; maybe he was as weary as they at listening to such an endless stream of complaints. He might have commended the diligence of the tenantry if his suspicion of them all did not lead him to believe such professions were 'spoyled wth sinester ends'.[68]

Deane amassed a list of opponents. Some of the aspirant yeomanry were probably taking a chance in a situation in which Buckingham's men had been unable to administer an estate for some years and evidence of rent or ownership had been lost or destroyed. Others had an opportunity to ingratiate themselves with the new lord whilst advancing their own position. Some resented Deane's arrival and their own loss of status, and some were no doubt irritated by his brusque and officious manner. Nevertheless, there were several reasons why Marten's position was open to challenge. Although he had been granted the manor by act of parliament,[69] the authority of that parliament was so challenged that even the most remote of parish yeomanry had some notion of its notoriety. The act was only binding whilst the parliament was considered to have authority. Either allegiance to the old lord, or doubt about the validity of the new, was sufficient to undermine Marten's control. Royalist John Parkes, of Brierley, was treated with some leniency by local justice of the peace Thomas Baskerville when caught digging and selling two loads of slate, contrary to his copyhold, because on 'finding that Tile not for his turne', he had sold it and bought ten loads for house repairs. Deane, however, had misgivings. He was a liar and 'stricks [strikes] meanly at your right and titll here as an enimie'.[70]

Deane was a bore – he continuously 'thundered' letters at his master – but he was wise to try to secure Marten's tenure, both financially and legally. He instigated a new survey, but there had been no attempt to search out the former deeds. He did not have a rent roll.[71] Although there were 'other great affayres' that kept Marten in London, a journey to Herefordshire would have added personal weight to his claim to authority, confirmed by presiding over the assize courts. Marten travelled irregularly, did not usually hold court, and visited too long after he had taken control.

The Price of Infamy

Almost as soon as Marten had taken possession, the surveyors of the estates of delinquents toured the country. While Deane was trying to persuade Marten to purchase Lord Craven's estate at Uffington,[72] Miles Hill was concerned that he should know of the assessors' activities in Herefordshire. The assessors carried a letter to verify that Marten had been awarded Leominster by act of parliament, but they were less convinced that he was in rightful possession of all of the lands. Deane was in a quandary; if he allowed the state to survey, he would save himself the expense, but he would then face the risk of the authorities not accepting his claim and the state survey being used against him.[73] The state surveyed, Gabriel Whistler signed on the lord's behalf, but Marten annotated the survey with complaints that Walton's lands had been omitted, and several sites had been noted only as an acreage and not given a value.[74] Marten could not rely on support from the local corporation. Relations between the Foreign and the town of Leominster were strained. Marten visited in 1650; the only reference to him in the borough records is a chamberlain's account 'for wine and metheglin, bestowed on Coll. Marten. – 10s'.[75] By 1652 he was in dispute with the borough, which regarded the priory and its lands as part of the corporation; it had seized the priory and was calling on Marten's tenants to attend its court, to the detriment of Marten's authority. The corporation tried to assert its control whilst Marten was absent. Like his national career, he was a powerful figure only at times when, and in places where, he had the ability to marshal the power of the great and the good behind him. When Deane threatened legal action, the borough worthies backed down:

> I have given you to understand of the difference betweene the Towne of leominster and I concerning the monthly Asseasment for they have taxed the priory – The mansion house of the fforaine – as a member of their corporation. when the masters of the Towne sawe I had severd [served] the asseasors wth a warrant to put it to triall, they came to mee and answere mee that they would not contend wth Coll Marten but desired mee to stay my hand untell Coll Marten came in p[er]son, who should end the businesse himsellfe, so that if they prove honest you are lick to get the deshing of the matter yoursellfe, for upon these termes it is stayed, for I answered them that had I not found it to bee preiuditiall to your court Barron and priviledges of your fforraine I should a have beene silent.

Deane advised his lord to check the records of the estate in the Exchequer and Augmentations' office. Marten was characteristically dilatory, and the corporation made another attempt on the priory eighteen months later, intending to add the property to their own charter.[76] In November 1653 he had still not made a search of the records to ascertain the extent of his right in Leominster and Deane was powerless unless he did:

And why you tye my hands from these is you have not searched yet where you promised mee. on[e] search should serve for all. And for the coppy of the duckes Pattene [duke's patent], wch in my Judgment sayes it is more than nessessary, I would not bee so quiet with the Shreiffes officers in acting that in your liberty, did I p[er]fectly knowe you had power to prevent them.[77]

Towards the end of 1652 there was a further dispute about the payment of the fee farm rents, the rights to which had been part of a separate sale by the Commonwealth government.[78] In October Hill advised Marten to pay just one year, a decision with which Marten seemed to concur. In February 1653, however, Deane's counsel had more immediate leverage with the lord, as the steward had been summonsed to appear before the magistrates at Hereford. Through Deane, Marten was charged with arrears of fee farm rents dating back to 1642, the point at which they had ceased to be paid. This was, as Deane exasperatedly expressed it, 'six yeares before you had any right here and . . . I have nothing to doe wth that'. The reserved rents on the estate did not approach the total of fee farm rents owed. Deane made a stand, arguing that since Marten had not purchased the fee farm, his steward was not liable to collect the rents and if the creditor required them, then it was the responsibility of his agent, Mr Bull, to solicit for them. Marten's creditor was Arthur Samuel, a gentleman from the East Midlands, who, as one of the trustees for the sale of estates forfeited for treason, had profited in a quietly efficient way from the land redistribution policies of the Commonwealth, though he was investigated for possible bribery in this office in 1653.[79]

By the end of 1652 Marten's national status was waning and this had a corresponding effect on his ability to act as local lord. His political career was in ruins and his creditors had more leverage against him. At the turn of the year 1653/4, as the parliament of the saints was overtaken by the Protectorate of Cromwell, Deane wondered whether his master was privy to a 'hint of what hopes wee have of our sterne men how they are lick to guid our maine shipe to a happy ariveall'. This might be of some comfort to Deane, though none to Marten, who could expect little support from the Cromwellian regime. At the end of January, Deane rushed to see Marten, but was 'afrayed that the arreares of the ffee ffarme rents will not goe right on your side; it may so fall out that my iourney may countervaile the charge I shall put you to and I longe to see you and never more then when you are in trouble'.[80] Marten's creditors were given assistance by the Protectorate government, with the revival of the court of the Duchy of Lancaster, to facilitate the prosecution of outstanding cases, of which Marten's fee farm arrears was one.[81]

Deane professed himself on friendly terms with Bull, Samuel's agent, or at least thought him a reasonable man, but Samuel was not to be trusted. He was currying the favour of neighbouring aristocrat Sir James Croft (*see* plate 5), a man of high-church principles and impeccable royalist pedigree.[82] The Welsh marches, despite the vocal presence of gathered churches – and if Hill was representative, sectarian religion did not necessarily produce tenants well disposed to Marten's tenure – was also an area of disgruntled royalism.[83] Several larger landlords had a direct and long association with the crown. There were royalist yeomen, such as John Parkes of Brierley, who had been caught selling slate. Even the local puritan gentry, such as the neighbouring Harleys, had switched their allegiance once it became clear the extent to which the parliamentary radicals' programme was a threat to the established social order.[84] Croft was the figure-head of royalist resistance in the neighbourhood and if Samuel favoured Croft, it meant trouble for Marten, for as Deane posed it, 'if hee begin to shew favour to hee, [he] must bee an opposer of you'. Bull showed Deane a letter by which it appeared that Croft was returning the compliment to Samuel. This was to be the opening salvo in a long dispute with Croft, who from his castle just to the north of the Foreign, was, despite the political stain of royalism, fast re-establishing himself as the major social force in the area.[85] The case came to court in August 1654.[86] Of the four halmotes into which Leominster Foreign was divided, Croft laid claim to Ivington and, in this part of the Foreign, denied subjection to Marten's jurisdiction. Deane countered with highly detailed records designed to prove that Ivington had been part of the Foreign since the reign of Philip and Mary, and further, that Croft had failed to hold his three-weeks' court for such a long time that he had forfeited any right. Marten was advised to force Croft to show his written authority, otherwise 'this will prove an inlett for other things to passe upon bare notion'. A week before the case was due, Croft's party had retained six lawyers: Marten's side was still without legal representation, because the lawyers were 'somuch inclinable to the late Kings party that [they] would give away the cause if [they] could'.

By dint of poor judgement, sloth, and the sheer bad luck that washed in with the tide of national chaos, Marten was in a situation of exquisite social nicety. His politics had alienated him from the local, pro-monarchical aristocracy, and he was an outsider, whose estate had been conferred by a parliament for whom the aristocracy had nothing but contempt. He was a republican, a regicide, of notoriously loose morals and obscure lineage. His lack of breeding, in terms of both social standing and behaviour, made him a source of scurrilous royalist gossip and debilitating rumour. His servant, Deane, was certainly of humble stock, and a combination of Deane's lack of breeding and manners and Marten's absence alienated the yeomenry. There was a considerable list of those who had once had power and reputation on the estate, who felt ousted. One would learn from another how to undermine Marten's position.[87] Marten reassured Deane that he knew many 'thirsted' after the estate.[88] Young John Norgrave was one of those against whom they had to be vigilant: those who favoured Norgrave made an enemy of Marten.[89] Norgrave 'abuses both Mr Marten and his tenants and I doe thincke and knowe must bee contended w'h or no honest man shall live by him'.[90] Miles Hill reverted to the ranks of the mistrusted, particularly once Marten had lost national political power. In December 1653 Hill contested that he owed Marten any of the rents that he had collected, on the grounds that he had been losing a staggering £1 a day whilst in his employment. Deane, with his heightened sense of duteous loyalty, believed Hill was obliged to continue in his former post. Edmund Stephens was another who 'goes about to delude us'.[91] Marten's relations with this middling rank of local society were the most fraught.[92]

The result of alienating himself from the upper echelons of Herefordshire society was to have detrimental repercussions on Marten's relationship with the more humble tenants. Marten and his employees showed concern for the poor on their estates but, in losing their control and being unable to assert their authority, they left their tenants open to exploitation and manipulation by others. Hill had drawn attention to his careful treatment of 'the poore tennants' as a means of winning over his master.[93] Baskerville thought he was doing right in his lenient treatment of Parkes.[94] However, after two years in possession of the manor, Marten had lost the respect of his smaller tenants. They complained of his absence and the journey to London required to see him,[95] and by September, the difficulties involved in accumulating those small sums of rent money were adding to the major financial stringencies. The Michaelmas rents for 1652 were difficult to collect for 'they come by leasure'; the estate needed 'an hourly eye'. The tenants were unlikely to pay until Marten had given them a definitive indication of the rate at which their fines had been set. By the time Marten's national position was in decline, with its local repercussions, he had lost any chance of recovering his authority in Leominster. In January 1654 Deane was aware that 'non of your tenants [had] sworne theire fealty'.[96]

Too little, too late, the campaign began in earnest to recover the profitability of the Herefordshire award. A building programme, designed to symbolise the social role of the lord, was replaced by a regime to maximise profit. The priory ponds were stocked with fish. A tougher line was taken with the lease and copyhold renters. Deane hinted that he was unwilling to continue customary tenancies. The Bennets were a family from the eastern village of Kimbolton. John Bennet's wife having died, her side of the family wanted to add new lives to the lease when John followed her. He was then in middle age:

> yet I [Deane] shall stand for five yeares profite if the survey bee not to[o] lowe rated and this will not only move the rest to come in but to finde present monie to[o]. bennet come not at mee and I knowe no reason why I should stay my hand. how you approve of this I pray let mee knowe spedily. I desire not to returne it to the ayncient stock because they shall hold it as a rule, for I have informed them generally that you will not nor shall not bee engaged to that.

Deane was desperate to re-establish profitability and towards the end of 1653 and during 1654 he developed a particular concern with woodland management and mining.[97] In the summer of 1657 he imposed a moratorium on timber cutting, although wood was disappearing from Westwood Park and the tenants were thought to be burning charcoal. The royalist major Bennett Pryor was singled out[98] and William Pascall was held guilty of destroying young oak saplings that had been newly planted.[99] Wood was at a premium, not only for building, but also to supply the ironworks. The proximity of iron working was a mixed blessing. Deane bewailed the heavy rains that had raised the rivers to flood level: 'I have had much to doe wth your fish poole for to preserve your fish for I never saw Ire [iron] thicker in all my life at last Ilet [inlet] in parte of the river Pinsly'.[100] In October 1653 Deane announced that he was 'goeing forward wth mineing for coall'[101] and was optimistic of the prospects of lead deposits.[102] Neither was he averse to improving the agricultural land, though details of how this could be done were scanty.[103] During the year 1656/7, Pervin was planted with trees; the women were given the task of planting acorns, and these woods were enclosed, although Richard Savaker was apt to let his young game-birds loose in them (*see* plate 4b).[104]

A number of cases rocked Marten's hold over Herefordshire. Walter Pullen and his wife, Joan, were served with a writ for forcibly entering a tenancy at Ivington: Deane seized their barns and was paying for a watch over the corn. Joan had been imprisoned, but Marten's delay in issuing the papers against them made him vulnerable to a countersuit of wrongful arrest.[105] It was thought well to make an example of the Pullens, or else 'wee should a have beene chattered out of the manner'.[106] Marten was also in the process of suing one of the Caswalls.[107] In return, his tailor was suing him for unpaid bills and, more seriously, the sheriff's bailiffs had forcibly taken possession of his Herefordshire property. Deane had been absent in Derbyshire, and on his return could only demand production of a warrant, haul as much of the property as possible into the barns and bar the door. In the end, Deane regained possession, though he was lucky not to face more serious charges: 'I went and so handled them that they left the possession to mee allthough our swords were somthing nimble'.[108]

In the later 1650s Marten and Deane partially resolved the delicate social relations. They combined continued paternalist consideration for poor tenants with tougher action on the wealthier yeomanry. In May 1655 Marten declared himself exasperated with Norgrave, Stephens and Hill, and Deane knew 'that your occasions are great for monie and your patience much prest'. Marten announced a new, uncompromising line with Harry Birch, who must 'please himself w^{t} prateing. I am content he should say that he can help people to bargaines of my hand there in spight of my nose as well as yours. but now & then I make shift to disappoint those that think to make a prey of mee.'[109] John Norgrave was not to be allowed to enter the property until the crops had been harvested and would no longer 'make a young man of mee in taking his copyhold. for knowing him so subtle as I do, I alwayes stand upon my guard when I deal wt him.' He was not to be allowed to exert a disproportionate interest on the estate, which included his attempts to negotiate down his rents, 'I knoweinge no reason why it should be cheeper nowe then it was at [the time of the duke]'.[110] Tenants were informed that no bargains would be made unless there was a clear ability to pay.[111]

Poorer tenants were considered as much at the mercy of unscrupulous middle-ranking yeomen as Marten. Norgrave was not only an enemy because he endeavoured to undermine Marten's claim, but because he manipulated the undertenants to do so: 'I pray you as you love your tenants and those that belong to you deale as little as you can wth Norgrave and his confiderats'. Many of the tenants in Leominster Foreign were elderly, prey to unscrupulous landlords, and vulnerable when their leases were close to expiry. Marten still sought opportunities to help men such as Thomas Stiffe, 'who is a very honest man & very poor', even though he was not a native of Herefordshire[112] but there was both an altruistic and a cynical motive for Marten's concern for the poor. His consideration for the very poorest on his estates reminds us of 'honest Harry', but in a situation like that in Herefordshire, it was better to have a direct relationship with poor, honest and obligated tenants, than to be at the mercy of those whose material comfort made them aspirant to a social status that threatened Marten's own.

Derbyshire: the Pattern Repeated

Marten was also awarded a huge, quartered estate in Derbyshire, to the eastern side of the river Dove, running from the southern outskirts of Buxton in the north in a 14 mile curve towards Ashbourne. When Marten took it over in the spring of 1649, the Hartington manor in Derbyshire seemed better maintained than Leominster. The

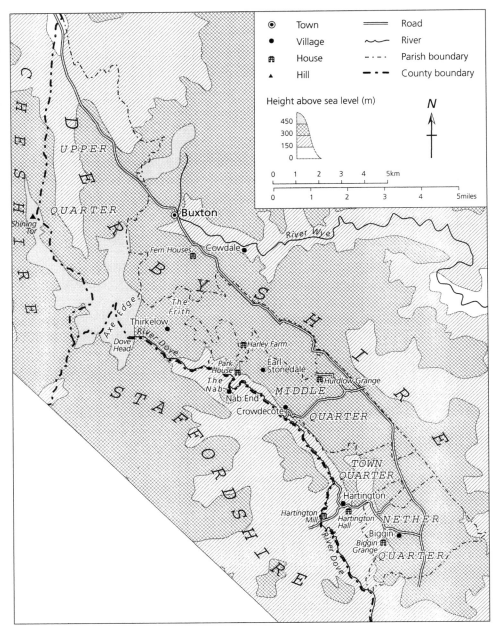

Legend:
- ⊙ Town
- ● Village
- 🏠 House
- ▲ Hill
- ═══ Road
- 〰 River
- – · – Parish boundary
- ▬ ▬ County boundary

Height above sea level (m)

450
300
150
0

N

0 1 2 3 4 5km
0 1 2 3 4 5miles

The parish of Hartington, Derbyshire

manor was under the administrative control of local bailiff William Wardle, who supplied a list of tenants, the rents they had paid in 1625, and a record of the improvements made to the estate.[113] Not only that, but as former Duchy of Lancaster land, the parish came under the influence of the honorary steward for Leicestershire, Marten's friend and political ally, Thomas, Lord Grey of Groby.[114] The following year, Marten's men were in place, with Maximilian Petty and William Wetton overseeing the Hartington affairs.[115] Petty was an improver, although his 'comrade' Wetton reported that his efforts were misunderstood. Nevertheless, as that year's Lady Day rents were collected, the tenants 'appeared with much cherefullnes' and asked that Wetton take over Harley Farm – which cost £350 and was worth £20 per annum to rent – formerly in possession of local worthy George Goodwin.[116] Wardle seemed amenable to Marten's control of the estate. A polite reply was made to Marten's enquiry after the state of the game at Hartington and a fair sample was delivered in pastry. The only dispute on the estate was between the tenants and Edward Pegg, of Fulham Meadows, Caldicot Mill and the Frith, over whether Pegg or the lord was due the rents of the mill. The tenants supported Marten's right.[117]

The tenants of Derbyshire were 'soe poore they have nothing to distrayne'. Their condition did not improve throughout the decade. The Naden family rented Earls Booth, a sizable property, and they were relatively secure yeomanry, paying £16 per half year for a sixth share. In 1655 a co-renter, one of Wardle's relatives, was paying only £7, 'which Cololl Marten was weling to accept by Reasone of poverty'. William and Anthony Whielden had considerably lower rents accepted for Turnerscliff and Gnotdale and several tenants' rents were abated.[118]

During 1655 Marten imposed a Berkshire servant in Derbyshire. At Hartington he appointed Richard Peters, a yeoman of Shefford, who had been in Marten's service at Beckett and had a position of responsibility in Marten's militia regiment.[119] Judging by the entertainingly inflected language, Peters was a man of more limited education than Deane, but his less obsequious correspondence arrived in lesser volume. Unlike Deane, who found himself among quarrelsome locals and inhospitable country, Peters was looked after by a gentleman, Rowland Heathcote, at his house in Cowdale, who 'Gives me a very sevel entartainment and pr[o]mis[e] hee will not sett the dice', liking his surroundings so well that 'you find it soe hard matar to gett me out of it', even though his child, remaining in Berkshire, was sick.[120]

The same administrative problems were nevertheless lurking beneath a more tranquil surface. Early in his appointment, Peters was forced to remind Marten of the need for written authority. Marten had corresponded with several tenants to alert them of Peters' arrival and to ensure that they did not pay their rents to anybody else. Nevertheless, Marten's London lawyer, Gabriel Whistler, wrote to Wardle and advised him to keep hold of the rents that he had collected. Until Peters received a letter of

authority, he remained a 'pawarles But faithfull servant'. The same advice was offered
by Wetton:

> yo[r] Tennants doe verie well resent yo[r] old servant Dicke Peeters, I am confident
> had you given him power [and] Instructions you would have had most of yo[r]
> busines done by this time [and] let mee tell you, y[t] the man is honest diligent and
> faithfull [and] able to serve you in these parts, indeede much more then I did
> expecte, but I see that a man y[t] loves you as hee doth you is a strong dictate to
> Instruct him in yo[r] affairs, and I am confident, if you doe speedily send him
> Instructions and power, hee wilbe an Instrument in doeing you very good service,
> many you have y[t] have p[ro]fest y[e] same, but for wante of true love they have
> diserted you, wch I am confident this man will never doe.[121]

Peters' honeymoon was shortlived. On 20 July he was confident of the support of
William Wardle. On 30 July Peters found Wardle had 'receved severall sumes of
severall Tenants more Then hee have Charged himself'. He had also fallen out with
the powerful Rowland Heathcote, having indicted him for coursing hares on Marten's
land. Regional gentlemen claimed hunting as a customary privilege, but although
Peters had seemed to follow the hounds at first, he subsequently directed threats of
'inveterate malice' against his former host and by July 1656 was daily issuing
'threatening thunder boults' against Heathcote.[122] Other major tenants were
undermining the authority of both Peters and his absentee master. By early 1656
Gabriel Whistler and John Loder were helping to administer the estates, because
Marten's debts tied him to the Rules of Southwark. Humphrey Needham despoiled the
estate by letting Cloyten's farm – which Marten had awarded to Peters – to a poor
drover – a lad 'whoe have not a peney in the worlde' – and two 'eidel wenches'. The
apple trees that Peters planted at Fearn wall, near the complex of houses to the south
of Buxton which Marten awarded to Peters to be the centre of his administration, were
destroyed by tenants. Heathcote and a Mr Higginbottom disputed Marten's right to
collect the goods of waifs, strays and felons, and the tenants were wasting their
copyholds.[123] The problem was deemed to be recurrent. Although the poorer tenants
were willing to treat for lives on their leases,[124] Peters had not 'soe much a parrld
[parleyed] with them Concerning termes, for that you did not give me Any Rule [in] it
a Cording to that you promised me. but if you have dealt with Rowland heathcot and
Georg naden, you have Given youar tenants A Rule to deale, by which I fear will
prove much to youar dameg.' Peters was regarded as a 'mortal Enemey' by greater
yeomen and lesser gentry. Even more sinister was the letter sent to Peters by Arthur
Samuel, whose agent in Derbyshire, Captain William Gent, would be calling to collect
fee farm rents of £97 17s. 6d., plus another 17s. 6d. in arrears. Wardle had not been

paying Samuel the rents, had been forbidden by Samuel from dealing with his affairs and Peters felt the need to warn Marten's tenants to have nothing to do with him.[125]

Marten started to act in 1655. He announced plans to discharge his debts, and should he be unable to do so 'about selling my land every where [in] parcells or otherwise – if that not neither, get leave of my creditors to be at liberty for 1 year'. A map of the estate was in progress and the lord of the manor intended to visit in person in April 1657.[126] He attempted to alienate land in Hartington, making a small lease to his common law wife, Mary Ward, possibly as a means of providing for her welfare, Marten being then fifty-four years old.[127] In July 1657, however, he alienated all the land, living up to his promise to 'go speedily about setling my estate in trustees', by granting Mary a total of 752 acres.[128] There was some talk of improving the agricultural land, but it was not land with which one could do very much. Peters was a great supporter of the use of rabbits, which he was sure was the only improvement, for the land was 'drie innufe'.[129] He was reluctant to let the lead mines or collieries around Hartington, though the lead mines were worth a mere £6 6s. 8d. a year, and in 1657 the mines and the right to hold the Barmote court and appoint barmasters, combined, would only fetch £10. The coal mines were subject to the same delays and difficulties as the agricultural land:

> Sr you may see by this rentall you mad noe certen bargen for the Cole mines, but Left it to Geor Naden to sett it indefrant bee twext you and the Colears. you asked 6ˡ and thay bad 3ˡ as thay say soe, in regard of the Great Charg thay have benn at this yeare, parswades me to take 4ˡ 10ˢ. theiar tyme in it is out at mickelmas.[130]

In Derbyshire, Marten's chief opponent was Mr Savile, who appeared as the financial saviour who would purchase the estate, but

> I should be Glad to hear of aney way you [Marten] have found out to save The seling of this . . . for as Things stand now, Thay doe not stecke [stick] to say you will bee Glad to take 12 years purches in a whil. [T]rust mr savell as fare as you cane Throwe him for hee That have benn youar Greatest enemey all a Long in this buisnes cannot soe sudanly bee youar Cordell frend. I have Tould you all reddey I have sespected Combinacion bee twext him and othars of our neibars in my Last [letter] but one the which I stell bee Leve to be True. [I]f Thinges were quiat ons I Could stell bee Raising of money besids rents and prettey fast too, by which you should know it is Like a Trid hors.[131]

By December 1658 Marten's tenants were paying their rents to Savile, despite Peters' protestations that the Hartington rents were among Marten's best and would be well paid if the present 'Trobles' were over.[132] Marten again alienated the upper echelons of local society, and was too lenient with the poor. He imposed strangers as estate managers and gave them no authority. He was slow to act.

Marten's family ties were also part of his undoing. In his early days as an MP, Marten had mortgaged land to the royalist MP, his brother-in-law, Sir George Stonehouse, who held it in trust for Marten's mother-in-law, Lady Lovelace.[133] By 1653, among other personal creditors, Marten owed John, Lord Lovelace, Baron Hurley, a total of £8,000. Proceedings in Chancery began against him in November. The date is significant. Marten had supported moves to end the freedom from prosecution for debt, which was the privilege of members of parliament. Throughout his career in the Rump, therefore, many to whom he owed large sums could have brought him down. Nevertheless, it was not until the Rump had fallen that Marten's creditors moved in. Legal immunity from prosecution was not the issue. Rather, it was the power that a prominent member of the Rump could bring to bear, and the hesitancy with which known malignants moved against republicans, which had kept Marten from the courts. Life under the Lord Protector did not just mean a betrayal of republican principles, but government by a man who would not protect him. When Deane wrote from Leominster in 1658 to 'confesse you are somuch indebted to the lord protector', he was not making a political statement but giving thanks for Oliver's death, which had timely removed a personal pressure from their continuing financial problems.[134]

On 24 November 1653 Marten appeared at the court of Chancery and acknowledged his debt to Lovelace. By the time the sheriff of Middlesex came to proceed against Marten, however, the debtor had disappeared and Lovelace chose to levy goods in Derbyshire. Should the goods not fetch £8,000, the estate would be sold.[135] '[M]y brother Marten and my son Wildman' put forward several schemes for satisfying the debt, to which Lovelace was willing to accede, but the lands were inventoried and invested in Lovelace in August 1657, until such time as the debt could be recovered.[136] Thomas Deane was solicited for advice on clearing the bills and counselled that the news of Marten's liability to Lovelace remain secret in Herefordshire, in case it proved detrimental to Marten's right. Personally, he was preoccupied that he might have to leave the priory. Deane advised Marten to continue to hold the lands and prudently send up rents.[137] In December 1658 Sir John Harpur disputed the boundaries of the Hartington estate. Both Harpur and Marten used the traditional method of perambulation, and Marten made sufficient impression on the Hartington tenants for John Naden to remember his right when Harpur again challenged the boundary on the Staffordshire side in 1674. Naden had known the boundaries for the past thirty years, '[a]nd that Henry Martin then reputed lord of Hartington Mannor did p[er]ambulate the said bounds . . . about seaventeene or eighteene yeares agoe [1658/9] And that hee

1. Sir Henry Marten, artist unknown

2. *A Description of the Coleny of Surranam in Guiana*, 1667, showing the settlement shortly before its cessation to the Dutch

3a. Margaret Onely, daughter of Margaret Lovelace Staunton and step-daughter of Henry Marten, by J.M. Wright

3b. Edward Onely of Catesby, Northamptonshire, husband of Margaret Onely, by J.M. Wright

4a. The Priory buildings, Leominster, Herefordshire, centre of the Marten administration of Leominster Foreign

4b. Pervin Farm, one of the properties that was part of the estate of Leominster Foreign

5. Colonel Sir James Croft, of Croft Castle, Herefordshire, Marten's rival in Leominster

Last quarter the 18 day, at 10 and 39 min. morn:
New moon the 25 day, at 11 and 32 min. morn.

D.	h. m.	Sun setting.
1	7 42	
2	7 44	
3	7 45	
4	7 47	
5	7 49	
6	7 51	
7	7 53	
8	7 54	
9	7 56	
10	7 57	
11	7 58	
12	8 0	
13	8 1	
14	8 2	
15	8 3	
16	8 4	
27	8 5	
18	8 7	
19	8 8	
20	8 9	
21	8 10	
22	8 11	
23	8 12	
24	8 13	
25	8 14	
26	8 15	
27	8 16	
28	8 17	
29	8 18	
30	8 18	
31	8 19	

B 5

6. A page from Marten's almanack of 1655

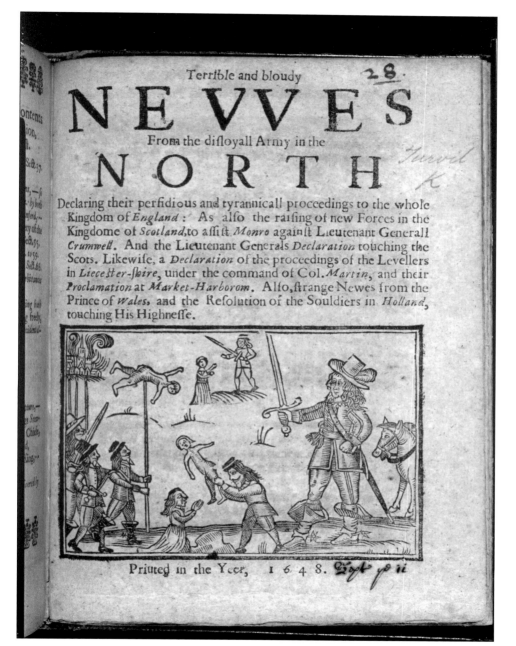

Terrible and bloudy

NEVVES

From the disloyall Army in the

NORTH

Declaring their perfidious and tyrannicall proceedings to the whole Kingdom of *England* : As also the raising of new Forces in the Kingdome of *Scotland*, to assist *Monro* against Lieutenant Generall *Crumwell*. And the Lieutenant Generals *Declaration* touching the Scots. Likewise, a *Declaration* of the proceedings of the Levellers in *Liecester-shire*, under the command of Col. *Martin*, and their *Proclamation* at *Market-Harborom*. Also, strange Newes from the Prince of *Wales*, and the Resolution of the Souldiers in *Holland*, touching His Highnesse.

Printed in the Yeer, 1 6 4 8.

7. The frontispiece of *Terrible and bloudy Newes*, showing Marten's Leveller troops outside Market Harborough, 1648

A PLEA for the
PEOPLE
in aunswer
to their late Adversary
Mr Prynne

the said Henry Martin did ride the same bounds publiquely and without disturbance'.[138]

Marten visited Hartington at this time to reassert his traditional right because, according to his steward, his name was almost forgotten and his tenants were reluctant to pay him their rents.[139] The manuscripts relating to Hartington end with a draft and a fair copy, in Marten's hand, of a proposal to sell the manor to Mr Savile, first valued at £10,000, subsequently amended to £9,000, 'which price . . . I make thus low, that I may have all my money together'. Savile offered £6,000, for which Marten was prepared to part with those farms that were then let at the highest possible rate – rack-rented. There was a certain note of bitterness in Marten's first draft which had become suitably respectful by the second:

If you please to buy ye farmes onely that are racked including Park-house, & ye copy & freehold rents, leaving mee ye rest. viz: ye Manor, Reversions & Leapedg 6000ˡ I will take your sixe thousand pounds.

If you please to turn ye tables & be content wᵗ the Manor & reversions leaving mee ye farmes & rents abovesaid 3500ˡ I shall expect no lesse then three thousand & five hundred.

With his parting shot, he wished Savile 'as much good wᵗ it, as my self wᵗ ye money'.[140] In 1670 the Lovelace family attempted to recover the lands by petition to Charles II, submitted by John Lovelace, now deceased, and his father, 'in consideration of his constant affection to his Royal ffather and himselfe and his sufferings for the same and in consideration of those great Sumes of money which hee had paid for the said Henry Marten'.[141]

The Social Revolutionary

Marten was not simply a wanton libertine. Not all of his misfortunes were of his own making. He clearly enjoyed the fine things that riches could procure and retained bills to vintners, cooks, tailors, and apothacaries, who supplied potions to cure the effects of his excesses. The same languor that left pamphlets and speeches unfinished let him down when it came to the cumbersome and time-consuming detail of land management, particularly when his estates were so distant.

Marten ignored social hierarchy, installing agents who were of obscure background and alien dialect. Little can be traced of the background of most of Marten's local servants,[142] the one illustrative exception being Thomas Deane. Deane was from Uffingdon, a parish in which he retained a lifelong interest despite taking up residence in Herefordshire. Thomas was probably the son of Thomas and Agnes Deane. The will of his father in the autumn of 1626 reveals that Thomas had not yet reached his majority, but would then be possessed of £27, a bed, chest, cupboard, coffers and some brass pots. He had a brother, Richard, and a sister, Jane. Thomas Deane senior was by no means poor, but he was humble. He left a total estate valued at £62 13s. 8d. and he could not sign his name.[143] His son, however, was educated to a level at which he could administer huge landed estates and could pen interminable letters. Deane's manner, obeisant concern for his employer and officious care of his duties may well have reflected the duty and gratitude due from one of humble birth whose education and elevation was the responsibility of the local lord. Marten earnt the gratitude, love and loyalty of his closest servants, but they in turn, alienated others, who felt they had more right to office.

There were several references to Marten's fairweather friends. He was a poor judge of character. Mr Ewer, who gave evidence against him at his trial, was either his servant from Shrivenham or one of the Ewers he had estranged in Leominster.[144] While Marten earnt the slavish love of some, he alienated those with firmer local contacts and thus greater power. He was a paternalist landlord and surprisingly traditional. His concern for the ordinary person, however, manifest itself in his care for the poor on his estate and his reluctance to enter into improvements, such as enclosure, which might radically alter their parochial status. But it was hardly a strategy designed to maximise profits and was another way in which those at yeomanry and gentry level were excluded from the community he built.

Marten was forced to rely on others to extricate him from his financial disasters. John Loder quietly accumulated parts of the manors and in 1654 received £613 2s. 10d. from Marten to end litigation against him.[145] John Loder senior died a yeoman in 1662, but his son claimed to be a gentleman.[146] Loder often worked in tandem with John Wildman, who successfully purchased sequestered royalist land and could help his friend out of his monetary difficulties: he purchased the home farm and manor house at Beckett in May 1657, for a total of £9,300.[147] Wildman's interest in the estate was passed on to his posterity, and his son erected a fine, classically inspired memorial to his father in the church at Shrivenham. Wildman's son dying without issue, the line passed to the boy he had 'adopted', in approval of the 'Roman custom', and John Shute of the Inner Temple became the first Lord Barrington.

The turmoil of the seventeenth century, the disruption of the war and the radical philosophies it engendered was forged into quieter eighteenth-century manners. Whilst John Wildman junior was a man 'whos excellent Natural parts and Manly dispositions had been happily cultivated by a Liberal Education', the Martens slipped into parochial obscurity. Marten's wife, Margaret, remaining in Longworth, died just before her husband in 1680. They left a son, also Henry, who inherited a tiny fraction of the once magnificent landed empire, though they did still possess some land in

Hinton,[148] and the younger Henry Marten was still able to send his son to Oxford. Marten the wit would have undoubtedly enjoyed the irony that while others got rich at the expense of his estate, the name Marten still appears on churches, buildings and roads in the villages of Berkshire, despite a mere forty-year tenure. In the end, however, there can be no other person to blame for the loss of the estate but Marten himself. As Marten joked to Wildman – who was a complex but potent combination of kinsman, friend, colleague and creditor – in an aphorism he coined for himself in 1655, he had been imprudent. He produced a play on the words of Horace:

> A. (Wildman) Rusticus expectat &ct.
> O. (Marten) Stultorn incurate vigor malus ulcera vexat.

For Marten, 'a false appearance of working hard exacerbate[d] the uncured sores of foolishness'.[149]

VI
Trade and the Sea

Despite the land that Sir Henry Marten bought, the Marten family were *parvenus* and had more connections with the financial, trading and shipping concerns of the City than with their aristocratic Berkshire neighbours.[1] Marten's maritime connections made his career and were one of the reasons for its premature collapse. In particular, Henry's brother, George, practised trade, and whilst his lifestyle was similar to Henry's, George's debts contributed to the collapse of his brother's political career.

During the 1620s and 1630s, Henry Marten was the owner of a merchant ship, called the *Marten*. This was a vessel of 532 tons, a considerable size.[2] When England appeared to be in danger, during 1640/1, Marten offered his ship towards the fleet that patrolled the coast – the summer watch. For these purposes, he attempted to have it rated at 700 tons – second rate – which was refused, but he continued to regard it as 600 tons.[3] Its lieutenant was called Hackinger, and it carried 210 men, making it the largest merchant vessel employed in the summer watch.[4] Henry Marten recorded a number of bills for a variety of purposes. He installed his younger brother, George, as the *Marten*'s captain, who proved as adept as Henry at running up debts. Some of these appear trivial, such as payment for messages carried ashore, and there were several for the not inconsiderable sum of £50 for casks delivered aboard.[5] During April 1642 the expenses seemed relatively innocuous. George ordered more drink and Henry paid £50 for new rigging. George passed on all of these expenses to his brother with the request 'Brother pray pay this some out off the first payment you receive ffrō the howse of Cōmons'.

If the ship was offered to the summer watch as a financial investment, there was no sign that it was a lucrative prospect. When Marten audited his accounts in the spring of 1642, calculating his expenditure and potential fee from the Commons, his ship was a loss-maker. During December 1641 he had borrowed £2,000 from Ralph Ingram, a citizen ironmonger of London, and £1,000 from a Mr Musgrave towards equipping the *Marten*.[6] There was a commanding crew of maybe twelve men, not counting the captain George, but including a Captain Harris.[7] Mr Merrill was in charge of providing sustenance for the crew and took receipt of such goods, mainly alcoholic, on board. William Green was responsible for the rigging, receiving new sails at a cost of £36. Both the men earned £50 each for their six-month engagement. The wage bill for the seamen was, however, only a fifth of Marten's total expenditure, and he had had to find a total of £5,500 in order to put to sea. The parliament having rated the *Marten* at 600 tons and employed it for six months (April to September 1642), he would be paid only £4,077. If he were to be employed until November, he could earn an additional £1,359, but it would still not cover his costs.[8]

The expenditure of maintaining a summer watch in April 1642 was innocuous enough. On 2 July it took the form of a well-planned coup.[9] Henry Marten presented a Commons' petition that called on Charles Stuart to appoint the Earl of Warwick as Admiral of the Fleet. Charles hesitated. George Marten was one of ten sea captains to join Admiral Warwick and Vice-Admiral Batten in the parliamentary council of war that therefore planned to make its own changes.[10] In August George offered advice to Warwick on the capture of the King's pinnace, the *Henrietta Maria*, off the coast of Portsmouth; an action for which he was offered the thanks of the House. The following month he was part of a detachment under Captain Swanley which tried to take Newport, Isle of Wight.[11]

Following the coup, the expenses that Henry Marten incurred were of a different nature. He was ordered by members of the Committee for the Defence of the Kingdom – Pym, Hampden, Holles, Saye and Sele, Fiennes, and Nicol – to pay a Mr Hill who had come to London with a 'catch' – a party of the King's captains. It had cost Hill £4 to feed them for a fortnight and Marten was to cover his costs. Again, the sums did not add up. Marten was asked to pay £18 5s., but the total costs incurred were £20 5s.[12] The captured men were the royalists Slingsby and Wake, who refused to obey a summons from the Earl of Warwick, as admiral of the now parliamentary-controlled fleet. The two captains were 'seized, taken, and carried by their own men to the earl, who immediately committed them to custody, and sent them up prisoners to the Parliament'.[13] Marten controlled the purse strings for the naval coup. Although the expenses that Marten incurred during the first few weeks of that watch appear to have been met, the rising costs of administering compensation to parliament's supporters and paying for intelligence during the summer far outweighed any 'wages' he received from the Commons.

In 1643 Henry Marten requested the Shipwrights' Company to verify the *Marten* at 532 tons, and called on the commissioners for the navy to send his account for the use of the ship in the summer watch of 1642. Not all of Marten's account had been paid. Nevertheless, the committee for the navy accepted his tender when he offered the *Marten* for the summer watch of 1643, carrying 159 men and 36 guns.[14] After its service to the state, Marten appears to have sold his ship – which was taken as prize by the *Tiger* in 1651 and may have been the ship with which Admiral Penn attacked Jamaica in 1655[15] – and it was put to good use by the Commonwealth state in mounting another summer guard.[16] This did not relieve Henry Marten of the financial burden of mounting an armed vessel. During 1654 Mary Wilson and Samuel Crisp, executors for the estate of the Ingram family, were forced to sue in the Upper Bench for the £2,000 which Marten had borrowed thirteen years earlier.[17] Marten, prosecuted by anonymous creditors,[18] failed to appear before the court, did not advance any case, and the issue was still troubling both Henry and George two years later.[19]

Marten's shipping interest catapulted him from relative county obscurity to a position on the Admiralty Committee, which fulfilled the functions of the Lord High Admiral until the formal appointment of the Earl of Warwick to the post in 1643. Marten sat with some heavyweight parliamentarians.[20] Kenneth Andrews has listed the shipping interests of members of the Admiralty and Navy committees and several MPs had connections with ships that were used by the parliamentary navy. Marten's was the largest, and if the income expended was proportionate to the influence one could exert, it may be the case that the sums he was prepared to spend entitled him to a say in the management of naval affairs. However, the balance sheet indicates that he made a loss on his ship during the summer watch and, as a man who was already running up debts, investing in an enterprise that one knew in advance would be loss-making would seem foolish to a point that even the feckless Henry Marten would recognise. Was it the case, therefore, that Marten displayed greater political guile than the reputation he has attracted and, seeing the direction of affairs during the crisis months of 164½, invested in political power and ensured his place at the centre? Andrews did not view him as a key figure during 1642, but his purchase of large numbers of 'intelligences' would indicate that he was a force behind the scenes and that his money bought power. Despite his political extremism, so out of tune with his fellow committeemen, Marten was indispensable.[21]

The Younger Brother

George Marten's background was more obscure than his brother. He was younger than Henry, possibly born in 1608, and, around 1638, married Frances Weld, daughter of the late Sir John Weld of Hertfordshire.[22] On his marriage, George came into possession of the lands that Sir Henry Marten had purchased from the bishop of Oxford. He was a wealthy man in his own right.[23] George and Frances had a daughter, also Frances. After George became captain of the *Marten* he becomes difficult to trace. He accumulated considerable debts, but he had been guilty of that prior to the outbreak of war. During April 1642, whilst the ship was being re-equipped for its state service, George computed a total of £8,200 of debts, 'wherein my Brother Marten is bound for mee'.[24] At some point prior to 1644, George Marten went to France, and during that year sent papers back to his brother.[25]

The first war ended in 1646 and with it George Marten's involvement. It left the brothers heavily in debt and searching for ways to recoup their losses. Henry's chance lay in the total defeat of the royalist forces and the possibility of preferment by the state. Around 1646 George Marten sailed for Barbados, joining an exodus to the English colonies. The Caribbean was a magnet for the ambitious, the reckless and the buccaneering: an ideal theatre for men prepared to take risks.[26]

There is no evidence that his wife or daughter accompanied him; the English Caribbean during the 1640s was a masculine community. The Caribbean islands lay 'beyond the line' – outside the area in which European treaties regulated the behaviour of sailors and merchants – and European norms of diplomatic and social conduct did not apply. Life was lazy, revolved around drink, fit for 'mettlesome gamblers'.[27] George Marten was little different: he captained a ship laden with drink and repeatedly called to his brother to furnish him with decent wine. At the height of Henry's financial problems, George was content only that he send him 'now & then a small Hamper of three or fowre dosen Glass quart bottles of excellent Canary'.[28]

The Caribbean life could also be extremely hard work. This was particularly so in the early days: land had to be cleared, usually using slash and burn techniques, and businesses erected, coming to terms with new conditions and new crops. Barbados was uninhabited when Europeans first disembarked and, as such, there was no resource of native labour whose expertise could be exploited. The settlers relied on the proficiency of other European colonists. An anonymous commentator declared, '[t]he island at first promised not so much as after experience taught its inhabitants to put a value on it, and by great encouragement of the Dutch, became a flourishing colony'.[29] The Barbadians grew tobacco, of such poor quality that it was virtually worthless in European markets. Nevertheless, there was potential for an Englishman with the right mentality: 'individualistic, competitive, and highly materialistic. Forswearing traditional notions of good lordship and medieval Christian values, [Barbadian society] was quite prepared to allow material interest to serve as a yardstick for acceptable and unacceptable social behaviour. The possibilities of amassing a large fortune brought men of this persuasion to Barbados.'[30]

Barbados was first settled in 1627, beset by political problems. Charles I initially granted title to Sir William Courteen, a member of a London financial interest with connections in the Netherlands, who was acting under the patronage of the Earl of Pembroke. Subsequently, Charles advanced the interests of Sir James Hay, first Earl of Carlisle, who ousted Courteen. The first investors were largely absentees and unwilling to commit huge capital grants to the colony. As such, initial farms on Barbados were small: between 10 and 30 acres.[31] In the first decade of the colony, Barbadian access to the home market was stifled by competition with Virginia, which produced superior tobacco. Therefore, in a dress rehearsal for a later fever, Barbadians turned to cotton. Sir Henry Colt, visiting the island in 1632, was on the whole of the opinion that the English planters were lazy and feckless, but was nevertheless pressed to note that 'trade in cotton fills them all with hope'.[32] It was not a success either. Although Caribbean sea-island cotton was of high quality and a long staple, the market was subject to wild fluctuations and the income it generated was not sufficient to maintain the colony, let alone power its advance. The islanders switched to indigo, a dyestuff that earned high prices on the European market. Still it was not sufficient to generate a thriving community.[33]

It was not until the late 1640s that the tiny island of Barbados established a relationship between the colony and the mother country which belied its size. The earlier plantation projects were finally beginning to bear fruit and the years after the end of the first English civil war brought a wave of vigorous settlers. The cessation of war offered new opportunities. The fresh arrivals were royalists, like Humphrey Walrond and Captain (later Colonel) Christopher Codrington, who had lost family fortunes in the ultimately doomed attempt to save Charles Stuart's cause, and younger sons, like George Marten, who saw a new theatre for investment and adventurism. Marten bought a going concern, producing tobacco, and it was in tobacco that he paid Codrington for 20 acres, in 1647. Marten thus began in a small way, growing a crop for which there was little demand.

He established himself in a house on the south side of the river Carlisle, near Bridgetown. This was possibly part of the 10,000 acres allocated to the London Merchant House in return for financial help to the plantation syndicate.[34] It is not clear whether Marten sailed to Barbados as the captain of the *Marten*, but the subsequent career of the ship seems to imply that his naval career was over. His letters give the impression that he had come to Barbados as a planter and settler and not as a merchant or trader. He abandoned more permanent interests in England and his messages to family, friends and creditors were delivered by other, more transitory residents. On 23 August 1647 he purchased a plantation of 179 acres in the parish of St John from the newly settled royalist, Humphrey Walrond.[35] The following year, he consolidated his estate, acquiring a further 20 acres from Codrington, and renting another 60.[36]

The settlers who arrived in Barbados after the civil war brought with them the factional scars of internecine division.[37] Marten, who had fought with the summer watch for parliament and who arrived in Barbados with his neighbour, Major Anthony Rous – 'my very kind & loving freind, and a person of as much honesty & honor, as I have ever mett with in these parts'[38] – was joined by disaffected royalists, granted their passage from England in lieu of composition fines. Barbados was to feed the careers of royalists who would become leading figures, such as Irish-born William Byam, the son of the precentor of Cloyne Cathedral. He had sailed to England at the start of the war, attained the rank of captain and was captured in July 1645 at the siege of Bridgwater. Humphrey Walrond was captured at the same engagement. Byam achieved his enlargement, provided he take the Walrond brothers to Barbados.[39]

The governor of Barbados, Philip Bell, remained resolutely neutral during the war, but things began to change with the flux of politics in England. Humphrey Walrond was the instigator of a plan to turn the General Assembly of the island into a permanent ruling council, and provoked planters' fear that servant rebellions were the first signs of plans by London to enslave them and turn the island over to schismatical enthusiasts.[40] With the island in a potentially explosive situation, the General Assembly tentatively welcomed the arrival of the new governor, neo-royalist Francis, Lord Willoughby of Parham. The thwarted Walrond tried to persuade the islanders that an apostate roundhead was an unreliable emissary of kingly authority, but the islanders who welcomed him were prepared to barter his potentially stabilising presence in return for an export duty on their goods.[41]

On 23 May 1650 the General Assembly banished and fined 122 Barbadian residents accused of being 'independents, non-conformist to the doctrine and discipline of the Church of England, and . . . aiders and abettors in the disturbance of the peace of the island'.[42] The men exiled ranged from the most successful and powerful planters, such as Colonel James Drax, to more moderate residents like Colonel John Fitzjames. The latter's information that Henry Ashton, governor of Antigua, would probably form an alliance with Willoughby was passed to Henry Marten on the Council of State.[43] Radical sectarians were ousted, along with those whose links with England made them suspect. The situation in England was no less secure and it became a matter of concern to the Commonwealth that it re-establish both the loyalty and the stability of their outposts, no matter how remote. Charles Stuart was proclaimed King, with the 'trumpeters receiving money and as much wine as they could drink from Governor Willoughby'.[44] The Commonwealth began to organise a fleet to reduce the island to obedience, but it was slow to mobilise. A fleet of seven ships, mounting 236 guns and carrying 820 men, was ready by January 1651 but did not sail until June, having first been employed in the Scilly Isles.[45] The fleet was commanded by the Surrey gentleman Sir George Ayscue, who initially found his tiny flotilla relatively unimpressive in comparison to the 8,000 armed islanders who turned out in response, but he finally reduced the island to obedience.[46]

The changing political circumstances in England and the prospect of an armed force arriving from the mother country concentrated the minds of Caribbean enterprisers on the profits in hand. The government in England directed the Committee of the Admiralty to check the ownership of Barbadian cargoes stored in London customs' houses, with the intention of seizing those goods that belonged to planters disaffected to the Commonwealth.[47] On Barbados, one group of islanders, opposing the ruling royalist group, proposed that the government send for Edward Winslow of New England, 'a person of approved fidelity to this Commonwealth', who would replace the royalist Willoughby as governor and turn the colony into an outpost of godly puritanism. But even the godliest of the settlers had a high regard for economic motivation. They proposed that Barbados be awarded the status of an incorporated town, with the rights, privileges and autonomy which that entailed.[48] Another similar view was put by John Bayes, the treasurer of Barbados, but he questioned the loyalty and credentials of the former group.[49] George Marten had said to him that the 'powers that do now govern in Barbados were not sensible that they had done anything against this commonwealth' but 'looked upon themselves as free people'.

George Marten's response was to organise London merchants and Barbados planters to petition for the right to continue trading with the island in five or six merchant vessels provided that, if they met with hostility from 'active incendiaries in the late troubles there', they could transform themselves into a fighting force. Their conditions of trade were that Willoughby repeal all acts that were to the dishonour of parliament, the islanders renounce their allegiance to Charles Stuart, and that those who had fled as a result of the royalists' coup be allowed to return to claim the lands of royalists, who would themselves be banished.[50] Willoughby and the General Assembly would then be allowed to remain. When the Council of State replied favourably to their petition, they followed up with another, requesting that they be allowed to join in the reduction of the island and that they should then be granted exemption from customs and excise, and the same privileges as were granted to the 'free people' of England.[51]

In 1651 George Marten arrived in England, an emissary from Barbados. He was playing a dangerous game and it is perhaps not surprising that he 'could hardly find footing att his first flight'.[52] London merchant John Paige reported to William Clerke: 'here is come an agent from the islanders to treat with our State, which as yet hath no audience. But it is hoped by many that there will be an accommodation; God grant it.'[53] Although it was George who transported the planters ousted by Willoughby, he was described in London as Willoughby's agent.[54] Economic advantage clouded issues of political loyalty, and George's intentions are far from clear. Having brought the fleeing 'parliamentarians' from Barbados, he appeared at the Council of State with an invitation to the escapees to return. George's band of merchants and planters lobbied the government. They would return to Barbados, help capture the island and secure it for the Commonwealth if the Commonwealth favoured them with advantageous conditions for planting and trade.[55]

Henry Marten sat on the Council and on 27 November he was appointed to a sub-committee to further the reduction of Barbados.[56] George could be expected to use the favour and protection of his powerful brother to further the interests of the Barbadian settlers and perhaps secure a settlement to the advantage of the majority. As such, he knew how to employ Levellerish and republican rhetoric to influence his brother's allies. So did his opponents. The group that had opposed Willoughby and proposed Edward Winslow instead, also brought the Levellerised language of individual liberties to bear:

[a]s freeborn Englishmen, we desire in Barbados that as all power in all places here in England do receive their immediate commissions for the exercise of all authority from the High Court of Parliament which is representative of the whole nation, so Barbados as a branch belonging to this commonwealth may be entirely incorporated into the same as any town, city, shire, or island thereto belongeth.[57]

This was language more likely to accord with Henry Marten's, and planter Sir Thomas Modyford reported that George had come close to being hanged for speaking out in favour of Lord Willoughby.[58] George may have placed a naïve faith in Willoughby, or seen the way of the tide and decided to follow the line taken by his brother. Whatever was the case, there is no evidence to describe him as a royalist, but as one of many anxious to secure the best economic advantage for themselves, and further their careers across the Atlantic, by gauging the political climate at home.[59] He returned to Barbados with Ayscue, and reported to his brother that the Admiral 'has performed the trust layd on him by ye Parmt with greate Honor Justice & wisdome, hee has delivered us from the Ld Willoughby & those that with him, meant to have caried theire fortunes upon or by the crimes[?] of this place [and] has left us in a willinge & cherfull obedience to ye Pamt the supreme authoryte of England'.[60] John Hollond, one of the 'regulators' of the Navy Commission, brusquely informed Henry that his brother would be paid his 'groats' by the Treasurer of the Navy.[61]

One main aim of Marten's petitioning group was to persuade the English state to incorporate Barbados as if it was an English town. However, the effect of such a move would not be to tie the island more closely to the mainland but would guarantee privileges for the freemen, thereby signalling their autonomy. They spoke the rhetoric of 'freeborn Englishmen', but the freedom they wanted turned political individualism into material advantage. They reinterpreted the tendency for Barbadian politics to degenerate into faction, exploiting the language of the devolution of power. Calls not to let power rest in the same hands for too long effectively meant that the writer really wanted the power for himself.

George's dual concerns were the maintenance of a functioning – and profitable – community on Barbados, whilst maximising its fiscal potential to England. Another petition, *The humble Petition of diverse Merchants Planters Mariners, owners of shipps eceat*, probably also written during 1650, although this version may not have been published, was sent directly to Henry Marten.[62] The petitioners were well aware that the Caribbean had been 'planted at the Cost, and setled by the People, and by Authority of this Nation, which are and ought to be subordinate to, and dependent upon England',[63] but complained that although they were innocent of any political rising against the Commonwealth, they were the ones being punished by stiff financial penalties:

they being comanded not to fetch away their Estates, or to correspond with the Persons there trusted by them: and whatsoever is sent to them from thence, is exposed as Prize: and strangers doe upon their own tearmes engross that Trade: and in the mean while your Petitioners Goods and Estates must necessarily bee consumed; and those Islands [Barbados and Antigua] be hardned and strengthned . . . to an obstinat Disaffection of this Commonwealth.

The solution, according to the petitioners, was for the London government to show them its trust. In return for being allowed to reopen trade with England and for letters of marque to repel unlicensed traders, they 'may alsoe have oportunities to winne and Persuade the Islanders, to consider and understand their Dutye and Interests and to submitt to this Com[m]onwealth'. Thus what was, politically, to the 'honour and advantage of this State' was also, economically, for 'the Preservation of yr Petitioners'.

English policy responded to the assertiveness of rivals like the Dutch, who threatened both the political stability of England and its economic and trading interests. The state paid increasing attention to matters of commerce. The act 'for the advancing and regulating of the trade of this Commonwealth', passed on 1 August 1650, sent instructions to the council of trade, including, among other things, an exhortation to consider the American plantations and advise how they might best be supplied only with English goods and should themselves supply the mother country with the entirety of its needs.[64] In October 1651 this dictum was reinforced by the first of England's Navigation acts, which confined all English and English colonial trade to English registered shipping.[65]

The Trade in Sugar and Slaves

Tobacco, cotton and indigo failed: sugar did not. Barbados was beginning to experience the vice-like grip with which the prospect of huge profits from sugar cane seized the mind. Unfortunately for the interests of English planters in Barbados, the Navigation Act could be counterproductive. As the economy was rapidly changing, settlers switching their interests to sugar, constantly increasing the acreage under cultivation, the home country's Navigation Act had the effect of banning trade with the United Provinces and with it access to Dutch expertise, equipment and shipping. Trade with Spain, Portugal and their colonies, already major sugar producers in their own right, was excepted from the act. The Barbados planters gave an unenthusiastic welcome to one of the Commonwealth's most far-reaching pieces of legislation.[66]

George Marten's land was considered prime for the production of sugar. His estate, in the parish of St John on the east coast of Barbados, was buffeted by waves, stirred up by the winds off the Atlantic, keeping it relatively free from mosquitos and all their attendant diseases, and cooler in climate for English people frightened by the maddening effects of the tropical sun. It was also situated on an escarpment, known as the Cliff, an inland range formed from coral as the island emerged from the sea. The machinery and engineering required by the sugar refining process benefited from these conditions. The strong winds drove the windmills that provided the power. The slope of the cliff enabled the boiling house, where the sugar canes and water bubbled in the first stage of the process, to be situated at a higher level than the curing house and store houses, where the resulting molasses was crystallised. The pull of gravity transported the molasses to the next stage of refinement.

The Martens were eager for an opportunity to recoup their losses and re-establish the family fortune. Dreams, hopes and potential empires were constructed on the profits of fields of waving grass. Sugar was a potentially profitable crop, as the following century was to show, but not in the conditions of the mid-seventeenth century. It posed problems for inexperienced planters. Plants had to be brought from Brazil. Planters had to foster links with the Dutch and Portuguese in order to gain the expertise required to build machinery and introduce the processes. Early canes were cut when they appeared to have reached maturity but when, in fact, the sucrose had not yet developed. It required fifteen months before a sugar crop was ready to harvest and several years before production was sufficient to pay off the massive investment required. Sugar needed a greater acreage than tobacco or indigo, enormous injections of capital, and was both labour and capital intensive.[67] The early plantations incorporated indentured labourers. As the workers came to the end of their indenture-period, they could claim a small piece of land. The consequence of this indenture system was a patchwork of smallholdings, which was antithetical to sugar production. What was needed was cheap labour, and labourers to whom the planters felt no obligation to provide contracts, land or accommodation. Thus English merchants moved into new areas. Speculative fever gripped the island and the city of London, which made provision to expand into sugar and slaves.

Neither George nor his brother had the capital to invest on this scale: George borrowed on the open market. Financiers provided enough for slaves, equipment and machinery, and he began sugar production around 1649/50. By 1656 he was master of a plantation on the escarpment running through the parish of St John, in the prime territory near the church, measuring 209 acres above the Cliff and 50 below, of which 40 was lease-hold with eighteen years left to run.[68] He had 60 slaves – 25 men, 25 women, and 10 children – 4 asses, a working water-mill, boiling house, equipment and 1,000 large sugar pots.[69]

Initially, Marten produced muscovado sugar, which could be of varying quality, from scummy, impure and unmarketable to the 'good merchantable' quality that was the chief currency of trading. It was a difficult and skilled job to produce even muscovado sugar correctly, but increasingly sophisticated European palates were not content with 'bare Muscovadoes' and demanded refined white sugar, which involved further engineering to build curing houses in which the molasses sat in pots waiting for the refining process.[70] George wrote enthusiastically to Harry about the prospects of white sugar, and in the latter half of 1656 was constructing a two-storey curing house, 90 feet long and 30 feet wide, with the hope that it would be completed by Christmas.[71]

White sugar was produced by a slow and laborious process in which molasses was poured into the top of a series of terracotta jars, stacked one above another. The sugar crystals formed around the outside of the jar and the surplus liquid dripped into the jar below. The process was repeated until, finally, the remaining molasses would be captured in a bowl at ground level. The pots were sealed with clay, which drew out the impurities to leave white, refined sugar.[72] A total of 1,000 sugar pots made Marten the owner of a moderately sized plantation. The quantities of white sugar that he produced were small, and a long time in the making. He expected it to be the currency for wine sent by his brother: 'I will not promise you payment for it, but the next yeare I shall make white sug^r, and then if you find by yowre Accompt, that the wine you send hether is Ballanst by the sug^r you receave from herer, I hope you will not be offended at it'.[73] Henry Marten, in the depth of financial crisis, was therefore expected to pay for wine to maintain his brother's lifestyle – 'that I may not in drinkinge yowre health lose my owne' – for which he would be repaid, at some unspecified future date, in kind, with a product that it was not clear George was capable of producing, the manufacture of which had in turn involved him in significant debts. The letter of George Marten's does, however, confirm Dunn's thesis that Barbados was the only English island on which white sugar was being produced: it was more usual for muscovado to be shipped to Europe to be refined closer to home. It was manufactured on Barbados in very small quantities and could be carried home by individuals. George's neighbour, Mr Settle, was able to transport George's new wealth back to his brother by hand.[74]

Most of the larger planters began expediently to buy in slaves to solve the labour shortage. Although white settlers greatly outnumbered black slaves during the mid-century, steadily the numbers of Africans rose. The price of a male slave fluctuated during the period, between £22 and £30, whilst a female slave, primarily for domestic service, cost between £25 and £27.[75] Although life was cheap for the imported black labourers, Hilary Beckles has convincingly undermined many of the arguments advanced for switching from indentured to slave labour.[76] George Marten may have kept more, but we know that on his 259 acre St John plantation, he had fifty adult 'able working negroes'.[77] Their names are recorded – a mixture of English, African and bastardised, anglicised amalgams.[78] There were also ten children. The fact that

Marten kept equal numbers of men and women and the presence of children may have indicated that he was unusual in allowing his slaves to live in families. Beckles is doubtful that slaves were encouraged to have children on the mid-seventeenth-century plantations, 'believing that the opportunity cost and monetary outlay to rear juveniles was greater than the expected marginal revenue'.[79]

Marten's plantation was not heavily supplied with slaves.[80] Figures later in the century, when sugar production was in full flow, indicated that a 100 acre plantation functioned at an optimum level of fifty slaves and seven servants.[81] George Marten may, on the strictly relative scale that hindsight imposes, have been a liberal slave owner. Nevertheless, in a six month period during which we can reconstruct and compare the names of Marten's fifty slaves, the character of the population had altered considerably. Ten of the names of the men and six of the women were different. This may have been due to high mortality rates. Some studies conclude that 33 per cent of slaves would die within three years of their arrival in the Americas. New slaves may have been bought to replace runaways.[82] In the latter of the two indentures that listed the names of George's slaves, it was specified that 'if any of these Negroes here inserted shall dye or Runnaway that then Capt George Martine shall supply every negroe soe or by any other meanes wantinge with another of the same sex'.[83] The high turnover of labour on the land of a 'liberal' planter must make us question planters who laid claim to benign treatment. Although it was rare in the middle of the seventeenth century to hear voices raised against the use of black labour, it was also quite fashionable to claim generous treatment of servants and slaves. Humphrey Walrond was described by Richard Ligon as a man who 'got such love of his servants as they thought all too little they could do for him'.[84]

George Marten became an establishment name among the settlers of the east coast. He was a trustee of the vestry of St John's church, his own and his brother's reputation for unchristian conduct notwithstanding. In the future, accusations of atheism, blasphemy and debauchery would be as damaging to George's political career in the colonies as Henry's in England. During 1653 George was responsible for collecting the finance for a road building programme in the parish and he was still being named a parochial trustee five years later.[85] He was part of a clique, described by John Bayes as 'old, overgrown, desperate malignants who called themselves the representatives of the island, but if suffered . . . would in time become the sole power'.[86] In the years following the Commonwealth reconquest, these men set about reorganising the government. One of their first actions was to relieve Bayes of his post of 'public treasurer of the customs and excise' for unspecified 'crimes', which amounted to not supporting Ayscue. George sent the details of this debate to his brother on the Council of State.[87] They augmented the powers of the Assembly, choosing former roundhead Thomas Modyford[88] as Speaker, and slashed the powers of the governor.

In June 1653, after the fall of the Rump, Daniel Searle, who was sympathetic to the direction of the government in England, was confirmed as governor, and the constitution was changed again. The new assembly consisted of six nominees chosen by the governor and two members elected from each of the parishes.[89] George Marten sat on the General Assembly for the parish of St John. The Caribbean settlers re-enacted the English struggle between executive and legislative control over the militia and the extent of representative power. This, in turn, was a repeat of the petitioning debates of 1649 and 1650 and of Bayes' argument against the ruling junto. In many ways it anticipated the controversy that dogged the early years of the Cromwellian Protectorate in England. The Assembly attempted to institute annual elections and Searle dismissed it with the warning to England that the Assemblymen were 'unsatisfied with the constitution of England [and] would mould this little limb of the Commonwealth into a free state'. Despite the web of faction and the complexity of England's fluctuating interests, George Marten was a skilful politician and despite his brother's fall from grace in April 1653, rose to be Barbados's Speaker in the session of 1655.[90]

George was still anxious to use the influence of his brother to further his own and his allies' future on the island and advised Henry that the Council of State should anticipate petitions of complaint. The Assembly felt obliged to levy duties on the merchants and planters in order to defray the 'very many publick chardges' that the local administration was incurring in re-establishing peace and prosperity on the island.[91] Customs' levies of 4 per cent were charged on merchants exporting Barbadian goods, whilst planters were taxed at 2 per cent of their crop. Marten's constituency was the permanent residents – the planters – and not the merchants. Although merchants complained about the levy, Marten explained that they were able to circumvent its detrimental economic effects by using English government policy to inflate their prices, to the ruin of residents. The government's ban on trade with the Dutch had cut off what had previously been a lifeline for the planters. English merchants now had a monopoly of trade and

I dare sweare the merchant has not made this yeare less then 5 or 6 of one, which was never gott but of ye ignorant Indyans formerly, for now they are to[o] wise; but they know our rents & if I goe to buy an axe or any such thinge that I know the price in England to bee 20 pence or 2 shillinges, they will not take less . . . then the valew of twenty shillinges.

The only means of survival for planters like himself, he argued, was for them to ship all of their requirements from England at their own expense, something that barely 10 per cent of planters could afford. Henry Marten's government may have introduced the Navigation Act, but George Marten hoped his brother would use all his influence in parliament and council to minimise its effects. '[P]erfect freedom' meant economic self-management as well as a sense of republican citizenship.

George Marten enjoyed life in the Caribbean. The weather was to his liking. He possessed his elder brother's wit and facility with words, so it was with heavy irony that he thought of Henry 'in abundance of zeale & sobrietye'.[92] He described Henry's political misfortunes as having 'brought [his] hoggs to an ill markett' and tried to entice his brother to join him:

> I hope I can heere as Joseph was in Egipt onely to provide for you to serve you, if ever you shall have neede of mee in the world that I will not sacrifice in yowre service; Good Brother if ever you shall thinke it fit to quitt England, doe not thinke there is in the world a more helthfull, pleasant & plentifull place then this; & then I hope you will not scrupell cumminge hether, for truely I can entertayne you heere as well as ever you could mee att Beckett.[93]

He lived on credit: he had always done so.[94] Although the family was in decline, he was pleased to hear from Henry of an upturn in their affairs early in 1656: 'I am very glad to understand youre affaires are so well, as to be in a hopeful condition; for my part I wish not mine better, for I have lived upon that Accompt above these eight yeares, and if I can but keepe my hopes alive, I shall thinke (tho you are of another mind) that I have more reason to bragg then complaine of my condition'. He also followed his brother's example in keeping a household with a common law wife. George's Barbados wife was called Susan, or 'butter-box', by whom he probably had a child. However, Susan was a further drain on Henry's resources since he felt obligated to be responsible for her welfare whilst she was in England, and provided her with accommodation. More usefully, he gave her £30 with which to buy a passage back to the Caribbean, having some left over for victuals.[95] George wrote about her to his brother in as loving terms as Henry used about Mary Ward.[96] There is little evidence to concur with Lord Portland's description of the younger brother as 'dour George'.[97]

Despite his debts, George felt himself to be a man of independent means. This lasted only seven years. By 1653 he was in severe financial difficulties. Early investment by local planter Thomas Reeve, which had cost him £240 or 24,000 pounds of sugar, remained unpaid.[98] In October 1653 Christopher Codrington bought back the twenty-one year lease on his 60 acre holding. There were still fourteen years left to run.[99] The following month he was forced to mortgage the original 179 acres that he had purchased from Walrond in August 1646 to two Barbados merchants, Thomas Kendall and Thomas Bignell, who were acting on behalf of Captain Steven Thompson, a merchant in London.[100] Although George treated sceptically rumours from London that Henry had been imprisoned in the Tower, he dismissed the level of debt both were carrying. He claimed he was clear of his initial debts and that the Committee of the Navy had paid £1,000 to Ralph Ingram to cover his investment in the *Marten*. He complained that had Ingram not died whilst George was in France, the state would not have fallen into such confusion about his own and his brother's status.[101]

George was, however, hurtling towards bankruptcy; disguised by the sun and sugar-fever, but ultimately much the same as his brother. In 1656 he signed indentures with two London merchants, James White and Thomas Cooper, and he mortgaged his 259 acre estate in St John's parish for a total of 133,666 pounds of sugar. He contracted to make repayments on the mortgage over the next three years, at a total of £1,200 to White and £1,000 to Cooper, but should he default, the two merchants could take possession of half the plantation each, as a going concern, complete with plant, machinery and slaves. George failed to make the repayments, and after 1658 he disappears from the records of Barbados.

Starting Again

Around 1658 George Marten left Barbados and set sail for another English colony, Surinam. According to a contemporary computation, he was one of 2,400 men to leave Barbados for either Surinam or Virginia between 1646 and 1658.[102] Surinam, on the north-west coast of mainland south America, was the furthest afield of the so-called Caribee islands and just five degrees north of the equator. The settlement had been established in 1650, under the governor of the Caribee islands, Willoughby of Parham, on his eviction from Barbados, and the majority of the early settlers in Surinam were made up of those ejected from Barbados. They were joined in the later 1650s by a new wave of unsuccessful Barbadian planters, of which George Marten was one of the most prestigious in terms of political status, but as much a victim of financial collapse as any. He was unlikely to have taken much from Barbados, having sold his entire estate to White and Cooper, and the Marten name was not credit-worthy in 1658. Peter Campbell believes he may have been in Surinam as a manager, though descriptions of his status within the new colony belie this (*see* plate 2).[103]

Surinam lay within the south American rain forest, with wide creeks twisting like tree branches away from the sandbanks at the entrance to the Surinam and Commewigne rivers.[104] Settlements were spaced along the creeks for up to 30 miles inland, whilst the rivers were still navigable, but beyond that point lay rapids and waterfalls. There was a myriad of strange creatures – '[t]he Ant-eater is of the size of an ordinary pig' – there were black, spotted and red 'tigers', turtles, monkeys, sloths and birds declared the most beautiful in the world. The climate was humid, sultry and tropical, and many were laid low with illness, particularly yellow fever and venereal diseases. However, Adriaan van Berbel believed that '[t]he uniform warmth causes this country to be much more pleasant for old than for young people. Because it seems as if the country smiles at them, and rejuvenates their years: . . . [t]he young people . . . lose much of their strength here, and come to fall away earlier than in Northern countries'.[105] George Marten was around fifty when he arrived in the territory. It was a colony of contrasts, being both 'blessed by God, and has so many virtues', but also a 'sad and rough' country.[106]

Van Berbel, writing towards the end of the century, described a settlement – which had then been taken over by the Dutch – of around 300 plantation estates. There were small urban centres – of 50 to 60 houses at Paramaribo, and of about half that size at the area now known as Jodensavanna.[107] He reported that Surinam had previously had even fewer inhabitants, perhaps 500. Only 100 settlers had been sent by Willoughby in 1651 and at its strongest – around 1665 – there were still only 40 or 50 profitable estates, out of a total of 129,[108] and a population estimated at 1,500 Europeans, 3,000 slaves of African descent and 400 native Americans.[109] The conditions that had hampered Barbados – too many smallholders, all attempting to make a profitable living from a crop for which economies of scale were vital – did not apply on the Guianan coast. They planted sugar – they were near the Portuguese centre of Pernambuco – and it was accounted better quality than that of Barbados. Timber from the fringes of the forest, especially the hardwood known as 'specklewood', was shipped to Europe as a cabinet-wood.[110] It was reported in 1654 that since most of the houses of Barbados were wooden, timber from Surinam had a ready market.[111] Sir Thomas Modyford optimistically offered his opinion in 1652 that Willoughby and his settlers would develop 'one of the fertilest most spacious and beautifullest countryes'.[112]

The evidence for Marten's status when he arrived on Surinam is not clear. There is no extant record of his borrowing more London finance to restart his planting career, but a plantation bearing his name does feature on a map of the English colony, drawn in 1667.[113] Three tributaries were settled by the English. The majority of plantations lay on the Corapena and Surinam rivers and a lesser number in the interior, on the Commewigne (Commawena) and its tributary, the Mapauny or Willoughby river. Several names were recognisable from Barbados; there were merchants like de Casares, and friends of Marten such as Westropp[114] and Rous. There were also old adversaries such as Byam, now described as a lieutenant-general, who retained his landed interests in Barbados into the 1660s,[115] but who owned two plantations in Surinam, one close to Marten's own and another on the Surinam river to the north-west of the old capital, Toorarica. The two sites were linked by the river and a track cleared through the forest. Marten's own estate lay on the left bank as one sailed upstream on the Corapena, or Para river, about 20 miles inland from Paramaribo. It was approximately three days travel by boat from the capital.[116]

The behaviour of the English settlers in Surinam differed little from their behaviour in Barbados. Around 1667, an anonymous author accounted for the 1,500 English settlers who had left Barbados by remarking on the

> several factions among the planters (which are gentlemen of the country, and are almost every [one] considerable proprietors, either a colonel, lieutenant colonel, major, captain, or lieutenant) . . . there have been several governors . . . All these governors changed their favorites, put the militia into new hands, elected new councillors and judges, so that dependents upon each governor are, with their adherents, the many distinct factions to this day.[117]

This factional fighting was exportable and was to strangle the development of the settlement, for the new arrivals from Barbados merely transplanted their muddy politics and continued, in a bastardised form, the civil war viciousness of eight years before.

The brutal malignancy of English politics in Surinam formed the backdrop to the work of Aphra Behn. In 1688 she published *Oroonoko: or the Royal Slave*, a romance set in the English colony of Surinam, the unique selling point of which was the contrast between white and black and the baseness of the former in comparison with the gallantry and greatness of her African hero, Oroonoko. Behn claimed to have travelled to Surinam and witnessed the story of her romance, which she committed to paper 'in a few hours' up to twenty-five years after she had left, although the manuscript could have been written rather closer to the events. The prose is fresh and vigorous and the factual details that underpin her story are many and accurate. She may indeed have been in the colony – though not for the reason she claimed – or have heard directly from those who were.

As an historical source, however, *Oroonoko* must be treated with caution. Behn's slave hero was tutored by a Frenchman in Africa, who taught him history, literature, about 'the late civil wars in England, and the deplorable death of our great monarch', giving him a European voice with which to relay the 'whole transactions of his youth'.[118] As a quixotic hero, sympathetically drawn, Oroonoko's appearance was Europeanised: his face was not 'that brown rusty black which most of that nation are', but 'a perfect ebony, or polished jett . . . His nose was rising and Roman, instead of African and flat.' He did not have 'those great turn'd lips, which are so natural to the rest of the Negroes' and his hair was pulled and dressed to make it fall to his shoulders. Behn's sensitive piece about the plight of African slaves still had to caress an English readership.

Oroonoko was an African warrior general from Coramantien, who met and fell in love with Imoinda, the daughter of a fatally wounded opponent. Their mutual love was consumated, a practice Behn defended as more honest than European courtship. They married,[119] but Imoinda was summoned by the King of Coramantien, who wanted her himself. She refused to betray her husband and the King discovered that his general, Oroonoko, had married a woman of high birth without his permission. As punishment, the embittered King sold the pair into slavery. Separately, they were both transported to Surinam. Oroonoko was sold to Trefry, a Cornishman whom Willoughby had brought to Surinam and made his estate manager. Trefry recognised Oroonoko's intelligence and humanity: the manager was 'a very good mathematician, and a linguist; could speak French and Spanish' and regarded his new slave 'as his dearest brother'. He gave Oroonoko the slave name of Caesar.[120] The 'amorous' Trefry, however, was also taken by the beauty of Imoinda. The love story tells of Imoinda and Oroonoko's tragic struggle to be reunited.

Behn, her novel written as semi-autobiography, met Oroonoko/Caesar, and joined small scouting parties that ventured into the interior to watch the 'tigers' rear their cubs. One such group of six consisted of Behn, Oroonoko, three other women, and 'an English gentleman, brother to Harry Martin the great Oliverian'. On this particular escapade, they encountered an aggressive jaguar, which Oroonoko slew with George Marten's sword. Oroonoko had killed another, which had long eluded the English gentlemen, and thus protected the colony's sheep and oxen.[121] Though the survival of European sheep in the tropical climate was unlikely, 'because it seems that these beasts thrive better in a cold and dry country than in one hot and damp', there were cattle.[122] Van Berbel related that the jaguars were starting to move further into the interior with the arrival of Europeans, several having been killed by sword or musket, but he had 'never heard of more than 2 or 3 people being devoured, ever since the foundation of the Colony'.[123]

Oroonoko's comparatively liberated wanderings around the colony, his noble bearing, and status, made him at the same time a focus for envy and a symbol of unity among resentful captives. When he escaped, it signalled the start of a slave rebellion: 'all hands were against the Parhamites (as they called those of Parham-Plantation) because they did not in the first place love the Lord-Governour', believing, among other things, that Oroonoko had been badly treated. It was rumoured that 'some of the best in the country was of his council in the flight'[124] and the factionalism of Surinam made plausible the idea that disgruntled settlers would use the instigation of slave rebellion to undermine the administration. One of the most hard-line who pursued Oroonoko was William Byam, the lieutenant governor, 'a fellow, whose character is not fit to be mentioned with the worst of the slaves'. Imoinda, pregnant and close to term, stayed by her heroic lord and shot several Englishmen with a bow and arrow, wounding Byam in the shoulder. Having promised an accommodation with the rebels, Byam betrayed Oroonoko and had him flogged almost to death. Behn and the wounded Oroonoko

> met on the river with Colonel Martin, a man of great gallantry, wit, and goodness, and whom I have celebrated in a character of my new comedy, by his own name, in memory of so brave a man: he was wise and eloquent, and, from the fineness of his parts, bore great sway over the hearts of all the colony: he was a friend to Caesar [Oroonoko], and resented this false dealing with him very much. We carry'd him back to Parham, thinking to have made an accommodation.[125]

Oroonoko apparently respected Marten as a father. Imoinda and Oroonoko resolved to die in a bloody suicide pact, rather than live as slaves or die at an Englishman's vengeful hands. Oroonoko survived and was hacked to pieces by James Bannister, one of the council. Behn travelled to Marten, to whom was dispatched one quarter of Oroonoko's mutilated body. Marten refused to display it, declaring 'he had rather see the quarters of Banister, and the Governour himself, than those of Caesar, on his plantations; and that he could govern his Negroes, without terrifying and grieving them with frightful spectacles of a mangled King'.[126]

The records of the English settlement on Surinam are so scanty that it is now impossible to gauge the accuracy of Behn's account. Her pretext for witnessing these events was that her whole family were sailing to the territory where her 'father' had been nominated by Willoughby to be lieutenant-general. This would explain her hatred of Byam, the current incumbent.[127] It could have been a literary device. Nevertheless, she used the details of English infighting as a factual backdrop to a fictional romance. She was undeniably aware of the nastiness of Surinamese politics:

> The Governour [Byam] had no sooner recover'd, and had heard of the menaces of Caesar, but he called his council, who (not to disgrace them, or burlesque the government there) consisted of such notorious villains as Newgate never transported; and possibly, originally were such who understood neither the laws of God or man, and had no sort of principles, to make them worthy the name of man; but at the very council-table wou'd contradict and fight with one another, and swear so bloodily, that 'twas terrible to hear and see 'em.[128]

Several accounts of the factionalism which destroyed the English Guianan colony survive. In 1662 Lieutenant Colonel Robert Sanford, who owned a plantation almost at the furthest extent of the settlement along the Surinam river, wrote *Suriname Justice*.[129] This account gives precisely the opposite view of Marten's political allegiances in the Guianas. This claims that Marten and Byam acted together to engineer another settler's fine, both holding an implacable hatred of the man. While agreeing that Byam was a brutal governor, he was encouraged by 'the violent counsels of Marten, who offered himself the Hangman of any at the Governours single command' and who was 'so famous in nothing but his variety of councels: and it seems the *whole Government* must dance to the *changes* of his brain'.[130] This account of George Marten's rather fickle political will may well have been carried from Barbados, where he had followed an ambiguous line. Sanford believed George to be no more the Christian than Henry, corrupting the colony and amusing Byam with 'witty prophanations of the sacred Christian Religion, atheistically with scoffs . . . seldom sparing his God in his jest'.

It is possible that the romance of Oroonoko was an inversion of the story of John Allin, a Londoner who arrived in Surinam from Barbados in 1657. Allin's experince was related by Byam, who thought him a blasphemer, who 'disregarding Scripture, and scoffing at Piety, entertained his hours of leisure with Romances, and the Lives of some bold *Romans* and daring Valiant ones, which bred in him an admiration . . . how any man . . . would on any account suffer torment or publick ignominious death, when his own hands with a stab or poison could give him ease and remedy'.[131] When Willoughby arrived in person, the governor was made aware of Allin's atheistical tendencies, but Willoughby assured Allin that his person and property were secure. Allin felt betrayed when he heard that the Lord Proprietor had designs on his 'vineyard'. '[G]uided by an Atheistical Tenet', Allin 'designed a most inveterate revenge on his innocent Excellency, and his own death.'[132] He burst into the evening service at Parham House, lunged at Willoughby's head, severed the fingers of the governor's right hand, and turned the knife on himself. For six days, he lay injured and feverish but, once dead, was discovered to have taken poison. His body was dismembered, disembowelled, beheaded and quartered, 'and when dry-barbicued or dry-roasted, after the *Indian* manner, his Head . . . [was] . . . stuck on a pole at *Parham*, and his Quarters . . . put up at the most eminent places of the Colony'.[133] A letter from Allin to Willoughby was discovered after his capture, in which he claimed that he had

> too much of a *Roman* in me to possess my own life, when I cannot enjoy it with freedom and honour.
>
> . . . I had your life in my hand, my sword drawn, and as much courage as ever *Caesar* had . . . I will conclude that you intend to destroy me, or at the least put ignominies upon me, which I will never endure; I will renounce all Allegiance, revenge my self on all my Enemies, then kill my self. . .
>
> From the Woods, Tuesday
> Jan.3. 1664.[134]

Behn's black slave hero, the antithesis of Byam's white planter, was given the name of Caesar to reflect his noble bearing and Roman nose.[135] Behn sneered at the sanctimonious formalism of Surinam's Christianity, which had little to do with real Christian values: 'such ill morals are only practis'd in Christian countries, where they prefer the bare name of religion; and, without vertue or morality, think that sufficient'.[136] She was at pains to justify non-Christian morés, such as African polygamy. Oroonoko/Caesar was betrayed by the establishment, vowing revenge that ultimately could not be executed but which resulted in the brutal ignominy of summary justice. Allin's quartered body was sent out around the colony as a warning to others, as was Oroonoko's in the fictional version.

Behn may never have met George Marten, and we cannot tell whether her descriptions of his actions and character in Surinam were accurate. She did know William Scot, son of Thomas, the parliamentary intelligencer. William fled to Surinam at the Restoration and subsequently became her spying partner.[137] Scot had been stirring up republican unrest on Barbados and may have recounted tales of the colourful Marten brothers, who provided apposite characters for both her romances and her comedies of morals and politics.[138] She does, however, give an authentic taste of the nastiness of the favouritism which was rife within Surinamese politics under the English. This was so tangled as to make superimposing objectivity virtually impossible, but we may note that none of the characters emerge with much credit. Preoccupation with petty power struggles and personalised animosities weakened what could have been a thriving community. Byam added to the tension by pointing to 1665 as the zenith of Surinam's prosperity. The following year it came under attack from the Dutch, and the English scorched those estates that seemed worth capturing. Surinam was ceded to the United Provinces under the terms of the Treaty of Breda the following year. Fighting continued, led first by Byam and then by Willoughby's son, Henry, but the English finally surrendered to Admiral Abraham Cijnssen. The Dutch allowed English planters to remain, but there was little to stay for.[139] The English had destroyed their own colony through factionalism, lack of investment and their antagonism against the Dutch. In 1665 they had also suffered the loss of large numbers of colonists when disease swept the Guianan coast. This was the ignominious death of George Marten, recorded by William Byam as one of Surinam's plague victims in the year 1666.

VII

'An Ugly Rascal and a Whoremonger'

The importance of historical figures usually lies in their deeds or their writings. Henry Marten is known by reputation. A local historian compared Marten unfavourably with his father. Sir Henry was 'hardworking, financially astute, devoted to his king, upright in character and respected by all'. His son 'squandered his father's fortune in loose living and hated the monarchy'.[1] Henry Marten is described as a singular radical, an isolated example of a republican, a colourful rogue, extremist and wit, drunken and promiscuous.

Hexter's study of 'King Pym' magnified his hero, and castigated the man who made Pym's role more difficult. Marten was distinctive in 'an assembly aggressively pure in principle' for his 'disregard of marriage', and his degenerate character provided a metaphor for the collapse of political designs.[2] When he appeared in front of the London councillors, to promote a General Rising and a new army commander, 'the apotheosis of Sir William Waller by a notorious freethinker and loose-liver was in a way an appropriate climax to a celebration that behind its brave front concealed a scheme already crumbling from its inherent weaknesses'.[3] Russell is sceptical of the impact of Calvinist resistance theory: '[i]t would be a matter for considerable surprise if William Strode, Sir Henry Ludlow, or Henry Marten could be shown to be principled believers in non-resistance'.[4] Jonathan Scott's portrait of Algernon Sidney includes a clash between his 'moralistic and imperious' subject and the 'irreverent, irreligious, and anti-aristocratic' Marten.[5]

Marten's reputation was sealed by contemporaneous anecdotes and witticisms. It is necessary to examine how far they had substance. Some of Marten's reputation is undoubtedly deserved. Other aspects have been magnified by salacious gossip. His political opponents exaggerated his personal image in order to collapse his political pretentions, and aid their own personal or political cause. Some of his reputation was the effect of deliberate manipulation, but then Marten made much of his own reputation, for self-preservation.

Marten's reputation for drinking is borne out. His friend, neighbour and business partner, fellow MP Edward Bainton, praised his witty and hospitable company, but Marten's intolerance of alcohol and the quantites he drank made him quickly drunk and incapable. Alcohol sharpened his tongue and then sent him to sleep, tempting fellow MPs into the conclusion that the combination of beer and wit cheapened the parliamentary process. Aubrey related one occasion on which the dozing politician, possibly playing up to the gallery by pretending to sleep in the Commons' chamber, was woken by a motion from Alderman Atkins to have nodders ejected from the House. As if from the dead, Marten sprang to his feet, calling rather for the ejection of all of the noddees.[6] Marten's style and effectiveness as a politician, as his own morals were called into question, relied on exposing the hypocrisy of others. His retort was always that the House would be a thin gathering should it remove all those who set ethical standards but failed to live up to them. He was making a serious point – that of universal fallibility – though he was not, by nature, a serious man. Should he fail to judge the mood of the House, MPs were liable to conclude that he did not take his post seriously.

He enjoyed good living. He attended the races, was the friend of scholars and playwrights, ate and drank well, and tended towards dandyism. Lely portrayed a serious, but sumptuously dressed politician, whose plain white collar and dark cloak were embellished with fur trim and jet pin. On 2 December 1649 Marten paid Christopher Smith £17 8s. 5d. to design and make a cloak, lined with lace and buttoning at the neck, a suit faced with taffeta, and hose lined with calico, which bear some resemblance to the clothes in which he was immortalised on canvas.[7] His tailors' bills evidence a love of finery and eye-catching display. That month, 'M[ists] Marten' could be seen around London in scarlet gown with silk and gold frogging.[8] Nearly a year later he purchased two pairs of silk hose in sky blue and scarlet, together with satin ribbon, 'fancis' and 2 yards of lace.[9] These bills reflect the income and possible grandeur of a member of the government – no puritan – but his expensive taste was not tempered in the 1650s when he lost power and income.[10] He did not let his sartorial aspect or his sophisticated palate suffer, as the extensive list of victuals provided for him during November 1654 testifies.[11] Whilst he was consuming dressed veal, goose, tongue, tripe, roast beef, capon, pork, mutton, cheese, mince pies and turnips, the bill became due for 'ale and Beere delivered for the use of the Right honourable Coll: Henry Martin' during the previous twelve months.[12] Twenty-two barrels of 6th beer, 3 kinderkins of 16th ale and 1 barrel of strong beer, at a cost of £9 7s. 2d., if averaged over the year, was more than 20 pints of beer a day. He procured a ready supply of wines from the Canaries, and his servants and tenants delivered cider from Herefordshire. His younger brother, whilst failing to make much money from sugar production, shipped home the secondary product of dark rum.

Extravagance and panache made Marten many friends, not all of whom were fair-weather. Neither did it seem to damage his ability to work with those whose political aims he shared, but whose objectives or rationale were markedly different. Pious republicans from the scriptural tradition, such as Grey of Groby and Edmund Ludlow, liked and respected him.[13] His licence was overlooked by fellow republicans but was a destructive weapon in the hands of the traditional social elite and those of a more censorious nature. When Marten attacked royalist aristocrats, they could reply with tales of excess that reduced the verbal terrorist to a Bacchanalian irrelevance. If he criticised Cromwell for his over-hasty recourse to breast-beating piety, Cromwell could exact his revenge on 'that broad fac'd . . . sott'.[14] Ironically, however, by the time William Parker established a tavern in Bow Street, Covent Garden, in which Wildman, Nevile, and other disgruntled republicans could decry their fall from grace, plot their return, and debate their politics in relative safety, amidst smoke and ale, Marten's extravagance had contributed to a sojourn in the Upper Bench prison, which effectively removed him from politics.[15]

Marten's Wife

Marten's notoriety as a drunk was a pale image beside that of 'a great lover of pretty girles', a description supplied by his neighbour, John Aubrey.[16] Aubrey's measured prose contrasts with others' lurid tales of promiscuity that went into grotesque and baroque detail. Marten had the dubious honour to have been branded a whoremonger by both Charles Stuart and Oliver Cromwell. The former, watching horses racing around The Ring in Hyde Park, caught sight of Marten and ordered he be ejected from the park because he was spoiling the King's enjoyment of the sport. Charles, a fastidious, moralistic and aloof man, was offended by Marten's drunken, flirtatious and noisy revelling. The King's outburst was said to have rallied Berkshire behind Marten to the extent of returning him *nemine contradicente* to the county seat. It was also believed to have fuelled his hatred of monarchy. Those who subscribed to the view that the politics of change was powered by envy were always keen to ascribe unworthy impulses to the republicans, but although many of the republican circle were said to have lived uproarious lives, promiscuity was an insufficient explanation for a political tenet with such dramatic consequences. Marten was not a republican because the King was disgusted by his morals.

Cromwell was equally scathing. On 20 April 1653 his soldiers escorted the Rumpers from the Commons' chamber. He addressed the members who refused to be cowed by a display of righteous military force, branding them for their immorality. He charged them with using their position to advance their friends and families and line their own pockets, believing they were grimly determined to cling to power despite the realisation that the Commonwealth was a failed experiment and they, a politically spent force. There were those who were drunkards and whoremongers, claimed the General, and looked over in the direction of Marten and his friend and republican colleague, Sir Peter Wentworth.[17] The imputation of a slap, which he must often have received from other hands, seems to have wounded Marten when meted out by the General, for he referred to this incident during the summer of 1653 in the draft of a pamphlet, in which he attacked Cromwell's role in the dissolution of the Rump.

Marten attracted and was attractive to many women throughout his long life, despite his far from gallant appearance. The face drawn by Lely is small, rude and framed with thin hair. In middle age he sported a wispy beard. Most agreed that even if he were not ugly, this was a plain man. Nevertheless, royalist circles hummed with scandalous tales of the womanising republican. The letters collected in the Clarendon State Papers, for example, are spiced with stories of his wanton behaviour. One woman claimed to have been woken by the drunken politician hammering on her door. Having sold her a story that he had nowhere to stay, he asked for a bed for the night. She took pity, but Marten informed her he would have to leave her again for a short while. He returned after about half an hour accompanied by a prostitute, solicited in the alleyways of the capital. The horrified and scandalised woman immediately shooed him back out into the street.[18] Audacity was certainly Marten's hallmark, but we should question the authenticity of the anecdote. If Marten had such a reputation, surely the woman would have been aware of it and her belatedly shocked outbursts have a hollow ring to them. Marten was possessed of a house in London, as were all of his parliamentary colleagues.[19] Why would he then go to the effort of scandalising a woman who seemed to have rather good contacts with the upper echelons of the royalist camp?

Henry Marten married Margaret Lovelace Staunton, the daughter of Richard, the first Lord Lovelace, and the widow of William Staunton, a wealthy London merchant. The marriage was arranged by his father, who had, in one woman, provided the social cachet of aristocracy whilst maintaining his close ties with the commercial wealth of the City. The Stauntons were close to Sir Henry, who had a regard for them more familiar than that which he held for most of his own kin.[20] If we assume that they were married in 1635, Margaret was thirty-one, her husband thirty-two or three.[21] She already had a daughter, also called Margaret. The daughter married Northamptonshire knight Edward Onely (see plates 3a and 3b) in February 1638, and in 1641 Sir Henry bequeathed them £100, describing her as one 'whom I have long kept with mee as my owne'.[22] Sir Henry's son thought differently: he married Margaret 'something unwillingly'.[23] They had two daughters before the birth of their only son, Henry, who was baptised in June 1639.[24] According to genealogists, they had two more daughters, Frances and Rebecca.[25]

After 1640 Marten 'lived from his wife a long time . . . shee was something distempered by his unkindnesse to her'.[26] Margaret remained on the estate in Berkshire, where she was described as 'the old one' and the 'old woman of

Longworth'.[27] Marten's concern for her after the birth of their son appears to have been confined to the maintenance of his estate and some financial provision to run the household, though his daughters complained that this was insufficient. Margaret fell ill during Marten's imprisonment in the 1660s, but her husband's worry was that 'if she should have died ere the K[ing]'s title had been purchased, it would have raised the market 200l.' The charge of hypocrisy might be levelled at Marten, who drafted a response to the Scottish Commissioners in which he likened the relationship between the English army and the Scots to a marriage:

You marry a wife & so become one with her in name & in flesh, at bed & boord. shee hath a starr in estate however you come by it, & you have ye like in her children for such a bond there is betwixt you as was sealed in heaven is allowed on earth & must not be cancelled till your departure or hers out of this troublesome world.[28]

Considering his treatment of Margaret Staunton, it is remarkable how long-suffering was the second Lord Lovelace's indulgence of his fallible brother-in-law.

Marten's main relationship was founded on love. He lived most of his life with Mary Ward, unerringly known as 'my deare' or 'my D'. Ward was from London, probably Southwark. She may have been Marten's cousin.[29] A series of Wardes are listed in the rate book for the parishes of Southwark between 1653 and 1661, but none mention a Mary by name. A niece of Henry's, Penelope Edmonds, married a Philip Ward, who was probably from Cheshire, but there is no obvious link with the Southwark Wards. Colonel Job Ward, who commanded the parliamentary fort at Tilbury, was likely Mary's brother. By an agreement of 10 August 1652, Marten and Edward Barker of Wandsworth made over the lease of Marten's land at Kimbolton, Leominster, to Job Ward, then described as a gentleman of the City of London.[30] Mary also had a sister, Frances.

Mary Ward referred to herself as Mary Marten, and there is a touching series of doodles among the Marten manuscripts in which she practised writing her two, alternative names and designed a cipher for herself – a pair of intertwining Ms. When, during 1660, Mary was allowed to visit Henry in the Tower, she was advised to give the guards both of the names by which she was known.[31] In view of this habitual use of an alternative 'married' name, the most tantalising reference comes from the *Commons' Journals*, as early as 22 November 1642. 'Mrs *Mary Marten*', accompanied by 'Four Children, and Two Servants', was given the Speaker's warrant to go down from London to Abingdon.[32] 'Mary' could have been a reference to Henry's sister, but she had married Sir Richard Rogers of Bristol in 1623, and although widowed in 1635, was always known as Dame Mary Rogers. Marten certainly referred to 'sister Rogers'.[33] It may have been a mistaken reference to Margaret Marten but, if so, it is worth asking why the name with which she was confused was Mary. Speaker William Lenthall was Marten's near neighbour who would have been well aware of the name of Marten's wife. If the relationship with Mary Ward was already established, he would also have known about it. If this is a reference to Mary Ward, therefore, they were already a well-established couple. The single fact that makes it seem the less believable is the active connivance of the Commons to refer to Marten's mistress as if she were his wife and to call her by her adopted name. By 1649, however, the Commonwealth worthies connived at their relationship. In a neat confirmation that Marten's excessive tailors' bills were to procure sumptuous frocks for Mary, Thomas Gower wrote to John Langley of a party held by Heert, the Spanish ambassador, who was 'discontented at the carriage of most of the English ladies who were at his entertainment, and they as much at him, for giving the chief place and respect to Col. H. Martin's mistress . . . they were also much displeased at her for being finer and more bejewelled than any'.[34]

Within the houses in which they functioned as husband and wife, they kept their own liveried servants and Mary controlled the household in her husband's absence. The degree to which the relationship between Ward and Marten was open to the scrutiny of all, irrespective of rank, is illustrated by Marten's concern for Derby House. This was an adulterous couple who lived in the house rented out to the most important government committees. As Gower confirmed, Marten, at the height of his power, was able to circumvent and override the ordinary rules of polite society. "'Tis no small argument', he concluded, 'of the greatness of the "Hogen Mogen Heeren Staten" of England that the Ambassador of the great Monarch of Spain should make such an entertainment for such a property belonging to one of the Parliament of England.' After the fall of the Rump, Cromwell continued to rent rooms in Derby House for the committees of the Protectorate. Mary had a house in Westminster, probably the same one. If so, we are encouraged into the speculative but nevertheless delicious day-dream of the meetings between the pious Cromwell and the red-skirted mistress of his bankrupt former colleague.[35]

In the mid-1650s, after his release from the Upper Bench prison, Mary and Henry lived at the Southwark house of Mary's sister, Frances. Around 1654 Frances lived in 'the Thatched house in the Rules', the Rules being the area of Southwark around St George's Fields which housed those who had paid a fine to be released from incarceration in the prison itself. Later Marten wrote to his Herefordshire agent, Tom Deane, that he was living in his own house in the same area - 'Rules, but no rules' – since he was released from the pervasive and generally malign influence of the governor, Sir John Lenthall, brother of the casuistic parliamentary Speaker.[36] In the eighteenth century a Southwark charity set up for the relief of debtors acquired the name of the 'Thatched House Society'.[37] In the course of 1657 Henry and Mary appeared to have escaped Southwark, since Mary was busy trying to find lodgings for them both in Epsom,[38] and towards the end of the 1650s Marten attempted either to provide for Mary, in the event that his wealth would disappear altogether, or to alienate land to her, in order to prevent the debts attaching to him, by making over the vast majority of his holdings in Hartington.[39] The couple had three children, all girls, the last of whom was still a babe in arms when Henry was incarcerated in the Tower in 1660. An earlier letter sent from the Tower made mention of only two 'brats'. There were signs that the couple retained some material possessions even after Marten's arrest, since Mary was advised to move all their belongings from Whitehall and Chelsea. John Loder, who had been the chief beneficiary of the sale of Marten's estates, was recommended as a middleman for the sale of the heavier items such as pewter, brass and iron.[40] The remainder of the Ward family moved south to Kennington.[41]

Marten the Adulterer

Mary Ward was an alternative wife, denied her proper status by the obligation to obey Sir Henry's wishes regarding marriage and the likely financial benefits that would accrue. It was a love match, and the extraordinarily tender letters that they exchanged are powerful literary manuscripts in their own right. Marten's and Ward's relationship lasted for at least thirty years, probably over forty, and survived enormous pressures. In describing the women with whom the republicans lived, Aubrey uses the term 'concubine'. But theirs was a relationship that went far beyond the normal keeping of a mistress or mistresses. In the fragment of a defence of polygamy, in Marten's possession, the voice of conscience, O, counsels the Marten character, T, that civil law prohibits bigamy on pain of death:

O. The whole world hath believed bigamy to be unlawfull, neither can any man take sundry wives without the great offence of men, wch all ought to eschew. Besides, God would have us obey Magistrates, [and] they are so far fro[m] approving polygamy, that they will inflict death on him that shall marry more wives than one.

T. But not if he have sundry concubines. If any man should be stirred up by God to take sundry wives, should he so do, it would be a scandal taken, (as they say) not given. Besides it would bee lawful for him, that he might avoid scandall, [and] the punishment of the magistrate, privily to take another.

O. But . . . should he be often seen in company of the second wife, men would not without offence think that she was his concubine. Wherefore I will ever exhort all men to shun polygamy, [and] accordingly exhort you to do the same.[42]

Contrary to O's contention that no people had ever permitted polygamy, ancient Judaic and Islamic texts had apparently described their concubines as a 'secondary wife', whose position remained inferior to that of the first wife but who, nevertheless, had some status in law.[43] T countered with a reference to ancient Rome, where barrenness had been punished; virtù being proven by delivering to 'posterity no worthier memory of himselfe, then by leaving children adorned with vertues'.[44] Mark Noble related, albeit 150 years after the event, that Marten had attempted to counter moves in the Rump to make incest, adultery and fornication punishable by death. His argument was that the punishment would encourage the crime, for it would push it into dark corners, and make people more circumspect. The severest punishment would make men cautious; failure to discover the guilty because they were discreet would 'embolden' them and thus the offence would be committed all the more.[45] The bill passed, but was revoked the following year, 'chiefly by his procurement . . . from the fear he should be the first example of the severity of it, for a more dissolute character it was impossible to find'.[46] Marten's scandal was not that he committed a crime, but that he blatantly and shamelessly paraded it; his mistress in red satin, him at the heart of the state. He was continually aware that this open relationship caused a scandal in the way that the secret keeping of a mistress or resort to the brothel would not. In the later 1650s, when his affairs, in the fullest sense, became perilous, and especially after 1660, when his affairs became traitorous, there was a new need for secrecy, ill-fitting a man known for his candour.

Mary's and Henry's frequent letters to and from the Tower were retrieved by a rival for Mary's affections, Richard Pettingall. He was probably a relation of Bartholomew Pettingall, with whom Marten transacted business.[47] They were given or sold to the royalist publisher Edmund Gayton, who hoped to further discredit Marten by revealing the nature of his adulterous relationship and to profit from the salacious fascination that Marten's private life held for the public.[48] In the end, his dual aims were thwarted. Both characters emerge sympathetically from the letters and the depth of their relationship was exposed. They reveal the conditions of the Tower at the time and give a glimpse of the tension that gripped London as the Houses tried to decide the fate of the regicides.

The couple's affection for each other and the changing fortunes of Henry Marten were woven together in their texts. The man who ten years before had spoken boldly and found a ready audience was now a cowed figure whose world remained as active but which was entirely contained within himself. 'The Skill', he adduced, was

not in being weather-wise, but weather-proof. In one thing, the storms I mean, are contrary to those the clouds pour upon us: for in that case it is best to keep all our clothes about us, and houses over our heads; in my case, to throw off all we can, and snugg like a snaile within our selves, that is our mindes, which nobody can touch.[49]

The relationship with his 'Monkey-face', 'houswife' and 'hussie' was the only remaining thing that gave Marten status. He managed to smuggle Mary and their children in to see him and arranged more orthodox visits with the connivance of a kindly gentleman porter. These were precious occasions; the expectation buoying up his failing spirits, for 'monday will come, you Chits-face you, therefore I won't be jeer'd for a beggarly rogue'.[50] The land that was being confiscated from him had ended the couple's hopes of material comfort along with a political career. Echoing his statement of 1646 to the Scottish Commissioners, Marten counselled Mary to

> Look upon my little brats, and see if thy Deare be not among them; has not one of 'um his face, another his braines, another his mirth? and look thou most upon that, for it is just the best thing in this world, and a thing that could not be taken from me, when Lemster [Leominster] was, when all the remainder of my Estate and thine was; nor when my liberty and the assurance of my life was, nor when thy company was.[51]

The creditors were still hounding him and the constant menace of bailiffs and royalists was now shadowing Mary. Henry made several attempts to ensure that she and their children were sent to safety in the country[52] 'because the whole tribe of Bay liffs and Catch-poles will be exasperated against thee, and have thee by hook or by crook'. In a series of metaphors, Marten revealed that his existence had, for some time, been from hand to mouth. The comfort of practising ideology in wealth had been replaced by the uncertainty of disguising his life in poverty.[53] Every material hope having been taken away from him there were also threats to his love: letter forty-two revealed Mary's offer, presumably of marriage, from Pettingall. Marten burnt Mary's letter to him as instructed, declared his love and his selfless wish for her happiness, and counselled that if she could achieve fulfilment with Pettingall, then he must be content to give her up. He had little now to offer her and she must take happiness where she could find it, for 'the world is grown so false'.[54]

With increasing scrutiny into his public affairs, Marten needed to disguise his private life. When the republicans had been in power, they had encouraged open declarations of loyalty, because they feared that the English people were in thrall to monarchy. Now the republicans were a cowed band, Marten relied on petty officialdom. He needed the discretion of minor public servants to hatch plots and schemes by which Mary could be smuggled into the Tower. Once that ceased to be feasible, Mary was bundled away to the country, for 'it needs be chargeable and dangerous, and every way unpleasant, to abide long where thou art, and to remove without a disguise, and to get a disguise without money is as hard'.[55] The private world of Mary and Henry took the place of the public. The renown accorded to a London politician and country gentleman was now only revealed in the intimate celebration of his features in the faces of his illegitimate children. The civic world of Henry Marten was undergoing something of a change while he chose to examine 'how I came to deserve . . . the rigours I undergo in the losse of that reputation and estate I left behind me'.[56] When he contemplated his future, he swung from optimism – as messages came from court that banishment was intended – to fatalism at the seeming inevitability of an end on the gallows. He believed that he could show good reasons why he should not be executed, but if his judges thought otherwise, 'who can help it?'.[57]

Marten's relationship with Mary Ward was adulterous, blatant and scandalous, but there is little to substantiate the more lurid tales of his sexual encounters. There was the exasperated tone of his father's record that 'my sonne oweth', but little evidence to corroborate the claim that, at time of his death, Sir Henry Marten subsidised his son's mistresses to the tune of £1,000 a year. There is no extant material that would confirm the tales that his house at Shrivenham was the scene of orgiastic and drunken revels,[58] or that he spend much of his time in London frequenting the stews. When, in 1648, his irregular republican band was scandalising the public's political sensibilities, a pamphleteer mentioned a Mrs Dunce, whom he would have to have left *bellum interruptus* in event of a second civil war. The MP returned for Berkshire in 1660 was Hungerford Dunce, and there was also a family by the name of Dunch in the region.[59] There is no evidence that Marten had a relationship with Mrs Dunce. In 1651 a claim to paternity was made by Ann Caitline, who wrote asking Marten to meet a minister, Mr Ingram, the following week, 'since it pleased yo[u] to make mee so far ingaged to yo[r] honor as to give my Grand sone a name'. The letter was dated 14 February and remains the only documentation of this type. It may have been an attempt to cash in on Marten's nefarious reputation, although Peter Ingram was the minister presented to Longworth in 1663/4.[60] Even if this were evidence of a third woman, it was not sufficient to account for the volume of tales of Marten's womanising, which were the toast of London society and provided the ammunition for numerous jokes and scurrilous stories.

The nastiest satire was directed at Mary Ward. *Fortunate Rising: or, The Rump Upward* made capital from referring to the name of the parliament and the '*Rump of Harry Martins Whore*'. A *Free Parliament Letany* called on carousers to sing to '*Harry Martins Whore*, that was neither Sound nor Pretty'.[61] A *Lenten Litany* referred to 'the zeal of Old *Harry* lock'd up with a Whore'. This was Harry Marten's whore in the singular. A man who had the propensity to such scandalous and sinful behaviour, however, did not merit restraint in the comments made against him, nor was sin considered something that could be moderated. On the contrary, those who had sinned had amply demonstrated their lack of self control. It therefore made no difference to the scandal sheets whether Marten was accredited with one adulterous relationship or hundreds. References that specifically referred to Mary Ward were expanded to allude in a more general way to lustfulness and sin, along with the claim that these were the driving force behind Marten's actions.

It was a powerful weapon with which to prick Marten's pretensions to act according to reason or conscience. His mind was reflected in his body, so 'addled' that his treason would be unpunishable by hanging; the corpse would crumble on the rope.[62] He would be no better purified in the flames: 'To bring 'em to th' stake as in order they lye,/ *Harry Martyn* the next place must occupy;/ 'Twas expected in vain he should blaze, for he swore,/ That he had been burnt to the stumps before.'[63] The Rump's necessity to levy heavy taxes was described as keeping the people poor whilst Marten had 'the power to Plunder and Whore',[64] and *The Bloody Bed-roll or Treason displayed in its Colours* introduced:

Here comes SIR HENRY MARTYN
As good as ever pist,
This wenching beast
Had Whores at least
A thousand on his list:
This made the Devils laugh,
So good a friend to see.[65]

Marten was indiscriminately accused of the sin of lust.[66] In the minds of those who were against sin, for whom there was no difference between momentary lapse and continuous transgression, Marten's actions were evidence of a flawed character that demonstrated his unfitness for government. As the 'Man in the Moon' laughed in 1649, a madam who had provided the Rump junto with prostitutes, selling them as virgins, had, by giving Marten another dose of the clap, 'disabled' him from fulfilling his attendance at the House.[67] No matter how loving, tender or faithful the relationship between Henry and Mary, Marten's openness had placed himself outside standard moral bounds. Once the bonds of self-restraint were broken, immorality would be free, unfettered and rampant. A single example was sufficient evidence from which to embellish a much more active reputation for adultery. Marten's whore became Marten's whores.

The Personal and the Political

Sexual licence and political revolution were most clearly linked during 1648. Birth, predominantly illegitimate, provided a recurrent theme in the writings of Norfolk gentleman, Thomas Knyvett, but he found ample opportunity to combine references to politics with others to fornication when describing the pamphlets that Marten issued against the Scottish Commissioners and a personal treaty with Charles. He confided his frustrations to fellow Norfolk royalist, Sir John Hobart of Blickling:

This week brought to my view a declaration in the King's name . . . I wish forty thousand stout well-armed men had but the same sense of it. But to divert this passion, up starts a babe of grace of this week's production, 'Mr. Martin's Defence of the Parliament's late Votes against the King and the Scots' Commissioners'. I have read it, and can say no more but that I look upon it not as the spurious issue of his brain, but as the sense of the saint-like houses: yet brave Harry hath the better on't, to beget the bastard, and make the honourable state to father it; else, sure, it durst never have peeped abroad.[68]

Similar concerns were expressed in the satire *Mr: Henry Martin his Speech in the House of Commons before his Departure hence*. It pursued the most effective form of attack. It took something for which there was some shred of evidence and embellished this small truth to imply much grander follies with as much veracity. Marten and his colleagues in the Commons were, up to a point, accurately portrayed, but scattering the tract with references to prostitution brought ridicule on the whole. The radicalism of Marten's politics was undermined by the addition of scandal; the threatening implications of his political programme neutralised, because they were implemented by a figure of fun.

This mock speech had supposedly been delivered to the House prior to Marten's return to Berkshire, where he raised a regiment to defend his home in case royalist forces made a new war on his estates. Marten combined his pamphleteering for parochial, anti-monarchical and virulently anti-Scottish causes with military power, raising a regiment on republican lines. In doing so, he upset all of the English elite. Already the scourge of royalists and noble commanders, he was pursued around the country by the officers of an irate General Fairfax, who, with the full approval of the moderate-dominated parliament, was intent on disbanding a force given no authorisation from above. Marten claimed no greater authority than the people of England.[69] Those who were already scandalised by his attitude towards the institution of matrimony were primed to expect the same disregard for any social or moral authority.

The regiment was largely made up of tenants from Marten's estates and soldiers enticed from official regiments with promises of republican democracy. This was to be a regiment of his 'Creatures', a reference both to his tenants' loyalty and affection and to women whose loyalty and affection were bought. His republicanism was described with relish and with a sufficient measure of truth to convince the reader. He had always been forward in speaking treason. Now the satirist put words into his mouth – 'I have troubled Israel and glory in it' – which one could well imagine Marten saying to his friends and drinking companions.

> I know, Mr. Speaker, [this pamphleteer had him say] the King loves me better then he doth *Vane*, or *Perpoint*, or *Mildmay*, or *Haslerigg*, or *Evillin*, or *St. John*, or *Wild*, or yourself, because I am plaine with him, and tell him and the World the truth of our intentions; I keepe me to my principles, and scorne to deale underhand like a Judas.

Marten was certainly known for his honesty, plain-speaking and tactlessness. It was unlikely that Charles appreciated such virtues. According to the writer, had Marten received his thirty pieces of silver he would have 'gone with it straight to a Bawdy house, and have had a gallant yong Wench for it'. When he had achieved his republican aims, and confiscated the King's revenues, he would spend his fortune in 'a famous Stewes in the City of London'.

Marten's theory of constitutional balance was reinterpreted in a way that destroyed its profundity as a viable, or at least interesting, political theory: 'When the King had power equall with ours, I durst teare his Proclamation: nay if I were sure I could doe it, I durst teare his heart out of his body, and drinke healths of his bloud to my little creature in Drury Lane.' Another thrust revealed an attack on the power of the army and its constant demand for arrears, which accorded with Marten's views. His concern that the soldiers were seeking to minimise the role of the parliament and to control civil politics was here given a masterly twist: soldiers sought to use up the revenue that Marten would have spent elsewhere. There was accurate satire of Speaker Lenthall, whose family had risen from relative obscurity by buying up monastic lands and who was then living in splendour in the priory at Burford. 'Mr. Speaker', Marten was reputed to have said, 'do you think ever to enjoy your lands, bought since this Reformation, if the King come home? Or doe you thinke I shall goe any more to a Bawdy house, or will my Wenches be suffered to come to me, when I have no money, and lie in prison?'[70] Marten was to spend much of the 1650s in the Upper Bench prison, living down this prophetic line. The lands that the parliament granted to him came too late and were insufficient to cover his debts, though had the House awarded him £10,000 it would 'furnish me with a Doctor and Drugs, to keep and preserve my life; which if it bee denyed me, the French scab will eat out my bowels'.[71]

Marten's reputation as a libertine was used to destroy the danger for the royalists, the establishment, and the wealthy, which lurked behind his views: a passion for political liberty could be neutralised by concentrating on a reputation for sexual freedom. Sir John Maynard was ejected from the chamber, either for personal attacks on a single member or for going against the general direction of Commons' policy, but Maynard's speech may well have provided a model for anonymous scandalmongering. Maynard claimed that Marten would introduce

the Democraticall Element, and is all for parity and Anarchy, and I conceive his end is to bring all to confusion, that he may be chosen one of the Tribunes of the People, or a John of Leiden: and then new kings new lawes, and likely the first Act will bee for a Bigamy or a Coraglia [seraglio?].[72]

During 1648 the presses roared to good effect to ensure that readers received the worst possible picture of Marten and his republican troops. The word 'Leveller' could be used to put fear and suspicion into the hearts of English people, particularly in the regions where the radicalisation of London was a distant rumour and not an exciting reality. In September 1648 Thomason received a copy of *Terrible and bloudy Newes from the disloyall Army in the North*, which was one of several news-sheets to emerge with information on the progress of the second civil war in the north of England and Scotland. The frontispiece included a woodcut containing all the stock images with which the seventeenth century portrayed violence. Women pleaded on their knees to soldiers who were smashing the brains of their babies onto the rocks or parading infants on the end of pike-staffs. Other women prayed whilst the soldiers ran them through. In the background, their community went up in flames. Dismounted from his horse and brandishing his sword stood the soldiers' commander, Henry Marten. The town was Market Harborough and this was a description of the actions of his notorious republican regiment of 'Levellers' in Leicestershire (*see* plate 7). Inside, a correspondent – ejected minister William Turvil – described the 'great terrour and amazement of all his Majesties liege People' at Marten's forces.[73] Marten's regiment was made up of those who were 'of desperate fortune, and mean condition'. '[T]he basest and vilest' resorted to his regiment because Marten had lured them with 'strange, politick and subtle delusions', presumably the thought of power in his republic.[74]

This was, however, sensationalist journalism. The illustration on the frontispiece was a device to persuade people to buy the newsbook on the basis of the scandal of the contents. The letter from Turvil was couched in language that sought to induce fear and alarm throughout the Midlands and among the literate classes of London. It was both an exercise in maximising circulation and discrediting its subject. Feeding on prejudices about Marten's wildness and extremism, and on the popular fear of levelling, not to mention gratuitous violence, the author and publisher created an image of Marten designed to capture readers' imagination. Turvil went on to say that the troops 'rob and plunder exceedingly . . . but we hear that Col. *Martin* hath given command, That no souldier whatsoever shall dare to plunder or use violence against any, but that they behave themselves civilly, executing nothing contrary to order.' When a party of Marten's soldiers arrived at Market Harborough, the townspeople scattered in fear, but 'the Levellers perceiving this, made *Proclamation* neer the Swan, and at the Crosse, *That no violence or wrong should be executed upon any, neither would they in the least disturb or hinder the Market*'. They stayed at the Crown and departed peaceably. It is more unusual, perhaps, that the author printed the true along with the salacious and exaggerated version, but by the time the readers had reached the denouement, it was too late for Marten's reputation. The image of the wild republican had stuck.

The events of 1648 are vital to an understanding of Marten's politics and why he failed. That year saw the culmination of the action in which he had been engaged for ten years. In the past, however, his campaigning had been covert, or confined to the relative safety of the House of Commons. Only on occasions, such as his suspension from the Commons in 1643, did news of his activities or views leak to a wider audience. The best way in which royalists could belittle Marten's role prior to 1648 was to feed on the rumours of his relationships with women and laugh in their salons and garrisons at the politician who spread the 'French fire' around the capital. After 1648 Marten's political radicalism was exposed. There was no longer any need to speculate on the nature of his republicanism or his anarchic means of securing power, or to confine satirical barbs to personal demeanour. Now all three could be blended into an attack that, at one and the same time, revealed the fear with which certain sections of society viewed the prospect of Marten in power and successfully hampered the possibility that he could put his proposals into practice. Marten and his allies would not have come to power had they not – among other things – set up unauthorised regiments. The extra-military pressure exerted by these local militias was a valuable lever to ensure that after November 1648 power did not come to rest in the hands of the New Model's Council of War. The republican soldiers' reputation for levelling and their commander's for licentiousness, however, ensured that they were mistrusted by the grandees and many sections of the Commons, not merely feared and despised by the royalists. When Marten was at his fieriest, his personal reputation could drench the flames.

In the 1650s the compound of Marten's personal and political lives produced a different reaction. When Marten was powerful, language could be manipulated by others to lessen his reputation. During periods of political impotence, Marten's own language contributed to his marginalisation. Although his influence had been on the wane for several months, his loss of political office in April 1653 sealed his fall from power. Cromwell's star was in the ascendant, first behind the scenes of Barebone's parliament and subsequently as Lord Protector. Marten drafted a pamphlet in the form of a satirical letter to Cromwell, declining a seat in the assembly of the saints and John Wildman combined with republican officers to bring down the Protectorate. Marten's wit compares with Wildman's invective, but although Marten's piece is more graceful, circumstances dictated that, even had it reached the presses, its effect would have been the lesser. Wildman's petition of the three colonels was given added potency by the prospect of mutiny and rebellion from within the New Model, and the attendant danger that it would bring down the Cromwellian regime. Marten's piece was an effective exposé of hypocrisy amongst the new elite but it failed to hit its target because Marten was no longer a threat. The jokes had a tendency to turn and bite their master.

The collapse of the cause of radical republicanism ran parallel to, and was to a certain extent the product of, Marten's increasing slide towards bankruptcy, though the debts were far from newly accumulated. Henry and George Marten were jointly bound for £6,000 in 1641,[75] and by 1642 the debts of George Marten alone, for which Henry was responsible, amounted to £6,750.[76] Henry had amassed a further £3,000 of debt a year later and George's debts had grown to £7,000 by the time he left for Barbados around 1646.[77] Henry Marten was largely responsible for financing his brother's merchant adventures. It is hardly surprising, in view of the massive debt that he had to service, that both became dependent on the idea that sugar planting would reap profits disproportionate to the sums invested. In the early 1650s Marten's creditors were increasingly restless. A combination of extravagant living, money expended on backing the parliamentarian war effort and directing the course of politics, financing his brother's extravagances and his investment hopes, and servicing crippling interest rates resulted in Henry's arrest for debt in 1654. Marten was committed to the Upper Bench prison next to St George's church in Southwark some time during 1655, with total debts of approximately £35,000. This was some eighteen months after the committee in charge of the Upper Bench prison calculated a total indebtedness of over £900,000 held by 393 prisoners.[78] Should these figures have remained the same in 1655, the average debt would have been just over £2,250 per person. Marten's sum represented 4 per cent of the total Upper Bench debt, or fifteen times the average debt per person. Whilst enduring the overcrowded and insanitary conditions of the Upper Bench, Marten attempted to provide for his family with Margaret in Longworth, another with Mary in Southwark and George's continuing financial crises in Barbados. Early in January 1656 George Marten's interpretation of his elder brother's affairs was naïvely optimistic[79] and by September of that year, George was still refusing to accept the seriousness of the family's position:

Youres of the 9th of July with a Hamper of excellent sack I receaved the 7th of 9bris last, for which bee pleased to accept of my harty thankes till I shall bee able to make some better requittal: By a letter from M[r] Westropp of the 19th of Aug I understand you were very ill & by others of a later date that you were in the Tower for the first, tho I hope you have beene long ere this recovered, and tho I doe not beleeve the latter, yet till I shall bee well satisfyed both of yowre health and libertye, I shall not bee without a great deale of feere and trouble for you.[80]

Marten had three weapons of self-preservation; his brazenness, his wit and his resourcefulness – 'I have several strings to my bow; and one of 'um will take if luck serve'.[81] Together they made a unique, exasperating response to political issues. Marten's draft letter to Cromwell combined the three elements: witty cynicism at the idea that one such as he could be invited to be a member of the assembly of the saints; a vitriolic attack on Cromwell, which was both undermined and underpinned by the irony in which the attacks were couched; and the resourcefulness with which Marten extricated himself from an alliance with those who had been responsible for Pride's Purge, and realigned himself with those whose hopes of republican reform had been stymied by the army rather than the Rump. Cromwell's dismissal of the Rump was reinterpreted in the light of these three stylistic weapons:

it was observed by one p'sent in Parlt when you dismist it, that God almighty whose name you had been formerly bold w[th] in most of your designes would not permitt you to p'tend to it in that acco[u]n[t], but suffered you to bee driven furiously on by a Contrary Spirritt, that so there might be one eminent passage of your life, in which you might perfectly appeare your selfe; and though I doe not approve of this expression of his, or goe about to excuse him for it, yett knowing him to have ever been a faithfull freind to your Ex[cy] will acknowledge that their being sensible of it at last, and desire to putt a Cure to all by dissolving was not crime, and if it were, it was such a one as the Army and your selfe were most eminently guilty of.[82]

Marten drew attention to Cromwell's free use of Scriptural justification and undermined it with the barb that it had always been a pretence. Having stated that this was such an important event that the conscience of the General did not permit him to dissemble, he sabotaged Cromwell's virtuous image with the revelation that there had only ever been this one occasion on which he had revealed the true man. The whole edifice of the pious Lord General was further deflated by flattering the reader in the collusion that they had always known the true nature of Cromwell. Parliamentary dissolution was surely not a crime, since the members did not dissemble: they had acknowledged their faults. But if it were a crime, then the army was the guilty party. Hence, in the course of this passage, Marten revealed the full complexity of his style.

Every proposition was set up, only to be undermined, and every proposition which had been undermined was further diminished by the existence of a counter example. It was a style that owed much to a training in syllogistic discourse and a system of argument and counter-argument that he successfully used to counter churchmen's and politicians' claims to logic.

On 7 May 1659 Marten was restored to some semblance of power by the recall of the Rump, and was once again at liberty to employ his wit in the service of power, though to less effect since, as Ludlow related, his 'affectation of raillery in the house of commons' was only possible after 'he was restored from a prison upon its reassembling'.[83] The political situation was also less to his liking. Marten was now in alliance with a community of classical republicans that had formed around the taverns of Covent Garden and the philosophical ideas of James Harrington. The group of ill-matched politicians that produced *The Armies Dutie* in May 1659 included Marten, but no longer as a creator of republican thought. Marten's notion of balance had given way to Harringtonianism and Marten's collaborative effort was to add the touches of sarcasm. In particular, he was bitter at the provision of land for the army. In a tract that was an uneasy mixture of religious fervour, Harringtonian political science and attempts to shame Fleetwood into supporting the republic, Marten's contribution was undoubtedly to the last of these. Having reiterated the arguments shaped by Scripture, echoing those employed in 1648, the style changed, and was recognisably Marten:

Now, My Lord, if we would plead with you by worldly Arguments or motives, that concern your self, it were easie to evince, that safetie, honour, and greatness to your self, and familie, can be certainlie compassed by no other means, then by returning to the Principles from whence you are fallen.[84]

Marten was still a part of the political scene, but was a symbolic link with the past, rather than someone whose method mapped out the future.

A Wit Without an Estate

Once imprisoned for High Treason at the Restoration, Marten was forced into isolation. He honed his style composing his prison defence. The grand scale of the courtroom, the state trial, judgement by the world and its law and the 'report of the crimes charged upon me [which] overtakes me wheresoever I go', found correspondences in the microcosm of the 'home' to which Marten was confined, so 'that of that leisure I now have, I might well employ some time in arraigning my selfe at the bar of my own conscience'. Marten admitted regicide. He outlined the complicity of himself and his fellows and their fitness to be tried by a state court, in statements shot through with sarcasm. The 'persons who had the boldness to make an example' of the royalists' 'Ring-leader' would be a sacrifice, to 'appease the ghost of their often soiled cause'. Having tried himself, Marten found himself innocent, and then demolished his own defence by admitting his partiality for one side of the argument. He confirmed that he sat on the High Court of Justice and signed a warrant for Charles' execution; 'whereupon I believe he was afterwards executed'. He backtracked on the position that he had taken in 1649. He would not have started to fight had he known the price the war would exact. He would not have executed the King had he known he was paving the way for King Cromwell. He represented himself as the ally of the Levellers and accepted the complaint that Charles had made so forcibly at his trial – the High Court had had no legal authority or right to try a man without a jury. Finally, Marten's resourcefulness enabled him to twist the legality of the charge made against him, agreeing that he 'judged' the King, but not that he 'murdered' him.

Marten deployed words stylishly, in pamphlets and on the public stage, like a gentleman who knew how to use his oratorical education to find debating points that possessed elegance, precision and finesse. At the height of his power, he used his pen and his tongue with devastating effect to demolish the pretensions of an opponent. His one-liners made the pompous look small and the socially powerful humble. Aubrey paid testimony to his ability to turn the stance taken by the whole House with one short, but well-crafted and pithy contribution.[85] Spiking a piece with more bald and earthy references was a way of startling an elite audience; juxtaposing sophisticated allusion with bold, unambiguous punch-lines, which mutually reinforced the simplicity of the argument and the complex way in which it could be expressed. On the other hand, a complex political notion could be made comprehensible to a wider and usually less educated audience by the use of simple phrases and recognisable narratives. Marten could employ the rhetorical flourishes, learning and verbal dexterity of the elite and bring them to the aid of the commoner. In contrast to the majority of political writers of the period, who used Biblical and classical allusions as parallels of the contemporary situation, Marten treated them as anecdotes that were illustrative of a rationalised and secularised debate. He presented a rational argument, stripped it to its essential qualities, and then reinserted the historical illustrations in order to make the abstract more widely comprehensible. He tipped his elegantly flighted arrows with barbs of pure vitriol.

This style was a result of Marten's use of rationalistic, syllogistic logic. As a humanist, he revered the commoner because commoners could see through the obvious hypocrisy or manoeuvrings of more exalted politicians. The truth was simple. It could be stated simply and illustrated with a commoner's example. Philosophical arguments of abstract principle were illuminated with an example of parallel logic, couched in every-day terms. An example can be found in one of his many attacks on the Scottish Commissioners. During 1648 the Commissioners were demanding a say in the peace negotiations. Marten sought to exclude them, whilst being forced to admit that they had previously been invited in and were of help to the English. His parallel was both a piece of subtle logic and an easily comprehended example:

> For instance, the Law of this Land that gives me leave to pull down my neighbours house when it is on fire, in order to the quenching of it for the securing of my own, will not authorize me against his will, to set my foot within his threshold, when the fire is out, though I make it my errand to direct him in the rebuilding of his house, and pretend the teaching him so to contrive his Chimneyes as may in all probability prevent for the future a like losse to him, a like danger to my selfe.[86]

Later, he turned the knife still further: '[o]nly I would have it confessed, that the fire we talked of, was of your Countrymans kindling, began to burn at your house, to be quenched at ours, and by our hands'.[87] Ludlow cited another example. Marten was attacked at his trial with the charge that the regicidal High Court of Justice was representative of only a fraction of one of the three estates. His response was that if a property consisted of a tenement and common land, and the tenement burnt down, the proprietorship of the commons would be unchanged, though the tenement was now a single stick of wood. Size did not matter to authority.[88] Sometimes he overdid the use of metaphorical illustration. He drove home the point that the English had clung to their Scottish allies too long: 'we have kept such thornes thus long in our sides, then to return with the dog to the same vomit, and with the laxy Sow, scarce clensed of her former wallowing to bemire our selves again'.[89]

He rarely used classical allusions, especially in his published work, in which he was addressing an audience without his education. He invoked Biblical examples more frequently but in the same way, to illustrate an abstract, rationalistic argument. They did not carry any particular, special or parabolic truth. When he turned again on the Scottish Commissioners, addressing ordinary but literate people who hovered around the edges of political activity, especially in the environs of the capital, he employed a similar style, illustrating logical deconstruction with comprehensible imagery. The Commissioners had wanted Charles to be admitted to London to negotiate a personal treaty. Marten wanted to reply that to do so would be to restore Charles to sufficient power to crush them and thus make it impossible to lay any terms on him, even though he was the vanquished. Employing the image of both balance and logic against the Scottish Commissioners, the people were asked to 'weigh their reason':

Then (allowing it true against us . . .) the consequence thereof will hang thus; My groom being drunk, and falling asleep with a candle by him, hath set my stable on fire, and burnt it down to the ground; therefore his awaking and coming to himself will set it up again. Because *Agag* by drawing his sword, had made many women childless, it seemed to be *Sauls* opinion, That the putting up his sword again would restore the children to their mothers.[90]

Marten's delivery and the structure of his discourse was a vital part of his political success. It also provided a measure of his political failure. His authority as a speaker was integrally dependant on the political power that lay behind it. Wit without power was buffoonery and since one of Marten's chief parliamentary weapons was his cutting language, the way he spoke was likely to exclude him during those periods in which his influence was low and magnify him at times when he could bring real political leverage to bear. His devastating language was not a sufficient political weapon in itself: without power it was merely entertainment. Aubrey had cited the force of his reasoning, not elegant turns of phrase. The syllogistic style was simple in structure, however, and could therefore devastate the pretensions of spuriously sophisticated proposals that tried to reconcile antagonistic ideas through tortuous compromise. Marten's politics were simple, adversarial and not designed for arbitration. Thus, when the political scene was ripe for radicalism, Marten was its star. When what was needed was moderation, Marten lacked the words.

Of all the accounts of the regicides at their trials in 1660, only Marten's name was linked to his character. Others were disgraced by their supposedly lowly births or by religious views that could not be tolerated by the stability-minded Restoration regime. Although his greatest crime had been the presumption to try his King, Marten was described as 'Colonel of a regiment of Horse – [his unofficial band formed in 1648] –, and (somesay) of a Regiment of Whores: having sold his Estate three times over, he lay a long time under a bad Reputation'.[91] The link between radical politics, extravagance and licentiousness was exploited to the full in Mark Noble's *Lives of the English Regicides*.[92] Noble listed the lands of the Duke of Buckingham, which Marten had received in satisfaction of a debt of £25,000 owed to him by the parliament. This recompense was, according to Noble, despite the fact that the members of the House had noted the link between character and politics as early as 1643, when Marten had defended John Saltmarsh. The move to send him to the Tower took account of the connection between financial and political excess, because he revealed 'the extreme profligacy of his life, and the very dangerous tendency of his answer'.[93] His debts left him an isolated individual, without the protection of parliament; he was 'sunk so low in character, consequence and fortune'.[94]

At their trials, many regicides, including Marten, declared no malice against the King's person, but rather a desire to curb the excesses of his office. Marten's contribution combined a sound grasp of legal technicalities with straightforward ribaldry. Examples of venom that had once been employed in the service of the state were quickly replaced by self-preservational buffoonery. On being arraigned and shown the Act of Indemnity, he pointed out that he could not plead, because he was not the person named in the charge. Marten was very keen that his name was spelt with an e, and when arraigned and shown an act exempting 'Henry Martin' from pardon, he claimed mistaken identity, for he was solely and universally known as Harry Marten. Unfortunately, undermining the authority of the court in this way was no longer a viable option for him. Everybody knew who he was, the nature of his reputation, and the farce of such literalism. Besides, the court produced a precedent.[95]

Marten nevertheless continued on the same tack. Having rehearsed his arguments in his letters to Mary Ward, with some refinement they reappeared in his trial statements. The charge included an intention clause: the regicides were guilty of 'treason, for a malicious, traitorous, compassing and imagining the King's death'.[96] Marten quibbled with the word 'malicious', as he had previously quibbled with 'murder', and claimed that the nature of the law was dictated by the circumstance in which it was committed. Such attempts at legalism were used against him, for in seeking to deny malicious intent towards the King, Marten left himself open to the response of the Solicitor General: 'he does think a man may sit upon the death of a king, sentence him to death, sign a warrant for his execution, *meekly, innocently, charitably*, and *honestly*.'[97] The prosecution proceded with witnesses who testified to Marten's serious intent to kill the King – in itself an anti-christian act – which defined him as a dangerous subversive, whilst he had done so in a frivolous way. Marten's self-image was therefore used to undermine that which Charles' judges had sought to project; that they had declared a solemn judgement on a king who had broken the trust between himself and his people. The court produced Mr Ewer, described as one of Marten's servants,[98] who was the witness who gave history the anecdote that Cromwell and Marten had cheerily spattered each other's faces as they signed the death warrant. The relationship between Cromwell and Marten was certainly in a short period of thaw at the end of 1648. The Lieutenant General seems to have possessed a playful side to his character, but it is unlikely that he committed himself to judicial execution with a glad heart.[99] Neither does the incident ring true for Marten, though they may, in fact, have been 'marking' each other in recognition of their action's serious consequences. Sir Purbeck Temple told the court that he had overheard Cromwell ask on what authority Charles would be tried, and Marten told him 'in the name of the commons and the parliament assembled, and all the good people of England'. Thus, Marten was trapped by his own style, portrayed as both the brains behind this profound change in the nation's constitution and as 'merry . . . at this sport'.[100]

Ironically, Marten was deemed to have escaped not because of his wit, but because of his lasciviousness. Falkland joked that since the execution of the regicides should be a sacrifice, the object of which was pure, there was no point in undermining the glory of the royal restoration by making a martyr of such a rogue.[101] Bishop Burnet reiterated the point:

One person escaped, as was reported, merely by his vices: Henry Marten, who had been a most violent enemy to monarchy, but all that he moved for was upon Greek and Roman principles. He never entered into matters of religion, but on design to laugh both at them and at all morality; for he was both an impious and vicious man, and now in his imprisonment he delivered himself up unto vice and blasphemy. It was said that this helped him to so many friends, that upon that very account he was spared.[102]

Henry's relationship with his brother contributed to his reputation. George Marten was known to Aphra Behn, and she framed posterity's image of both brothers. She claimed to have been so impressed by the gallant captain George Marten that she would name him in her next production. True to her word, *The Younger Brother; or, the Amorous Jilt* provided a leading role for the younger brother himself, now called George Marteen. The parallel with the Marten family stretched beyond the similarity of the name of the eponymous hero. The leading protagonists were three men: the father, Sir Rowland Marteen, and his two sons; the elder, Sir Merlin, and the younger, George. The patriarch, Sir Rowland, was a dour, sober, respected and hard-working character, so scandalised by the profane behaviour of his elder son that he threatened to disinherit him, to the benefit of George. The character of George, on the other hand, was exiled to a life in the merchant fleet and the colonies:

Geo: I'm a *Cadet*, that Out-cast of my Family, and born to that curse of our old *English* Custom. Whereas in other Countries, younger Brothers are train'd up to the Exercise of Arms, where Honour and Renown attend the Brave; we basely bind our youngest out to Slavery, to lazy Trades, idly confin'd to Shops or Merchant Books.[103]

The irony of the younger brother was that whilst George pleased his father by seeming to plod in a respectable trade, he was, in fact, leading a double life as a dandy gentleman about town. In this he spent as much as his elder, dissolute brother, but prudently kept it from his puritan father. As the real Henry Marten cited in a parable to James Harrington:

what cares a younger brother whose father hath settled a fair estate upon him, & putt him in possession, though his elder brother bring a wholl chamber full of women to proove that hee who is outed of ye Inheritance was born before ye other. [N]ay doth it not add to ye honnour of ye youth, that ye old man should see cause for his sake to invert ye ordinary course of things [then leave his worth unrewarded?].[104]

In the first scene, the character of 'Henry' Marteen is hearsay. Reference is made to his likely disinheritance as a 'celebrated Rake-hell, as well as Gamester'. Sir Merlin Marteen does not appear until act one, scene two. The scene as it was written by Behn, however, does not survive. It was rewritten by the publisher Charles Gildon – himself a libertinistic atheist – for the 1696 production. Behn's original, in which most of the political jokes had been placed in the mouth of Sir Merlin Marteen, was considered to have passed out of popular currency by the time the play was performed. Instead, Gildon wrote out the politics – 'that old bustle about *Whigg* and *Tory*'[105] – and magnified the character of the rake-hell. A song commissioned from Mr Motteux, to introduce the character of Sir Merlin, echoed the complaint of Sir John Maynard in 1648. Marten was 'He, [who] like the Great Turk, has his Favourite She;/ But the Town's his Seraglio, and still he lives free'.[106] In the taverns and coffee-houses of Covent Garden, where in the 1650s William Wetton had his city house and Will Parker his republican ale-house, Marteen's life was 'Mirth, Musick and Wine', interspersed with wenching and vandalism. His country cousin, Sir Morgan Blunder, complained that Merlin's city life of 'Blousing and Politics', in which he talked 'downright treason' and of 'Guelphs and Gibelins', disagreed with his rustic constitution.[107] Such behaviour was held to be an enemy to fame, fortune and power. Sir Rowland Marteen moralised that

A Rake-hell is a Man that defies Law and good Manners, nay, and good Sense too; hates both Morality and Religion, and that not for any Reason (for hee never thinks) but merely because he don't understand 'em: He's the Whore's Protection and Punishment, the Baud's Tool, the Sharper's Bubble, the Vintner's Property, the Drawer's Terror, the Glasier's Benefactor; in short, a roaring, thoughtless, heedless, ridiculous universal Coxcomb,[108]

and Sir Morgan prophetically warned Sir Merlin that 'a Wit with an Estate is like a Prisoner among the Cannibals'.[109] The echoes of Harry Marten are unmistakable.

It was Gildon's professional opinion that theatre-goers in the 1690s would no longer recognise Marten's life or his politics. Nevertheless, his infamy remained a sharp memory several years after Marten's seclusion and death. In 1682 the tie between lasciviousness and political radicalism was still being lampooned. A character called Harvey was 'not so much for levelling the Men, as *Martin* the Women'. Two years after the 'great Turk's' death, 'all the Women in the City are with Child by *Martin*, and so longed for Levellers'.[110] Gildon dedicated his 1696 edition of *The Younger Brother* to Colonel Christopher Codrington, from whose father George Marten had purchased the majority of his estate. By 1690 the Codringtons had established themselves as one of the foremost families in the Caribbean. They must surely have known and remembered the Martens.[111]

Late seventeenth-century England combined bawdy tavern humour with a tone of stern moralising. After the Restoration and, more particularly, after 1688, republicanism was banished from the spectrum of acceptable political ideas. Marten was upheld as an example of the character that republicanism bred and the personal and political chaos that resulted from its implementation. Neither had Marten left sufficient reputation to act as an idol for those who engineered spates of republican revivalism. By the time of Monmouth's rebellion in 1685, he had been dead just five years, dying no martyr's death on the gallows, but in poverty and exiled obscurity in Wales. He was now a moral lesson to all those tempted to abuse their position and gifts. According to Noble, Marten died in 'such wretched poverty and abjectness, both in spirit and fortune, that he was glad to receive a cup of ale from any who would give it him':

Such was the end of the gay, the licentious, debauched, abandoned, Harry Marten, who could play his jests, whilst sacrificing his royal master to the aggrandizement of the rebellious army. – Such were the last sad days and years of this man, whose quickness of thought, elegance of manners, vivacity, wit, and charming gaiety, had often fascinated, not only the convivial board, but the grave, austere, dour, republican chiefs in the house of commons, who often chose him their manager and director. Who, after spending a noble paternal inheritance, vast sums gained by plunder, or the lavish grants of the parliament, was reduced to a lower station than his most menial servant; and whom, if he had not been supported as a criminal, must have been as a prisoner for debt.

Such a character is an awful lesson to the rich and thoughtless, to the man of genius, to such who are favoured with peculiar blessings of mind and fortune, that they may restrain themselves by checking those propensities to which both their tempers and the specious temptations of their station allure, – lest, like Harry Marten, they become monuments of their own ruin, and the public objects of scorn, contempt, and abhorrence.[112]

Noble's age found moral lessons irresistible, adorning monuments with tales of heroicism, charity, patience, constancy and duty. Marten's wit, his lifestyle and his politics were the making of a popular hero, but he found how easily the same characteristics could destroy him. Whilst on the top of the ladder he was the gilded bird which adorned the republic: a thinker, a rake, a jovial host and the defender of the people's interests. Once the ladder had been toppled, he could no longer shake off the gilding to reveal the man of substance beneath.

Postscript
The Immortality of Fashion

Marten's reputation was, however, kept alive. Archdeacon Coxe, pillar of the Established Church, royalist, lover of the balanced eighteenth-century constitution, nevertheless wrote a detailed and objective summary of Marten's career. He muddied the distinctions between different types of republicanism and religious viewpoint, but Coxe opined that

> [t]he dissoluteness of his life and immorality of his conduct led Marten to reject that pure religion which enjoins the controul of the passions. Hence he united with Harrington, Sydney, Wildman, Nevill, and others, who supposed themselves more enlightened than the rest of mankind, and denied the truth of revelation. The same licentiousness of opinion, which delivered him from the restraints of religion, influenced his sentiments on politics: warmed with the glowing images of Greek and Roman classics, he panted for a perfect commonwealth, a republic of representatives chosen by the people, and wholly governed by public opinion, which admitted no distinction, but superiority of genius, talent, or science.[1]

Marten was portrayed as a man who had aspired to use the army, whilst the army got the better of him. He was recognised as a supporter of the Levellers, especially in Grey of Groby's county of Leicester, where Turvil had given such an unfavourable account of his 1648 regiment.[2]

Bradney, on the other hand, was convinced that '[m]ore notice has been taken of him in local books and pamphlets than he deserves' and held the poet Robert Southey culpable. The young Romantics emerged from Oxbridge in the 1790s, full of revolutionary fervour, and revived, in the light of the French Revolutionary regicide, a rhetoric of heroic and quixotic republicanism. French Revolutionary radicals found Marten's type of republicanism more congenial than that of Sidney and Harrington, whose vision of patriotic liberty had been an element of American revolutionary thinking.[3] Romantic reinterpreters embraced the violence of revolution and the killing of kings.[4] Literary commentators put new life into the reputations of the heroes of the 1640s.[5] The most remembered line of Shelley's *The Mask of Anarchy* is the attack on

Castlereagh – 'I met Murder on the way' – but the real villain is the figure of anarchy:

> And he wore a kingly crown;
> And in his grasp a sceptre shone;
> On his brow this mark I saw -
> 'I AM GOD, AND KING, AND LAW!'[6]

For the purposes of martyrology, however, Marten, having been spared the gallows, spent the post-Restoration years in jail, and was in need of some further romanticisation. Denied the death of a patriot hero – he choked on his supper – it was necessary, in order to keep the faith alive, for Marten's captivity to have been more gruelling than the reality. The length of time that he spent in captivity was extended. Southey's work appeared in several Jacobin-influenced magazines and in November 1797 he published a short piece inspired by a trip to Wales from his home in Bristol. At Chepstow castle, he encountered Marten's Tower. According to Southey's account, Marten was incarcerated there for thirty years; eighteen years longer than the reality. The poem, printed in John Aitin's *Monthly Review*, managed to confuse, within sixteen short lines, the classical, Biblical, millenarian, and libertarian strands within the republican tradition:

> For thirty years secluded from mankind
> Here MARTEN linger'd. Often have these walls
> Echoed his footsteps, as with even tread
> He pac'd around his prison; not to him
> Did Nature's fair varieties exist;
> He never saw the Sun's delightful beams;
> Save when thro' yon high bars he pour'd a sad
> And broken splendour. Dost thou ask his crime?
> He had REBELL'D AGAINST THE KING, AND SAT
> IN JUDGEMENT ON HIM; for his ardent mind
> Shap'd goodliest plans of happiness on earth,
> And Peace and Liberty. Wild dreams! but such
> As PLATO lov'd; such as with holy zeal
> Our MILTON worshipp'd. Blessed hopes! a while
> From man with-held, even to the latter days
> When CHRIST shall come, and all things be fulfill'd![7]

This poem brought Southey's revolutionary politics to the attention of the *Anti-Jacobin*, which under the influence of George Canning, among others, began to publish deflamatory pastiches of the kind at which Marten excelled.[8]

Fifty years later, the image of Marten as a republican icon became a tool for those who sought to embed republican rhetoric within the campaign for the universal franchise. William Linton started his career as a wood engraver, providing images for the *Illustrated London News*. He launched his own career as a publisher and editor, however, where his premises in Hatton Garden became a republican meeting-house during the 1840s, much as two centuries before radical ideas were encouraged by Will Parker's ale. In 1850 he contributed to *The Red Republic* and the following year began *The English Republic*.[9] By 1865 Linton was disillusioned. His interests turned from prose to poetry and he made plans to emigrate to America. His first collection of poems, led by one titled 'Claribel', included 'Harry Marten's Dungeon Thoughts'.[10] The sixteenth and seventeenth centuries provided him with numerous examples of English heroism – Raleigh in the Indies and another on the battle of Newbury: Marten had taken a minor, unlauded part in the latter. Since Marten's dungeon was supposed to be Chepstow, the relatively comfortable surroundings again underwent derenovation. Linton's poem is insufficiently meritorious to dwell on its lines. He took the sentiment attributed to Marten – that he would think and act the same, given his life again – and embroidered it with a rallying cry of patriotic liberty. An unlikely foursome of Vane, Milton, Scot and Marten struggled to persuade the English. In 1865 Linton felt the stifled air of political debate in England reflected in the four walls that had surrounded Marten: 'Difference between/ Chepstow and England is not much, I ween./ 'Tis but a cell a few more paces wide.'[11]

The tradition of reinterpreting Henry Marten for contemporary purposes continues. In November 1993 Sir Keith Thomas unveiled a plaque to mark the house in Oxford considered to be Marten's birthplace. The building in Merton Street is now part of Corpus Christi College. The sea-green of the Levellers was commemorated in dyed flowers, hung beneath the plaque, and the Mayor of Oxford and one of his Labour Party colleagues at Westminster made speeches that celebrated Marten as a champion of the oppressed. Marten's legacy had been to reunite the politically diverse traditions of Oxford's town (parliamentarian) and gown (royalist). Leveller Association members paraded the 1648 banner – 'For the People, against all Tyrants whatsoever' – through the streets and gave three 'huzzahs'. There were Morris dancers and Irish folk music, played by those who subsequently chose to rename themselves 'Henry Marten's Ghost'.

Appendix
Pieces written by Marten

The following is a list of published works by Marten, those attributed to Marten on grounds of style or content, and major manuscripts written by Marten but not sent to the press. When a pamphlet number is given it is the reference to the copy held in the Thomason Collection, British Library, London.

2 August 1643	*Three Speeches delivered at a Common Hall . . . at the reading of a Proclamation from the King*, 28 July 1643, a pamphlet; Marten's speech is the third.
(Oct?) 1646	*A Reply to ye aunswer without a name pretending animadversions upon Mr CHALLONER'S speech published by* – groom to ye same Mr Challoner, BL Add. MSS 71534. ff. 89–90. A draft of a pamphlet as part of Marten's support for Chaloner in the Speech without Doors campaign.
26 Oct. 1646	*A Corrector of the Answerer to the Speech out of Doores*, E364(9). A printed pamphlet, confirmed by Marten because of the overlap with the manuscript version above. False imprimatur of Evan Tyler, Edinburgh.
(Oct?) 1646	*A Resolve of the Person of the King*, Wing Short Title Catalogue M824A, another version of *A Corrector*, above, also printed with Tyler's imprimatur.
16 Nov. 1646	*An Answer to a Speech without Doores: or Animadversions*, E362(9), a printed pamphlet.
30 Nov. 1646	*An Vnhappie game at Scotch and English*, E364(3). A further contribution to the Speech without Doors campaign, shown to be by Marten because of stylistic similarities and the bogus claim to have been printed by Evan Tyler, Edinburgh.
1646	'An additional instruction for ye Ld Lieutt of Ireland to be sent after him', policy on Ireland to be implemented by Lord Lisle, ML v78/11.
1647	A draft of a reply to John Selden, originally written in 1642, to which he returned in 1647 as a reply to 'The privileges of ye

	Baronage of England when they sitt in Parliament', BL Add. MSS 71532, ff. 5–6.
after May 1647	'Rash censures uncharitable', ML v78/1–2v, and the other at BL Add. MSS 71532 ff. 14 and 14v. Manuscript fragments of a draft reply to John Lilburne, *Rash Oaths Unwarrantable: and the breaking of them as inexcusable . . . being an Epistle written by Lieutenant-Colonell John Lilburne to Colonell Henry Marten, . . .* May 1647.
11 Jan. 1648	*The Independency of England endeavoured to be maintained*, E422(16), authorship claimed by Marten, a pamphlet attacking the role of the Scottish Commissioners.
[7 Feb.] 1648	*The Parliaments Proceedings Justified*, E426(2), another claimed attack on the Scottish Commissioners.
6 Jan. 1649	*A Word to Mr Wil. Prynne Esq*, E537(16), shown to be by Marten on grounds of style, argument and content. Prynne was a constant sparring-partner.
[Feb.] 1649	*Opinions offerd by H.M.*, ML v78/10, a manuscript draft, consisting of title-page, dedicatory epistle, and the first line.
[22 March] 1649	*A declaration of the parliament of England, expressing the grounds of their late proceedings, and of setting the present Government in the way of a Free State*, E548(12).
c. 1649	'An answere to ye Author of ye Captious Questions', BL Add. MSS 71532, f. 15v.
1649	'A plea for the people in answer to their late adversary Mr Prynne', BL Add. MSS 17534, ff. 10–11v.
1650(?)	'Wee ye P. of ye C. of E', manuscript draft, justifying the war against Scotland, BL Add. MSS 71534, ff. 20–21v.
1652(?)	*Les Maximes de bien gouvener pour maintenie la LIBERTIE dans l'obeissance*, ML 64/137. A manuscript fragment draft of an 'Agreement of the People' for the Frondeurs.
1653	'H.M. his vindication', BL Add. MSS 71532, ff. 24–24v.
(June?) 1653	ML 93/39–40v and 2–4v, a full draft (not in Marten's hand, possibly a fair copy) of Marten's refusal to accept a (bogus) invitation to join Barebone's Parliament, beginning 'My Lord'.
[1654?]	Mock heroic poem, composed in Latin, on Cromwell's assumption of the 'throne', in manuscript: BL Add. MSS 71532, f. 16.
1655	A Latin poem about Sir Philip Sidney, signed Henricius Martinius and printed and published in William Duggard's edition of *The*

Countess of Pembroke's Arcadia (10th edn, London, 1655), sigs. C8v-d1. It only appears in, and seems to have been purposely composed for, this edition. This reference was found by Ian McLellan, and I am grateful to him for his permission to include it here.

1655   A reply to Harrington's *Commonwealth of Oceana*, BL Add. MSS 71532, ff. 9–10v.

1655   *Justice Would-bee, that made himself a Ranter Last week in opposition to those hee calls QUAKERS*, ML v78/6–8.

2 May 1659   H[enry] M[arten], HN, IL, IW, II, SM, *The Armies Dutie, or faithfull advice to the souldiers*, E980(12). A compositely authored pamphlet as part of the Good Old Cause.

1662   *Coll. Henry Marten's Familiar Letters to his Lady of Delight*, 1662, published by Edmund Gayton. Marten's letters to Mary Ward, from the Tower of London. Published without his permission.

Abbreviations

A&O	C.H. Firth and R.S. Rait, *Acts and Ordinances of the Interregnum* (3 vols) (London, 1911)
Aubrey, *Brief Lives*	John Aubrey, *Aubrey's Brief Lives* (ed. Oliver Lawson Dick) (London, 1987 edn)
BDA	Barbados Department of Archives
BIHR	*Bulletin of the Institute of Historical Research,* later *Historical Research*
BRO	Berkshire Record Office
CJ	*Journal of the House of Commons*
Clarke Papers	*The Clarke Papers: Selections from the Papers of William Clarke* (ed. C.H. Firth) (4 vols) (Camden Society, London, vol. i, 1891; vol. ii, 1894; vol. iii, 1899; vol. iv, 1901), with vols i and ii reissued by the Royal Historical Society (Woodbridge, Suffolk, 1992)
Clarendon, *History*	Edward Hyde, Earl of Clarendon, *The History of the Rebellion and Civil Wars in England* (ed. W. Dunn Macray) (6 vols) (Oxford, 1888)
CSPD	*Calendar of the State Papers Domestic*
CSP Col	*Calendar of the State Papers Colonial*
DRO	Derbyshire Record Office
EHR	*English Historical Review*
GCD	Samuel Rawson Gardiner, *Constitutional Documents of the Puritan Revolution, 1625-1660* (Oxford, references to the 1979 edn)
Gardiner, *History*	S.R. Gardiner, *History of the Great Civil War* (4 vols) (Windrush Press reprint, 1987)
Gardiner, *Commonwealth and Protectorate*	S.R. Gardiner, *History of the Commonwealth and Protectorate* (4 vols) (Windrush Press reprint, 1988)
GWO	Gwent Record Office
HJ	*Historical Journal*
HLRO	House of Lords Record Office
HMC	*Historical Manuscripts Commission*

HR	*Historical Research*
HRO	Herefordshire Record Office
JBMHS	*Journal of the Barbados Musuem and History Society*
	Note that some articles in the *JBMHS* do not cite an author
LJ	*Journal of the House of Lords*
ML	Marten Loder Manuscripts, held in the Brotherton Collection, University of Leeds; see below
Oxon RO	Oxfordshire Record Office
TWNC	*Transactions of the Woolhope Naturalists Club*
Snow and Young, *Journals*	Sir Simons D'Ewes, *The Private Journals of the Long Parliament* (ed. Vernon F. Snow and Anne Steele Young) (Yale, 1987)
Williams 'Anatomy'	C.M. Williams, 'The anatomy of a radical gentleman, Henry Marten', in D. Pennington and K. Thomas (eds), *Puritans and Revolutionaries* (Oxford, 1978)
Williams, 'Career'	C.M. Williams, 'The political career of Henry Marten, with special reference to the origins of republicanism in the Long Parliament', D.Phil. Oxford, 1954
Whitelocke, *Memorials*	Bulstrode Whitelocke, *Memorials of the English Affairs* (4 vols) (Oxford, 1853)
Worden, *Rump Parliament*	Blair Worden, *The Rump Parliament, 1648–1653* (Cambridge, 1974)

A note on the manuscripts relating to Henry Marten

Major repositories of Marten manuscripts are:

Berkshire Record Office (chiefly Marten's almanack of 1655);

The British Library (Add. MSS). These are predominantly political papers of Sir Henry and Henry Marten, previously held by the Fairfax family and purchased by the British Library in 1995;

The Brotherton Collection, University of Leeds.

The Brotherton Collection, University of Leeds

The Marten Loder Manuscripts consist of 68 boxes of documents and 122 volumes of bound documents. Not all directly relate to Marten: some relate to the Loder family and many of the manuscripts are eighteenth century. The papers relating to the Marten family include papers not only of Henry, but also of Sir Henry and George Marten.

The items are, at the time of writing, not listed or catalogued. Some documents have not been given a folio number, including items within boxes of manuscripts that have otherwise been foliated.

After box 68, the bound volumes often appear shelved by description rather than by volume number. A corresponding volume number has, however, been added, and appears on the inside folio of each volume. These refer mainly to items such as, for example, 'Henry Marten Papers: Political and Miscellaneous I' (i.e., vol. 92), 'George Marten Letters' (84), 'Henry Marten Letters, 1626–1658' (88). Where possible, the volume number had been cited.

A large number of the bound volumes are arranged as First, Second and Third Series. These are numbered sequentially throughout, continuing to the volumes not described as part of a series. Occasionally, it proves necessary to pin-point material to cite the series number and a volume number within the series. Most volumes within the series are, however, single wills or indentures.

The papers were read in the 1950s by Professor C.M. Williams, and, occasionally, material on the same subject has been moved from one box/volume to another, in order to keep similar or contiguous material together. Hence, the draft open letter to Cromwell (1653) consists of ff. 39–40v, bound within volume 93, along with eight loose pages, moved from elsewhere, numbered 2–4v.

The full reference to these manuscripts should read University of Leeds, Brotherton Collection, Marten Loder MSS, but for ease, this has been abbreviated throughout to ML. Boxes are referred to as MLb and volume numbers as MLv.

A note on the pamphlets cited

Unless stated, all pamphlet references are to the Thomason Tract collection of pamphlets held by the British Library, London. A useful, but not necessarily reliable, catalogue of these printed sources is G.K. Fortescue, *Catalogue of the Pamphlets, Books, Newspapers, and Manuscripts relating to the Civil War, the Commonwealth, and Restoration, collected by George Thomason, 1640–1661* (2 vols) (London, 1903). The reference number given (usually prefixed by E) is that given in the British Library. When the date of the tract is printed, it is given. Thomason noted on the frontispiece, in manuscript, the date on which he received a tract and, in cases in which that provides the evidence of dating, the date is shown in square brackets; hence, E457(6), [7 Feb.] 1649.

Notes

Chapter I The Rise of the Republicans

1. University of Leeds, Marten-Loder MSS, (ML) 7/158-181.
2. Judith Maltby (ed.), *The Short Parliament Diary of Sir Thomas Aston* (London, Camden Society, 4th ser., vol. 35, 1988), p. 43.
3. Clarendon, *History*, i, pp. 182–3.
4. Ibid., i, p. 210.
5. *CJ*, ii, p. 8, 21 Apr. 1640; *CSPD* 1640–1, p. 197; Clarendon, *History*, i, p. 273.
6. *CJ*, ii, pp. 10, 12, 14.
7. *CSPD* 1641–3, p. 92.
8. *CSPD* 1640–1, p. 479, Feb. 1641.
9. *CSPD* 1641–3, pp. 126, 131. Sir Henry died on 26 Sep. 1641.
10. *CJ*, ii, pp. 51, 58, 64, 81, 91, 92; Williams, 'Anatomy', pp. 118–38.
11. Conrad Russell, *The Fall of the British Monachies, 1637–1641* (Oxford, 1991), pp. 280–302.
12. *CJ*, ii, pp. 99, 105, 107, 111, 112, 125, 129.
13. *GCD*, pp. 155–6; *CJ*, ii, p. 132; Russell, *Fall*, p. 299.
14. *CJ*, ii, p. 188.
15. *CJ*, ii, pp. 261, 288.
16. *CJ*, ii, p. 344.
17. *CJ*, ii, p. 330.
18. *CJ*, ii, p. 352, 21 Dec. 1641. See Marten's ribald comments on the Scots being evicted from their London houses in his *The Independency of England Endeavoured to be Maintained*, 11 Jan. 1648, E422(16) p. 21.
19. *CJ*, ii, p. 468.
20. *CJ*, ii, p. 408.
21. *CJ*, ii, pp. 456–8. Williams' colourful if ambiguous phrase for Marten's action with his ship was that he 'insinuated' it into state service.
22. *CJ*, ii, p. 464.
23. *CJ*, ii, pp. 650–63.
24. ML v78/5; b40/28. See Hill's petition, 24 Jan. 1642, *CJ*, ii, p. 390.
25. *A true Copy of the Petition of the Gentlewomen* (London, 1642), *Harleian Miscellany*, v, p. 271; Valerie Pearl, *London and the Outbreak of the Puritan Revolution: City Government and National Politics, 1625–43* (Oxford, 1964), p. 226.
26. ML b67/19.
27. ML b40/50, 29 July 1642; on the order of the Committee for the Defence of the Kingdom, 6 July 1642, *CJ*, ii, p. 656. Receivers of these goods were Tempest Milner and Maurice Gethin, both commissioners for the assessment of London for Cordwainer ward.
28. Snow and Young, *Journals*, p. 91.

29. *CJ*, ii, p. 595.

30. ML b40/19.

31. ML b40/15, b40/28, b40/51, b40/63.

32. ML b40/43, b40/58.

33. ML b40/28.

34. Snow and Young, *Journals*, p. 292; *CJ*, ii, pp. 563–4.

35 Ibid., p. 362; *CJ*, ii, p. 583; Snow and Young, *Journals*, p. xiii.

36 Ibid., p. 120; *CJ*, ii, p. 508.

37. Snow and Young, *Journals*, pp. 191–2. Marten had opposed a bill for impressment after the Irish rebellion, on the grounds that it infringed the liberty of the subject: Russell, *Fall*, pp. 341, 417.

38. Cited in Russell, *Fall*, p. 518.

39. Such as Sir John Culpepper and Sir John Strangeways, *CJ*, ii, pp. 739, 750; Mary Freer Keeler, *The Long Parliament, 1640–1641: a biographical Study of its Members* (Philadelphia, 1954), pp. 239–40.

40. *CJ*, ii, pp. 507, 666, 682. Southby subsequently sat with Marten on the Berkshire militia committee of July 1659; *A&O*, ii, p. 1320.

41. Husbands, *Votes and Ordinances* (1643), p. 550, cited *DNB*, p. 1148.

42. J.H. Hexter, *The Reign of King Pym* (Harvard, 1941), p. 49.

43. Ibid., p. 57.

44. Williams, 'Career', pp. 47–53 and *passim*; Russell, *Fall*, pp. 518–19.

45. *CJ*, ii, p. 838.

46. *CJ*, ii, pp. 840, 845, 847.

47. *An Humble Proposal of Safety to the Parliament and Citie*, [25 May] 1643; *Instructions and Propositions containing incouragements to all good men to subscribe for the raising of an Army of ten thousand*, [8 July] 1643; *An humble Pettition of thousands of well-affected Inhabitants of the Citie of London and Westminster and the Suburbs thereof*, 1643; *CJ*, iii, pp. 176, 187; Pearl, *London*, pp. 268–73.

48. *CJ*, iii, p. 176; Hexter, *King Pym*, p. 123.

49. The choice of site may well also reflect Marten's commercial interests in the City. The draper, Tempest Milner, who had supplied the soldiers uniforms to the Hull detachments, was elected to the committee from the Londoners' side, Williams, 'Career', p. 101; ML b40/50; ML b67/82; Journal of the Common Council, ML b40/67; *Mercurius Aulicus*, 11 Sep. 1643; Pearl, *London*, p. 271.

50. Hexter, *King Pym*, pp. 122–9. For Williams' alternative explanation see 'Career', pp. 91–101.

51. *CJ*, iii, pp. 165, 171, 176–8.

52. *Three Speeches delivered at a Common-Hall . . . at the reading of a Proclamation from the King*, on 28 July; 2 August 1643, p. 18.

53. Hexter, *King Pym*, pp.125–6.

54. Thomas May's glancing account was conspicuous in mentioning London's fidelity both to Essex and to the new 'reserve' force of Waller, Thomas May, *The History of the Parliament of England* (London, 1812), p. 214.

55. Clarendon, *History* ii, pp. 388–9.

56. *CJ*, ii, p. 953, 3 Feb.1643; *CJ*, iii, p. 18; Hexter, *King Pym*, pp. 125–6.

57. ML b40/8-8ᵛ.

Item for 3 Armours New Gusseting lathering lining Nayling	4 - 4 - 0
Item for 2 New Crest	1 -10 - 0
Item for 1 back	0 - 8 - 0
Item for 3 New Culots	1 -16 - 0

Item for 3 New gauntlets	2 -15 - 0
Item for 1 headpeece New banding	0 - 2 - 6
Item for 1 peare of Cuffes New banding	0 - 2 - 6
Item for altering 1 back and crest	0 - 6 - 0
Item for Portring	0 - 3 - 0
The sum is	10 -17-[0]

58. May, *History*, p. 201.

59. *CJ*, iii, p. 48, 17 Apr. 1643; *CJ*, iii, pp. 68–9, 1 May 1643; *CJ*, iii, p. 152, 3 July 1643; *A&O*, i, pp. 215–19, 29 July 1643; 'Order to redress the abuses in taking horses for supply of the army', 10 May 1643, Ibid., pp.155–6.

60. *CJ*, iii, p. 109, 29 May 1643; *CJ*, iii, p. 164, 12 July 1643, to ensure they were employed by the state under the Lieutenant General.

61. *CJ*, iii, p. 206; Whitelocke, *Memorials*, i, p. 208, who noted it as 12 August.

62. Hexter, *King Pym*, pp. 59–60.

63. Gardiner, *History*, i, p. 202.

64. *CJ*, iii, p. 206.

65. To Lilburne, in *Rash censures unwarrantable*, ML v78.

66. Ibid.; ML b62/unfol.

67. *CJ*, iv, p. 397; Stonehouse was disabled on 6 Jan.1646, and on Ball's death in 1648, Marten's friend, Henry Nevile, was helped to the seat. After Ball's death, his republican, levellerish tract *The Power of Kings Discussed* was published, a reply to David Jenkins, a vocal opponent of Marten's, 30 Jan.1649, E340(21). On the links between Abingdon radicalism and Marten's power base, see chapter 4. For the recruiter elections, see David Underdown, 'Party management in the recruiter elections, 1645–48', *EHR* 83 (1968). Williams believed that Marten had been elected for Abingdon and having presented himself at the bar of the House, the Commons relented and allowed him to assume the county seat, but Stonehouse's disablement was not decided until after Marten returned to the chamber; Williams, 'Anatomy', p. 121. *CJ*, iv, pp. 384, 388; BL Add. 31116, f. 252v; Harley MS 165, f. 152.

68. *CJ*, iv, p. 551; Gardiner, *History*, iii, p. 106.

69. Sarah Barber, 'Ireland and Scotland under the Commonwealth: a question of loyalty', in Sarah Barber and Steven G. Ellis (eds.), *Conquest and Union: Fashioning a British State, 1485–1725* (Longman, London, 1995) and Sarah Barber, 'The attitude of the people of Northern England towards the Scots, 1639–1652: 'the lamb and the dragon cannot be reconciled'', *Northern History* xxxv (1999), 93–118.

70. Used with venom by George Wither to call for soldiers' rights and the confiscation of delinquents' estates in 1644; George Wither, *The Speech without Doore, delivered July 9 1644 in the absence of the Speaker and in the hearing of above 0000003 persons then present*, E4(30).

71. [Henry Marten], *A Corrector of the Answerer*, 26 Oct. 1646, E364(9); *An Vnhappie game at Scotch and English*, 30 Nov. 1646, E364(3).

72. [Henry Marten], *An Answer to a Speech without Doores*, 16 Nov. 1646, E362(9); BL Add. MSS 71534, ff. 89–90.

73. BL Add. MSS 71532, ff. 11–11v.

74. *CJ*, v, p. 129; Austin Woolrych, *Soldiers and Statesmen: the General Council of the Army and its Debates, 1647–1648* (Oxford, 1987), pp. 36–8.

75. Woolrych, *Soldiers and Statesmen*, p. 26.

76. Gardiner, *History*, i, p. 116; *LJ*, viii, pp. 127, 261.

77. ML v78/11, 'An additional instruction for yᵉ Lᵈ Lieutᵗ of Ireland to bee sent after him'.

78. ML v78/12.

79. ML v78/13.

80. H.N. Brailsford, *The Levellers and the English Revolution* (Nottingham, 1961), pp. 205–6.

81. Wildman carried the title of Major, but was always classed as a civilian.

82. BL Add. MSS 71532, f. 23.

83. 'Petter', would seem to be Maximilian Petty. It seems unlikely to have been Hugh Peter, the Independent divine.

84. ML v72/519.

85. Sexby in 1632, Petty in May 1634. Petty's uncle had been MP for Westbury, Wiltshire, in the parliament of 1628.

86. Starting as early as May 1641; *CJ*, ii, p. 134.

87. Brailsford, *Levellers*, pp. 240–1; Woolrych, *Soldiers and Statesmen*, pp. 1900–4; Pauline Gregg, *Freeborn John: a Biography of John Lilburne* (London, 1961), p. 195 and *passim*; John Lilburne, *Two Letters written by Lieut. Col. John Lilburne*, 13 and 15 Sep. 1647; Lilburne, *A Copy of a Letter written to Col. Henry Marten*, 20 July 1647, 669.f.11(46); E407(41) and *Rash Oaths unwarrantable and the breaking of them inexcusable*, 31 May 1647, E393(39).

88. ML v78/1-2ᵛ, f. 1.

89. Brailsford, *Levellers*, pp. 240–1.

90. Gardiner, *History*, iii, p. 366.

91. *CJ*, v, pp. 311, 314; Gardiner, *History*, pp. 366–8.

92. There were several agreements called an engagement. In order to distinguish the Engagement of 1647 between the Hamiltonian Scots and Charles I from the Engagement of loyalty to the Commonwealth Council of State (1649–51), the former is given in italic.

93. *GCD*, pp. 347–53.

94. *CJ*, v, pp. 415–16; *A Declaration of the Commons of England* E427(9); Gardiner, *History*, pp. 51–62; *GCD*, p. 356; Clement Walker, *Relations and Observations, hisatorical and politick, upon the Parliament begun . . . 1640* (London, 1648–1660), pp. 69–70.

95. Edmund Ludlow, *Memoirs* (ed. C.H. Firth) (2 vols) (Oxford, 1894), i, p. 182.

96. Henry Marten, *The Independency of England Endeavoured to be maintained*, [11 Jan.], 1648, E422(16), but clearly written as a reply to the King's answer to the Four Bills and therefore probably written between 28 Dec. and 3 Jan., E422(16).

97. Ibid., p. 15.

98. Ibid., p. 12.

99. 7 Feb. 1648; E426(2).

100. As I interpret 'Honorable drudges' and 'gallant champions'.

101. Ibid., pp. 4–6.

102. Ibid., p. 10.

103. Patricia Crawford, 'Charles Stuart: that man of blood', *Journal of British Studies* xvi.2 (1977), 41–61.

104. Bodleian Library, Oxford, Tanner MSS 57, f. 197.

105. Ayers' Common Plantation lies within Pusey. Ayers and Eyres are interchangable in this instance. Unfortunately, the Pusey records have been lost. Marten was said to have been a relative of the Yate family centred on Buckland.

106. The names Walrond and Waldron were considered interchangeable, which raises the interesting notion that John may have been related to George Marten's royalist enemy in Barbados, Humphrey Walrond: Worcester College, Oxford, Clarke MSS, cxiv, f. 67.

107. Sarah Barber, '"A bastard kind of militia": localism and tactics during the second civil war', in Ian Gentles, John Morrill, and Blair Worden (eds.), *Soldiers, Writers and Statesmen of the English Revolution* (Cambridge, 1998).

108. *Mercurius Pragmaticus* 22–29 Aug. 1648; see also *Clarke Papers*, ii, pp. 56–7; *Mercurius Pragmaticus* had been showing keen interest in Marten's troop since June, 6–13 June 1648, E447(5), as did *Mercurius Elenticus* 23–30 Aug. 1648, E461(20).

109. Thomas, Lord Grey of Groby, *Old English Blood boyling afresh in Leicestershire men*, [28 Aug.] 1648, E461(7); *Articles of Treason and high Misimeanours [sic], committed by John Pine of Curry-Mallet*, [2 Apr.] 1649, 669.f.14(15)/669.f.13(94); see Barber, '"A bastard kind of militia"'.

110. Christopher Durston, 'Henry Marten and the High Shoon of Berkshire: the Levellers in Berkshire in 1648', *Berkshire Archaeological Journal* 70 (1979–80), 87–95.

111. David Underdown, '"Honest" radicals in the counties, 1642–1649', in D. Pennington and K. Thomas (eds), *Puritans and Revolutionaries* (Oxford, 1978), pp. 186–205.

112. Bodl., Tanner MSS 57, f. 197, 15 Aug. 1648.

113. Bodl., Tanner MSS 57/1, ff. 197 and 199; Clarke MSS, cxiv, ff. 67 and 80; *Mercurius Pragmaticus* 22–29 Aug. 1648, E461(17); *CSPD*, 1648, p. 268.

114. Marten probably did not go to Ashby, but was certainly in Market Harborough, see *Terrible and bloody news from the disloyall army in the North*, 11 Sep. 1648, E462(28).

115. *CJ*, vi, p. 129, 2 Feb. 1649. This seems not to have come about.

116. David Underdown, *Pride's Purge: Politics in the Puritan Revolution* (Oxford, 1971), pp. 104–5.

117. Ludlow, *Memoirs*, i, pp. 203–5; Underdown, *Pride's Purge*, p. 108.

118. Clause iv; 'that the power of this, and all future Representatives of this nation is inferior only to theirs who choose them'.

119. John Lilburne, *Legal Fundamental Liberties* (1649), reprinted in A.S.P. Woodhouse, *Puritanism and Liberty: being the Army Council Debates* (1647–9) (London, 1986), pp. 342–55.

120. Barbara Taft, 'The Council of Officers' *Agreement of the People*, 1648/9', *HJ* 28.1 (1985), 189–97; see also *idem*, 'Voting lists of the Council of Officers, December 1648', *BIHR* lii (1979), 138–54.

121. Ludlow, *Memoirs*, i, p. 210; *CJ*, vi, p. 97.

122. ML v91/39.

123. Maurice Ashley, *John Wildman, Plotter and Postmaster: a study of the English Republican Movement in the Seventeenth century* (London, 1947), pp. 69–70; Richard Overton, July 1649; John Lilburne, July 1649.

124. [Henry Marten], *A Word to Mr Wil. Prynne Esq*, 6 Jan. 1649, E537(16), p. 15. This pamphlet was published anonymously, printed by Thomas Brewster. The style, particularly that of the *ad hominem*, caustic and sarcastic introduction, is reminiscent of Marten's known writing; he was drafting several pieces to William Prynne at the time; and Marten repeats several phrases in this printed piece which he had rehearsed in manuscript, such as the dog howling at the moon and the Billingsgate language. It was a reply to Prynne's of the previous day, entitled *Mr Pryn's last and finall Declaration to the Commons of England concerning the King, Parliament and Army; shewing that it is High Treason to compasse the deposition or death of King Charles*, E537(12).

125. Evil counsellors theory describes the phenomenon of attributing blame for England's crisis, and ultimately civil war, on the malign and self-interested influence of Charles' advisors rather than attaching blame to the King himself.

126. Ibid., p. 15. I am grateful to David Norbrook for drawing my attention to this reference.

127. *CJ*, vi, pp. 94–5.

128. Scottish Record Office, Hamilton Papers, GD 1/406/1/8277. My thanks to David Scott for this reference.

129. *CJ*, vi, p. 93.

130. Cornet Henry Denne, *The Levellers Designe Discovered*, [24 May] 1649, E556(11), p. 8; *Clarke Papers*, i, lix.

131. Lilburne, *Foundations of Freedom* (1648); *CJ*, vi, p. 122.

132. Marten, *Independency of England*, p. 21: 'So long as we needed the assistance of your Countrymen in the Field, we might have occasion to give you meetings at *Derby* House . . . whereas now since we are able . . . to protect our selves, we may surely . . . be sufficient to teach our selves how to go about our own business'.

133. *CJ*, vi, p. 102.

134. Marten attended eighteen sessions.

135. *CJ*, vi, p. 111.

136. *CJ*, vi, p. 115; Whitelocke, *Memorials*, ii, p. 492.

137. *CJ*, vi, pp. 124–5.

Chapter II Liberty: Restored and Forfeited

1. Sir William Davenant, ML 93/11.

2. ML b64/114, 30 Apr. 1650. The burning of Oxfordshire's harvest and the mistrust of Oxford people for the King (15 Apr. 1645) formed a plank of John Cook's prosecution of Charles; John Cook, *King Charls his Case*, [Feb] 1649, E542(3), p. 16.

3. ML b67/39.

4. ML b67/109, passed to Marten from the Council of State.

5. Leeds, ML b8/77, n.d.; ML b67/104, n.d.; ML v92/48, May 1649.

6. ML v92/76 and 78, Nov./Dec. 1650.

7. ML v93/11, 8 July 1652; Aubrey, *Brief Lives*, p. 179.

8. ML b8/50.

9. ML v93/17, London, 22 Nov. 1652. Debentures were vouchers given by the state, acknowledging goods or services supplied, which would be repaid with interest.

10. Aubrey, *Brief Lives*, p. 267; John 9.1, 'And as Jesus passed by, he saw a man which was blind from birth'.

11. *CJ*, vi, p. 96, 12 Dec. 1648.

12. HLRO, MS Commons' Journals, xxxiii, f. 625. On 5 March this task was devolved onto a smaller committee of Lisle, Scot, Ludlow, Holland and Robinson.

13. Underdown queried that Marten registered in December, though he was assuming Marten's signature on the death warrant and general radicalism would make him bound to be a fervent signatory of dissent.

14. Although Thomas Chaloner and Lord Grey were not named to the committee to register dissents on 29 December, they frequently 'reported from the committee' and did so themselves.

15. Worden, *Rump Parliament*, p. 177 and *passim*.

16. *A&O*, ii, pp. 2–4.

17. HLRO, MS Commons' Journals, xxxiii, ff. 732–4; Sarah Barber, 'The Engagement for the Council of State and the establishment of the Commonwealth government', *HR* 63.150 (1990), 44–57. The phrase cited here is that which Marten and Ireton attempted to reinsert a few days later, but we can deduce that the wording was similar.

18. Algernon Sidney to the earl of Leicester, unfortunately nine years after the event, Robert Willis Blencowe, *Sydney Papers: consisting of a Journal of the Earl of Leicester, and original Letters of Algernon Sydney* (London, 1825), p. 238; Gardiner, *History*, i, p. 5.

19. 'For our ancestors were of opinion that no bond was more effective in guaranteeing good faith than an oath', Cicero, *De Officiis* (Loeb Classical Library, 1975), bk. 3, ch. 31, section III.

20. The figures for MPs' ages, some of which are not known for certain, are taken from Underdown's *Pride's Purge*, appendix A.

21. *CJ*, vi, p. 109, 6 Feb. 1649.

22. *CJ*, vi, p. 133. The committee was Lisle, Marten, Whitelocke, Scot, Jones, Ireton, Grey, Nicholas, Sidney, Blagrave and Chaloner. Grey appears to have already been named to the committee on the Lords.

23. *A&O*, ii, pp. 18–20; ii, p. 24.

24. Aubrey, *Brief Lives*, pp. 266–7; *A Declaration of the Parliament of England, expressing the grounds of their late proceedings, and of setting the present Government in the way of a Free State*, [22 March] 1649, E548(12).

25. *Declaration of the Parliament of England*, p. 16.

26. Ibid., p. 24.

27. Lilburne, Overton and Prince, *The Picture of the Councel of State*, 11 Apr. 1649, E550(14); Lilburne, Overton, Walwyn, Prince, *A Manifestation*, 16 Apr. 1649, E550(25).

28. John Naylier, Richard Ellergood, John Marshall, *The Foxes Craft Discovered*, [2 Apr.] 1649, E549(7).

29. Ian Gentles, *The New Model Army in England, Ireland and Scotland, 1645–1653* (Oxford, 1992), pp. 343–4. It is still not certain whether there were two men called William Eyres with similar careers.

30. The officers' junto was defined as Cromwell, Ireton, Fairfax, Harrison, Fleetwood, Rich, Ingoldsby, Haselrig, Constable, Fenwick, Wauton and Allen.

31. Lilburne *et.al.*, *A Manifestation*, pp. 3, 7.

32. ML b8/82, 4 May 1650. Wetton may have hoped for Irish land or to have already had an investment in Ireland, but there is no evidence of his having invested adventure capital.

33. Wetton raised a regiment to go to Ireland, but there is no evidence that he, or his regiment embarked: C.H. Firth and Godfrey Davies, *The Regimental History of Cromwell's Army* (2 vols) (Oxford, 1940), ii, p. 641.

34. ML b2/unfol., 9 Apr. 1650; DRO 1235 (misc. papers relating to Hartington), p. 3, 5 Apr. 1650; that this is the same Maximilian Petty as the Leveller can be confirmed by comparing the signature with those in Oxon RO Li/XIII/ii/1 and Li/XIII/vii/b/1. Edmund Ludlow was referred to as a comrade by John Lilburne; Brailsford, *Levellers*, p. 349.

35. ML v78/51, 53, n.d. Wildman to Marten, 'My O, The sight of your desire to be with your A hath put life & health into him though he hath bene halfe dead with a vomiting fitt this night & I beleeve yᵉ fruition of my will be much better then yᵉ hopes of it, though nothing else is so, yet I doubt I am locked up by an inmate (unlesse I can deny importunity itself) from dining with my O but if that prove so I cannot be kept from you long after diner . . . This paper is happier then poore A because it comes to you sooner there, From my bedd'.

36. Ashley, *John Wildman*, pp. 68–81.

37. Joanna Savile to Henry Marten, 30 July 1652, ML v93/13.

38. ML v93/70.

39. Ian Gentles, 'London Levellers in the English Revolution: the Chidleys and their circle', *Journal of Ecclesiastical History* 29.3 (1978), p. 288.

40. Ibid., p. 298; G.E. Aylmer, *The State's Servants: The Civil Service of the English Republic, 1649–1660* (London, 1973), p. 59.

41. Sarah Barber, 'Irish undercurrents to the politics of April 1653', *HR* 65.158 (1992), 315–35.

42. ML 92/49, Bristol, 31 Oct. 1649; Aylmer, *State's Servants*, pp. 272–4; *Clarke Papers*, i, pp. 340, 383. At Putney, Bishop spoke up for John Saltmarsh and concluded that the cause of the disagreements on the Council was the continuing presence of the 'man of blood'.

43. William Cockayne, *The Foundations of Freedome Vindicated*, 7 Feb. 1648(9), E341(25).

44. Cockayne, *Foundations*, p. 7.

45. Ball was the author of several radical tracts: *Constituio Libreri Populi, or the Rule of a Free-born People*, 18 June 1646, E341(1); *The Power of Kings Discussed*, 30 Jan., 1649, E340(21); and *State-maxims or certain dangerous positions destructive to the very nature very natural Right and Liberty of mankind*, [5 Aug.] 1656, E886(6). The last two were published posthumously, although they appeared to be contemporareous responses to current pamphlets. Two theories are advanced to explain this. One is that there were two William Balls; one the MP and another a political theorist. The second idea is that Ball's work was entrusted to a friend (Marten?) who issued and re-issued it with suitable doctoring when it seemed timely.

46. Ball, *Power of Kings*; both Cockayne and Ball were published by John Harris of London.

47. The links between English and French radicalism are examined in Brailsford, *Levellers*, pp. 671–91.

48. ML 4/135.

49. ML 4/130, Orleans, 3 July 1650. This may have been the letter wrongly classified by HMC 13 report as being sent to Henry's brother. In fact, it is clear that the references to Marten's 'brother' and 'uncle(s)' are to other conspirators. Marten's uncle, William, was long dead.

50. ML v92/68-69v, Bordeaux, 30 June 1650.

51. ML b67/120, Rouen, 4 Feb. 1652; ML b67/122, Rouen, 25 Jan. 1652; ML b8/107, Rouen, 22 Mar. 1653.

52. Pierre Lenet to Barrière, 5 Oct. 1653: 'Vous avez bien sceu que M. de Saxeby a esté longtemps à Bordeaux et à la Rochelle; que luy et led[it] Sr. Arondelle . . .', Bib. Nat., Fonds Français, 6716, ff. 102–5.

53. Brailsford, *Levellers*, pp. 675–6. I am indebted to John Smith, University of Durham, for sharing his research on the Fronde.

54. Bib. Nat., Fonds Français, 6716, ff. 102–5 and cited in Victor Cousin, *Madam de Longueville pendant la Fronde, 1651–1653* (Paris, 1859 (?)), p. 465; S.A. Westrich, *The Ormée of Bordeaux: A Revolution during the Fronde* (Baltimore, 1972); Orest Ranum, *The Fronde: A French Revolution, 1648–1652* (London, 1993); Philip A. Knachel, *England and the Fronde: the Impact of the English Civil War and Revolution in France* (Ithica, NY, 1967); Jean Francois Paul de Gondi, *Memoirs of the Cardinal de Retz written by Himself* (ed. Ernest Rhys) (London, 1970).

55. That the agent who went by the name of Stephen Edwards was in fact Edward Sexby is confirmed by a letter from Pierre Lenet to Condé, 15 July 1652, concerning their London agent: 'M. de Barrière nous a donné avis qu'il y avoit icy un nommé Sixbi sous le nom D'Edouard qui nègotioit sous main – nous l'avons cherché par touttes voyes, sans en avoir peu apprendre aucunes nouvelles', Bib. Nat. Fonds Français, 6708, f. 66. The writer is pointing out that Sexby's pseudonym was Edward, not that his first name was Edward.

56. C.H. Firth, 'Thomas Scot's account of his actions as intelligencer during the Commonwealth', *English Historical Review* xii (1897), 116–26.

57. Also referred to by the correspondent who wrote in code from Orleans in July 1650, ML b4/130ᵛ.

58. ML v72/519, Lyme, 22 Sep. 1652; G.F. Warner (ed.), *Nicholas Papers* (Camden Society, new ser. 40, vol. iii, 1965), pp. 51–2.

59. ML v72/519.

60. Some punctuation has been added, to aid the sense.

61. ML b64/137, in Marten's hand.

62. There is no date on the *Maximes*, though a note on the reverse of the manuscript, on an entirely different subject, is dated 30 June 1652. If this is the date of the French piece, it was written around

the time at which the *Ormée* took control of Bordeaux, but the piece clearly belongs to the debate, of several months' duration, about the town's constitution, so the piece could have been written slightly later in the year.

63. Cousin, *Madam de Longueville pendant la Fronde*.

64. Worden, *Rump Parliament*, p. 38.

65. Ibid., pp. 218–19.

66. Ibid., p. 221; Aubrey, *Brief Lives*, p. 266.

67. Worden, *Rump Parliament*, p. 219.

68. Jonathan Scott, *Algernon Sidney and the English Republic, 1623–1677* (Cambridge, 1988), p. 94.

69. *A Declaration of the Parliament of England*, pp. 5, 27.

70. Ian Gentles, 'The debentures market and military purchase of crown land, 1649–1660', Ph.D. University of London, 1969; *idem*, 'The sales of Crown lands during the English Revolution', *Economic History Review* xxvi (1973), 614–35.

71. Steven C.A. Pincus, *Protestantism and Patriotism: Ideologies and the Making of English Foreign Policy, 1650–1668* (Cambridge, 1996), p. 52, by whom I am convinced, contra Brenner, that Marten and his allies were not the anti-Dutch war-mongers or in control of foreign policy. This is also borne out by Marten's role in Caribbean politics, see chapter 6; Robert Brenner, *Merchants and Revolution: Commercial Change, Political Conflict, and London's Overseas Traders, 1550–1653* (Princeton, 1993), p. 630.

72. Scott, *Algernon Sidney*, pp. 102–5.

73. Ludlow, *Memoirs*, i, p. 344.

74. Austin Woolrych, *Commonwealth to Protectorate* (Oxford, 1982); Blair Worden, 'The bill for a new representative', *EHR* lxxxvi (1971); Barber, 'Irish undercurrents'.

75. Worden, *Rump Parliament*, pp. 239–40; I am not as convinced as Pocock or Worden that Marten was associated with Nedham in 1652. Worden argued that Marten was associated with the editorials of *Mercurius Politicus* during 1650–1, but these editorials changed their tone after Dunbar, and Marten never advocated the glories of Venice (Worden, *Rump Parliament*, p. 252). See J.G.A. Pocock (ed.), *James Harrington: The Commonwealth of Oceana and A System of Politics* (Cambridge, 1992), p. xv.

76. ML v88/11; b32/unfol, the case against Marten got underway during 1654, see below.

77. ML b28/549; b28/633; b31/1298; Aylmer, *State's Servants*, pp. 13–14 and *passim*; *A&O*, ii, pp. 618–20, 'An Act for reviving a former Act of Relief of Persons upon Articles', 29 Sep. 1652.

78. ML v95/26, letter from Thomas Deane to Marten offering his excuse to Mr Baskerville, 25 Oct. 1652.

79. *A List of all the Prisoners in the Upper Bench Prison, remaining in custody the third of May 1653*, 12 May 1653, E213(8).

80. *A&O*, i, pp. 814–17, 7 Jan. 1646.

81. M.E.C. Walcott, *Westminster Memorials of the City* (London, 1849), p. 77; H.B. Wheatley, *London Past and Present* (London, 1891), p. 496; John Stow, *A Survey of the Cities of London and Westminster* (London, 1755), p. 641.

82. Westminster Local Library, Rate Book, Westminster St Margaret's, MF E165, 1651.

83. ML v78/15, 21 Dec. 1651; v78/51, 53, letters from Lucy Wildman to Marten, n.d. Again, punctuation is haphazard, especially full-stops, which were usually omitted in the original and have been inserted to aid the sense.

84. ML v95/7, 16 May 1652.

85. *Declaration by the Lord General and the Council on the Dissolution of the Long Parliament*, 22 Apr. 1653, reprinted in *GCD*, pp. 400–4, p. 401.

86. Whitelocke, *Memorials*, iv, p. 5.

87. Woolrych, *Commonwealth to Protectorate*; Worden, 'The Bill for a new Representative'; *idem*, *Rump Parliament*.

88. Barber, 'Irish undercurrents'.

89. Gardiner, *Commonwealth and Protectorate*, i, pp. 243–4; Underdown, *Pride's Purge*, p. 266.

90. *CJ*, vii, p. 37. Marten was not a member of any of the committees which discussed the elections.

91. Ludlow, *Memoirs*, i, p. 357; Worden, *Rump Parliament*, p. 341.

92. ML v95/31; v78/27; Westminster Local Library H435, 4 May 1653. He was no longer churchwarden by February 1654; Leeds, ML b16/164, 'Acrostic verses made at the parliments disolution by Gen: Cromwell and yᵉ army Aprill 20 1653'. George Thomason also copied down the verse, 'Lenthalls Lamentation', 10 May 1653, E694(11).

93. Summons to be a member of Barebone's Parliament, by Oliver Cromwell, 6 June 1653, *GCD*, p. 405.

94. The authorship is discussed by Worden, *Rump Parliament*, pp. 364–6, Woolrych, *Commonwealth to Protectorate*, pp. 81–2, 86.

95. ML v93/40/1.

96. Ibid., f. 2.

97. J. Richards, 'The Greys of Bradgate in the English Civil War: a study of Henry Grey, first earl of Stamford and his son and heir Thomas, lord Grey of Groby', *Transactions of the Leicestershire Archaeological and History Society* lxii (1988), 32–52, pp. 47–8.

98. Ashley, *John Wildman*, pp. 82–94; Barbara Taft, 'The Humble Petition of several Colonels of the Army', *Huntington Library Bulletin* xlii (1978), 15–41.

99. ML b32/unfol; b32/928, 21 Feb. 1654; b31/1284.

100. ML v78/62, 22 June 1654.

101. ML v89/1.

102. Gardiner, *Commonwealth and Protectorate*, iii, pp. 167–94.

103. *Survey of London*, London County Council, vol. xxv, p. 13. Living under rules was contrasted with confinement in the common jail, common prison or prison house.

104. Gardiner, *Commonwealth and Protectorate*, iv, pp. 257–71.

105. Deane to Marten, 5 Aug. 1656 (answered 12 Aug.), ML 78/97.

106. Punctuation added, spelling and capitalization retained.

107. ML v78/98, 8 Aug. 1656.

108. ML v99/7, Francis Tuckwell to Marten, from Longworth.

109. Woolrych, *Commonwealth to Protectorate*, pp. 139n, 140n; Woolrych prefers 'radical sectarian'.

110. Strype, *Survey of London*, vi, p. 93, cited in N.C. Brett James, *The Growth of Stuart London* (London, 1935), p. 171.

111. Westminster Local Library H438; H440; H441.

112. Ivor Waters (ed.), *Letters from the Tower of London 1660–62* (Chepstow, 1983), p. 4, (*Coll. Henry Marten's Familiar Letters to his Lady of Delight* (1662), published by Edmund Gayton, x, p. 14). Marten sent Mary Ward four bottles of 'Will Parkers Lemon Ale'.

113. *An appeale from the Court to the Country, Made by a Member of Parliament lawfully chosen, but secluded illegally by my L.Protector*, 27 Oct. 1656, E891(3), p. 1.

114. *A Commonwealth or Nothing: or, monarchy and oligarchy prov'd parallel in tyranny*, 14 June 1659, E986(17).

115. *The Dispersed United, or twelve healing questions*, 14 June 1659, E986(17*).

116. John Lisle, the regicide MP for Winchester, is an outside possibility, although he had been a stalwart supporter of the Cromwellian experiment, even the upper House.

117. HM, HN, IL, IW, II, SM, *The Armies Dutie, or faithfull advice to the souldiers*, 2 May 1659, E980(12), epistle to the reader.

118. Ibid., p. 6.

119. Ibid., p. 22; Scott, *Algernon Sidney*, p. 124.

120. Ludlow, *Memoirs*, ii, pp. 102, 224.

121. Revd O. Ogle and W.H. Bliss, *Calendar of the Clarendon state papers preserved in the British Library* (Oxford, 1872), iv, pp. 642, 671, dated towards the middle of April 1660.

122. Ibid., iv, p. 664.

123. Ivor Waters, *Henry Marten and the Long Parliament* (Chepstow, 1973), p. 65 and *idem, Letters from the Tower*.

124. *Familiar Letters*, ii, p. 7 and xxix, p. 26.

125. There are no records of this prisoner in either place. There was no corporation prison in Berwick, so Marten was either held in the castle in the town, or in the newly re-fortified bastion on Lindisfarne.

126. Waters, *Henry Marten*, p. 71.

127. Cited in Sir Joseph Bradney, *A History of Monmouthshire*, pt 1, vol. iv, 'The Hundred of Caldicot', (London, 1929), p. 17.

128. GRO, Kemeys Document M000(282.5), 19 Nov. 1678; Waters, *Henry Marten*, p. 72.

129. Now 'Marten's Tower'.

130. William Coxe, *Archdeacon Coxe's Historical Tour through Monmouthshire* (Brecon, 1904, new edn 1995, Cardiff), p. 304.

131. The popular reference has his servants' names as Catherine and Margaret Vick.

132. Coxe, *Historical Tour*, pp. 304, 311; Arthur Clark, *Chepstow, its Castle and Lordship* (Newport (?), Newport & Monmouthshire Historical Association, 1951).

133. Coxe, *Historical Tour*, p. 311.

134. The land, although jointly owned by a group of four men, was considerable, comprising 440 acres, three dwellings, three barns and three bakehouses.

135. GRO M120 5476 and M120 6119.

136. Coxe, *Historical Tour*, p. 311.

137. Andrew Clark, *The Life and Times of Anthony Wood* (5 vols) (Oxford, 1891–2), ii, pp. 504, 513. Wood was a cousin of Marten's friend, Maximilian Petty.

Chapter III Between Hobbes and Machiavel

1. J.C. Davis, 'Radicalism in a traditional society: the evaluation of radical thought in the English Commonwealth, 1649–1660', *History of Political Thought* III. 2 (1982), 193–213, p. 193.

2. David Wootton (ed.), *Divine Right and Democracy: an Anthology of Political Writing in Stuart England* (Penguin, London, 1986), p. 37.

3. Williams, 'Anatomy', p. 137. The comment on Marten's status was made by Clarendon.

4. Blair Worden, 'Classical republicanism and the Puritan Revolution', in Blair Worden *et al.* (eds), *From History to Imagination: essays presented to H.R. Trevor Roper* (London, 1981); Pocock, *Harrington*, pp. x and xv.

5. Scott, *Algernon Sidney*, p. 94.

6. Richard Tuck, *Philosophy and Government, 1572–1651* (Cambridge, 1993), p. 250.

7. Brian P. Levack, *The Civil Lawyers in England, 1603–1641: a political Study* (Oxford, 1973), p. 121. Levack has Sir Henry as an ally of fellow civilian radicals Dorislaus and Downing, who justified rebellion, a leading civil lawyer who was prepared to be heterodox.

8. Parliament, discovering the attempt by Charles to complete a design begun by James to curtail the

people's liberties, framed the Petition of Right, 'and the people of this Nation taught to claime their liberty, no longer from Magna Carta, but from the Peticon of Right': ML v93/40.

9. Ibid., ii, p.251. Marten was also prepared to defend military commissions issued under martial law during peacetime, on the grounds that it was necessity rather than law, an argument that brought him into sharp conflict with John Selden; ibid., pp.568–9, 572–3.

10. J.G.A. Pocock, *The Ancient Constitution and the Feudal Law: a Study of English historical thought in the seventeenth century* (Cambridge, 1957), p. 46.

11. Ibid., p. viii, n. 3; Christopher Hill, 'The Norman Yoke', in his *Puritanism and Revolution* (London, 1958, reprint 1969), pp. 58–125.

12. [John Lilburne], *Regall Tyrannie discovered: or, a discourse shewing that all lawfull (approbational) instituted power by God amongst men, is by common agreement*, [6 Jan.] 1647, E370(12); Brailsford, *Levellers*, p. 54 and *passim*. Brailsford accepted the Lilburne attribution, adding that he believes other hands added the more orderly passages, and noted that Wolfe and Pease did not question the attribution either. Brailsford also saw signs of co-operation between Lilburne and Marten, p. 140, n.29.

13. The exceptions being Tuck, *Philosophy and Government*, p. 259; and Robert Ashton, *Counter-revolution: the Second Civil War and its Origins, 1646–8* (Yale, 1994), pp. 311–12.

14. All three manuscript contributions are clearly in his hand, and the anonymous contributions, frequently claimed as Marten's on stylistic grounds, are now proved to be his by the inclusion in his papers of a draft entitled *A Reply to ye aunswer without a name pretending animadversions upon Mr CHALLONER'S speech published by – groom to ye same Mr Challoner*, BL Add. MSS 71534, ff. 89–90, which is a draft of an anonymous printed version, *An Answer to the Speech without Doores: or Animadversions*, [16 Nov.] 1646, E362(9). Similar phrases are repeated in *A Corrector of the Answerer to the Speech out of Doores*, [26 Oct.] 1646, E364(9).

15. Marten, *Corrector*, p. 13.

16. Ibid., p. 5.

17. Ibid., p. 8. This is the same self-nullifying argumentative process that was employed by his father in 1628.

18. BL Add. MSS 71314, f. 90; Marten, *Corrector*, p. 4.

19. Henry Marten, *The Independency of England Endeavored to be maintained*, [11 Jan.] 1648, E422(16), and *The Parliaments Proceedings Justified*, [7 Feb.] 1648, E426(2).

20. Marten, *Independency of England*, p. 11.

21. For a discussion of the Medieval concept of equity, see Robert Eccleshall, *Order and Reason in Politics* (Hull/Oxford, 1978), p. 56 and *passim*.

22. Marten, *Independency of England*, p. 5. A barque or bark was a three masted ship.

23. Marten, *Parliaments Proceedings*, p.10.

24. Ibid., p. 24. See also Marten, *Parliaments Proceedings*, p. 4 for a similar point about the Scottish Commissioners. John Lilburne, in his account of the drawing up of the second *Agreement of the People*, used the radical language of equitable balance to describe the Levellers' mistrust of the grandees. Better to leave the tyrants in place to balance one another out until the *Agreement* had secured an 'equal distribution' that would make all tyrants redundant. As Marten would even have tolerated the King until he had secured liberty for the English nation from the Scots, so Lilburne would tolerate individual tyrants until they could be expunged from the system by employing equity.

25. BL Add. MSS 71532, f. 15v, 'An answere to ye Author of ye Captious Questions', c. 1649.

26. Ibid., pp. 14–15.

27. Johann Sommerville, *Politics and Ideology in England, 1603–1640* (London, 1986), pp. 60–1.

28. BL Add. MSS 17534, f. 10. See also BL Add. MSS 71534, f. 11v, addressed to William Prynne (1649):

> Tell mee not what King Iua [John?] did
> Nor of Matilders waring
> Since some things from your self are had
> And some not worth your knowing
> I say not I am ye first slave
> But say I would be none
> Nor do I think you ye first lawyer
> Yet sure you should be one.

29. Hugo Grotius, *The Law of War and Peace: de Jure Belli ac Pacis Libri Tres*, trans. F.W. Kelsey (Bobbs Merrill Co, 1925); Scott, *Algernon Sidney*, p. 110.

30. Richard Tuck, *Natural Rights Theories: their origin and development* (Cambridge, 1979), pp. 63–5. Grotius' notion that individuals within the state were like atoms, but that the state possessed no rights of its own that were not formerly held by individuals, could provide a link both between Marten's political theory and his Epicurean notions of human nature.

31. Marten, *A Word to Mr Wil. Prynn Esq*, [6 Jan.] 1649, E537(16), pp. 14–15.

32. Marten claimed that he had always known the person/office distinction and the evil counsellors' theory to be bogus, see *A Word to Mr Wil. Prynn Esq*. This may help to explain the high proportion of the group of which Marten was part, albeit numerically small, elected as early as 1640.

33. Marten, *Independency of England*, p. 15.

34. BL Add. MSS 71534, f. 10.

35. BL Add. MSS 71532, f. 6.

36. Marten, *Independency of England*, p. 18. The phrase 'Nownsubstantive' was used to describe the honest party of the soldiery by John Lilburne, as part of the subtitle for *Englands Freedome, Souldiers Rights*, 14 Dec. 1647, E419(23), but unfortunately, he does not detail what he meant by his usage of 'noun substantive'.

37. Rainsborough at Putney (A.S.P. Woodhouse, *Puritanism and Liberty* (London, 3rd edn, 1986, pp. 56 and 67). Marten agreed to the notion, also aired by the radicals at Putney, that individual lords could be accepted as members of the Commons provided they stood for election in the proper manner. See also John Wildman at Putney (Woodhouse, p. 199). The Biblical phrase 'hewers of wood and drawers of water' (Deut. 29:11) indicated the inclusivity of Yahweh's covenant with Moses. It was a regular phrase to describe the common people within the commonweal, used at Putney.

38. Worden, *Rump Parliament*, p. 37, quoting *Lex Talionis* (1647), my emphasis; Underdown, '"Honest" radicals', pp. 186–205.

39. BL Add. MSS 71532, f. 23, in which the substitution of O for Marten and A for Wildman was used and which became their private form of correspondence for the future; W was Rainsborough. Richard A. Gleissner, 'The Levellers and natural law: the Putney debates of 1647', *Journal of British Studies* 19–20 (1979–80), 74–89, p. 77. This theory articulated '(1) that all men share an essential structure that determines certain fundamental human inclinations or tendencies; (2) that the good for all men is the realization or fulfilment of these inclinations; (3) that norms or moral laws are derived from man's nature and his efforts to achieve authentic fulfilment'.

40. Walwyn was B in the code.

41. *The Case of the Armie* is generally thought to have been composed by committee, though it has widely been regarded as having been drafted or organised by John Wildman. John Morrill suggests Edward Sexby as the author.

42. Woodhouse, *Puritanism and Liberty*, p. 2.

43. Marten, *Independency of England*, p. 15; Woodhouse, *Puritanism and Liberty*, p. 10. This point was taken up with vigour by Rainsborough.

44. Woodhouse, *Puritanism and Liberty*, p. 24. Marten was to make the same point to William Prynne: BL Add. MSS 71534, f. 11.

45. Gleissner, 'The Levellers', p. 85.

46. Wootton, *Divine Right and Democracy*, pp. 283–5.

47. Marten, *Independency of England*, p. 18.

48. BL Add. MSS 71532, ff. 5–6, a draft of a reply to John Selden, originally written in 1642, to which he returned in 1647 as a reply to 'The privileges of ye Baronage of England when they sitt in Parliament'.

49. George Wither, *Vox Pacifica*, cited by John Lilburne, *Englands Miserie and Remedie*, 14 Sep. 1645, and reproduced in Wootton, *Divine Right and Democracy*, p. 282.

50. BL Add. MSS 71534, f. 84, 16 Feb. 1646(7).

51. BL Add. MSS 71532, f .6.

52. Marten, *Independency of England*, p. 8, although the army must always be subordinate to God.

53. Lilburne, *Regall Tyrannie Discovered*, pp. 86–7.

54. BL Add. MSS 71534, ff. 10–11, 'A plea for the people in answer to their late adversary Mr Prynne'. In doing so, Marten was defending Richard Overton by name. He was to defend the Levellers in general; BL Add. MSS 71534, f. 19.

55. BL Add. MSS 71514, f. 19, fragment, untitled, n.d., but predating the execution of Charles I.

56. BL Add. MSS 71534, f. 11.

57. BL Add. MSS 71534, ff, 15–15v., n.d., probably 1647/8.

58. *CJ*, vi, p. 111.

59. *Mercurius Politicus*, no. 98, 15–22 Apr. 1652.

60. William Rainsborough at Putney, Woodhouse, *Puritanism and Liberty*, p. 52.

61. Woodhouse, *Puritanism and Liberty*, p. 53: 'I think that the poorest he that is in England hath a life to live, as the greatest he' is not the same point as 'I would fain know what the soldier hath fought for all this while'.

62. Justified in *Mercurius Politicus*, no. 36, 6–13 Feb. 1651.

63. This tension is that which reflects the distinction between a social and political contract: by the first, all people bound themselves to put themselves under the government; by the second, some got to choose who would constitute accountable magistracy.

64. See Barber, 'The Engagement'.

65. For Marten's belief that the Solemn League and Covenant was a 'cheat' and a 'snare', see *A Word to Mr. Wil. Prynn Esq*, p. 4.

66. John Lilburne, *The Engagement vindicated and explained*, [23 Jan.] 1650, E590(4); Barber, 'The Engagement', pp. 49–50.

67. BL Add. MSS 71534, ff. 20–21v, beginning 'Wee ye P. of ye C. of E', the usual and significant form of address chosen by the new rulers ('the parliament of the Commonwealth of England').

68. ML v93/40, f. 4.

69. Scott, *Algernon Sidney*, p. 110; Pocock, *Harrington*, p. x. There is no extant evidence that Marten ever used the phrase 'free state'.

70. Scott, *Algernon Sidney*, p. 110.

71. John Hall, *The Grounds and Reasons of Monarchy* (1651); *Mercurius Politicus*, no. 100, pp. 1569–70; For Nedham and Hall's contributions to political theory, see Scott, *Algernon Sidney*, pp. 110–12.

72. In many ways this was a parallel of the weakening of the republic advanced by the loyalist *de factoists*, entering government for the first time with the justification that despite a government's illegal usurpation of power, it was God's will that it be obeyed in the future, provided that it act legally. Such new thinkers were admitted to government's circles, with the aim of spreading the basis

of popular appeal for a government that had little. Instead, they introduced rival notions about the nature of republican government which were among the reasons that the government was brought down. For the long tradition of studies of *de factoism*, see James M. Wallace, *Destiny his Choice* (Cambridge, 1968); Quentin Skinner, 'Conquest and consent' in G.E. Aylmer, *The Interregnum* (London, 1974); Glenn Burgess, 'Usurpation, obligation and obedience in the thought of the Engagement controversy', *HJ* 29.3 (1986), 515–36; and Barber, 'The Engagement'.

73. Jonathan Scott, 'The rapture of motion: James Harrington's republicanism', in Nicholas Philipson and Quentin Skinner (eds.), *Political Discourse in early-modern Europe* (Cambridge, 1993); Marchamont Nedham, *The Case of the Commonwealth of England, stated*, p. 9; *Mercurius Politicus*, no. 98, 15–22 Apr. 1652. A theory of historical precedent is thus reintroduced to demonstrate that England was first a 'free-state' until the Normans 'yoked' it, replacing seven kingdoms with one.

74. Z.S. Fink, *The Classical Republicans: an essay in the Recovery of a Pattern of Thought in seventeenth-century England* (Northwestern UP, 1962 edn); Felix Raab, *The English Face of Machiavelli: a changing Interpretation, 1500–1700* (London, 1964); J.G.A. Pocock, *The Machiavellian Moment* (1975); Worden, 'Classical republicanism'; J.C. Davis, 'Pocock's perception of, Harrington: grace, nature and art in the classical republicanism of James Harrington', *HJ* 24.3 (1981), 683–97; Scott, *Algernon Sidney*.

75. Cicero's commitment to a republican government did not mitigate his interest in rescuing it from collapse by the interposition of a virtuous and heroic individual, a *rector*, for which post he probably had Pompey in mind.

76. Scott, *Algernon Sidney*, p. 14.

77. Cromwell's declaration on the reasons why the army dissolved the Rump Parliament, 22 Apr. 1653, in *GCD*, pp. 400–4.

78. Charles Blitzer, *An Immortal Commonwealth: the Political Thought of James Harrington* (New Haven, 1960), pp. 203–4.

79. Grey of Groby was subsequently to carry his religiously grounded form of republicanism as far as Fifth Monarchist activity against Cromwell, for which he lost his position in the army and was imprisoned.

80. David Norbrook, 'Lucan, Thomas May, and the emergence of a republican literary culture', in Kevin Sharpe and Peter Lake (eds.), *Culture and Politics in early Stuart England* (London, 1994), pp. 45–66; Susan Wiseman, '"Adam, the father of all flesh", porno-political rhetoric and political theory in and after the English civil war', *Prose Studies* 14.3 (1991), 134–57.

81. W.C. Abbott, *The Writings and Speeches of Oliver Cromwell* (4 vols) (Harvard, 1927–47), iii, p. 5; Worden, 'Bill for a new Representative'; Woolrych, *Commonwealth to Protectorate*.

82. 'The character of Sir Henry Vane by Algernon Sidney', Herts RO, D/EP F 45, cited in V.A. Rowe, *Sir Henry Vane the Younger* (London, 1970), Appendix F, p. 279.

83. Scott, *Algernon Sidney*, p. 105; and 'The rapture of motion'.

84. She died, aged 44, on 19 June 1618. Her 'mournful son', Henry, wrote:

> Stay passenger, and if thou art not stone,
> Weepe with Urania, whose nimph is gone:
> A nimph whom thou would sweare had been ye same
> Divine Urania, but for her name;
> And yet her name her nature well exprest.
> That in Gods temple built her careful nest.
> Thither to fly, that she ye easyer may
> Her yong ons teach, herselfe (loe.) leades ye waye.

Urania referred either to the muse of astrology or to an epithet of Aphrodite, the foam-born, Greek goddess of love, a love of a purer, higher, heavenly form.

85. The style of Marten's writing in this regard is examined in detail in chapter 7.

86. E.A. Havelock, *The Lyric Genius of Catullus* (London, 2nd edn, 1967), p. 20; Kenneth Quinn (ed.), *Catullus: The Poems* (London, 1970), p. 2. poem no. 3, pp. 96–100.

87. BL Add. MSS 71532, f. 16. I am grateful to David Shotter for help in pinning down this manuscript and the translation is his.

88. ML v93/39-40; HMC Report 13, Appendix iv, pp. 390–1.

89. BL Add. MSS 71532, f. 18.

90. Ibid., f. 39.

91. ML v93/40, f. 1.

92. ML b64/137.

93. ML v93/40, f. 4.

94. Both of Marten's examples eschew Rome. Lycurgus (*c.* 390BC) was reputed to have been the founder of the Spartan constitution, of whom Xenophon wrote that he had made Sparta 'the only city where being a gentleman was part of a national policy'. Solon (*c.* 600BC) was the statesman of Athens responsible for devising a system that freed the serfs, gave the people a measure of responsibility, and abolished the Draconian laws. The fact that he worked actively to relieve the people of the oppressions of debt may have weighed heavily with Marten at the end of 1653. Solon had also believed that all people should be equally committed to the constitution and wrestled with the problem that large numbers of the political elite had had to be excluded from power in order to protect the state; T.A. Sinclair, *A History of Greek Political Thought* (London, 1951).

95. ML v93/40, f. 4.

96. BL Add. MSS 71532, f. 15v.

97. [Edward Sexby], *Killing noe Murder*, printed in Wootton, *Divine Right and Democracy*, pp.360–88, p. 360.

98. *Tyrannus sine titulo and tyrannus exercitio*, ibid., p. 364.

99. Ibid., pp. 365, 375.

100. Ibid., p. 366.

101. Ashley, *John Wildman*, pp. 107–16.

102. Scott, *Algernon Sidney*, p. 28. White dedicated his piece to Kenelm Digby, a friend of Marten's and fellow enthusiast for Epicurean corporealism. This may have been evinced in passages of Sexby, *Killing no Murder*, p. 367. Richard Tuck provides interesting references in *Philosophy and Government* to the critique of White made by Thomas Hobbes in the early 1640s; see William Ball, *State-maxims or certain dangerous positions destructive to the very nature very natural Right and Liberty of mankind*, [5 Aug.] 1656, E886(6), by G. Dawson for T. Brewster; Beverley C. Southgate, *'Covetous of Truth': the Life and Work of Thomas White, 1593–1676* (Dordrecht, 1993), pp. 54–5.

103. BL Add. MSS 71532, ff. 9–10v. This reference to an atomistic theory of the state may have been one indication of Marten's acceptance of a materialist, atomistic and ultimately atheistic notion of existence.

104. Pocock, *Harrington*, p. 23, 'The Preliminaries, showing Principles of Government'.

105. BL Add. MSS 71532, f. 24.

106. BL Add. MSS 71532, f. 15v.

107. BL Add. MSS 71532, ff. 24–24v, 'H.M. his vindication', 1653.

Chapter IV Opinions on God

1. Nigel Smith, 'The charge of atheism and the language of radical speculation, 1640–1660' in Michael Hunter and David Wootton (eds), *Atheism from the Reformation to the Enlightenment* (Oxford, 1992), pp. 131–58; David Berman, *A History of Atheism in Britain: from Hobbes to Russell* (Beckenham, 1988).

2. *A&O*, ii, pp. 409–12.

3. ML 78/10.

4. Barbara J. Shapiro, *Probability and Certainty in Seventeenth-Century England: A Study of the Relationships between Natural Science, Religion, History, Law, and Literature* (Princeton, 1983), pp. 27–9 and *passim*.

5. Ibid., pp. 80–1.

6. But, as evidence of a degree of scepticism, one which a priori made religion no worse than any other form of knowledge.

7. Antony Flew, *A Dictionary of Philosophy* (London, 1979).

8. This dates the tract precisely to February 1649, between the execution of Charles Stuart and the death of Pile.

9. Woodhouse, *Puritanism and Liberty*, p. [80]; Gentles, *New Model Army*, p. 286ff. In these two works, the limited nature of toleration that was the product of the fragmentation of Protestantism is more correctly labelled 'liberty of conscience' or 'spiritual equality'.

10. Aubrey, *Brief Lives*, p. 266.

11. Ibid., pp.158, 269.

12. *Clarke Papers*, ii, p. 120.

13. Ibid., pp. 120–1. Wildman denied the magistrate the power to legislate in religious matters using the Martenesque notion of constitutional balance. A godly magistrate, given this power, would, at best, only be restraining what is evil. Given that the magistrate is only as fallible as those for whom he legislated, it was more likely that the power inherent in his office would result in his doing more harm than good. See also the gloss provided by Woodhouse, *Puritanism and Liberty*, p. [54].

14. Cited in J.C.A. Gaskin (ed.), *Varieties of Unbelief: from Epicurus to Satre* (New York and London, 1989), p. 51.

15. Aubrey, *Brief Lives*, pp. 235–6.

16. Gaskin, *Varieties of Unbelief*, p. 2.

17. Shapiro, *Probability and Certainty*, p. 93.

18. John Lilburne, *Rash oaths unwarrantable: And the breaking of them inexcusable*, May 1647, 25 June 1647, E393(39); a similar argument was made by Lilburne in *The Freemans freedom vindicated* 1646; Henry Marten, 'Rash censures uncharitable', ML v78/1–2 and the other at BL Add. MSS 71532, ff. 14 and 14v.

19. Lilburne, *Rash oaths unwarrantable*, pp. 14–15.

20. Matthew 5:17; 'think not that I am come to destroy the law, or the prophets: I am not come to destroy, but to fulfil'.

21. *CSPD* 1640–1, p. 479; BL Stowe Ms 743, f. 116, 22 Jan. 1635/6.

22. S.R. Gardiner (ed.), *Reports of Cases in the Courts of Star Chamber and High Commission* (London, Camden Society, vol. xxxix, 1886), pp. 181–5 and *passim*.

23. *CSPD* 1641–3, p. 531; *GCD*, pp. 103–5.

24. *CSPD* 1641, pp. 131–2, Sir John Lambe to Laud, 4 October 1641, which begins 'I hear Sir Henry Martin is dead'.

25. *CJ*, ii, pp. 91, 99, 105, 125, 129, 151.

26. Williams, 'Career', pp.103–4, 129; Gardiner, *History*, i p. 202; Whitelocke, *Memorials*, i, p. 208. Whitelocke was writing on 12 August, the day after Saltmarsh published *Examinations, or, a Discovery of some dangerous positions delivered in a sermon of Reformation preached by Thomas Fuller*. For Fuller's sermon, see Thomason Collection E36(8). For Saltmarsh's reply, E65(5). *Peace but no Pacification* was dated 23 Oct. E71(31). For Saltmarsh's religious views, see, among others, Nigel Smith, *Perfection Proclaimed: Language and Literature in English Radical Religion, 1640–1660* (Oxford, 1989), *passim*.

27. Barber, 'Ireland and Scotland under the Commonwealth', in Barber and Ellis (eds.) *Conquest and Union*, pp. 195–221; *idem*, 'Attitudes towards the Scots in the northern counties'.

28. Marten, *Corrector*, p. 12; probably in reply to *An Answer to the Speech without Doores: or Animadversions*, [16 Nov.] 1646. Contrast this with the language of Robert Blair's *A Letter from the General Assembly of the Kingdome of Scotland*, 18 June 1646 (London, 1646).

29. Marten, *Independency of England*, pp. 4, 7, 12.

30. ML v78/1–2v. The quote is given in full in chapter 1, p. 14.

31. ML v78/1–2v, 'Rash censures uncharitable', 1647.

32. The reference to God as a possible ghost is also pertinent here.

33. Brailsford, *Levellers*, pp. 252–3.

34. BRO D/A2 Berks. d.6., presentments to livings. Babb was a graduate of St Alban's Hall, Oxford, 7 Feb.1624; Andrew Clark, (ed.), *Register of the University of Oxford*, II (1571–1622), part iii (degrees), (Oxford, 1888), p. 428.

35. A.G. Matthews (ed.), *Calamy Revised* (Oxford, 1934), p. 557 Appendix I; during 1654 Robert Babb's wife, Mary, died aged only twenty-nine, and was buried in the church, a memorial being laid to the right of the communion table in the church of St John the Baptist, Inglesham.

36. Way was, however, very young, intruded in 1648, graduating from Christ Church, Oxford, in 1651; MA Oriel 1653.

37. BRO Ms Archd.pprs. d.7, f. 143.

38. BRO D/A2 c.185, f. 123 and another copy, f. 124, both dated 8 Oct. 1634. There is local folklore that holds that Harrowdown Hill was the base for a witches' sabbat. There is no evidence to confirm this, though there may have been some 'devilish' mischief in mocking church land.

39. A.C. Matthews, *Walker Revised* (Oxford, 1948), p. 69.

40. ML v93/55, n.d. The famous verse is:

> I do not like thee Dr Fell,
> The reason why I cannot tell,
> But this I know, and know full well,
> I do not like thee Dr Fell.

John Fell was also Dean of Christ Church and Bishop of Oxford.

41. BRO D/A2 Berks. d.7, f. 145, 31 Aug. 1662. Another minister allowed to remain in the vicarage after he had been sequestered was Joseph Wright, vicar of Buckland, who had been the minister for twenty years before being sequestered around November 1648; Matthews, *Walker Revised*, p. 72. Ingram may have fulfilled the role of minister during the 1650s, even if he was not officially sanctioned, since a Mr Ingram, a minister, was cited in a paternity suit against Marten in 1651; see chapter 7.

42. The Longworth congregation is the subject of a partial and romanticised account by John Stanley, *The Church in the Hop Garden* (London, *c.* 1920).

43. Ibid., pp. 66–70.

44. There may have been several people by the name of John Moulden in the area.

45. W.H. Summers, *History of the Congregational Churches in the Berkshire, South Oxfordshire and South Buckinghamshire Association* (Newbury, 1905).

46. Ernest A. Payne, *The Baptists of Berkshire* (London, 1951), pp. 24–5.

47. Ann Laurence, *Parliamentary Army Chaplains 1642–1651* (London, 1990) p. 162.

48. Payne, *The Baptists*, p. 35; B.R. White, 'John Pendarves, the Calvinistic Baptists and the Fifth Monarchy', *Baptist Quarterly* 25 (1973–4); Arthur E. Preston, *The Church of St Nicholas, Abingdon* (Oxford, 1895), pp. 116–18.

49. John Pendarves, *The fear of God: what it is and exhorted to*, a sermon preached to the Church of Christ meeting in Petty France, 10 June 1656 (London, 1657), 3 Apr. 1657, E907(3). Pendarves was also a lecturer at Wantage, where he was opposed by the more orthodox William Ley, who accused him of reviving the Donatist heresy; William Ley, *A Buckler for the Church of England against certaine queries propounded by Mr Pendarvis ... called Arrowes against Babylon* (Oxford, 1656), 12 June 1656, E882(1).

50. Stanley, *Church in the Hop Garden*, p. 69.

51. William Hughes, *Magistracy God's ministry or a Rule for the rulers and people's due correspondence*, a sermon at the Midsummer assizes in Abingdon (London, 1651) printed by George Calvert, June 1651, E664(7), dedication to the reader.

52. Ibid., pp. 4, 11–12.

53. Ibid., p. 2.

54. Ibid., p. 5.

55. Ibid., pp. 7, 9–10.

56. Ibid., p. 15.

57. William Hughes, *Munster and Abingdon* (Oxford, by Henry Hall for Robert Blagrave, 1657), Wing STC H3344; Payne, *The Baptists*, pp. 29–30.

58. David Underdown, *Royalist Conspiracy in England 1649–60* (New Haven, 1960), pp. 266–7.

59. Matthews, *Calamy Revised*, p. 282.

60. For example, periods of political republicanism could be echoed by religious radicalism. Anthony Wood noted 'a great meeting of the Anabaptists att Abendon, in order to make a disturbance in the nation', on 2 June 1659; Clark, *Anthony Wood*, i, p. 279.

61. BRO D/A2/c.160, f. 345, dated 24 Mar. 1662. The tax was levied at 13*s.* 4*d.* per yardland: ML 49/unfol.

62. For example, the career of Miles Hill in Leominster, chapter 5.

63. Ashley, *John Wildman*, pp. 100–1; Bodleian Library, Oxford, Rawlinson MSS 57, pp. 403, 409.

64. BRO D/A2/c.186, ff. 13–14, 21 Sep. 1634; BRO D/A2/c.185, ff. 123–4, 8 Oct. 1634.

65. ML v93/13, 30 July 1652. Chidley had also been campaigning for soldiers' arrears.

66. ML v93/3, Nixon claimed to be a kinsman of Marten's, 9 Apr. 1651.

67. ML v94/11, letter from John Stuvesse (?) to Marten dated 17 July 1652.

68. ML v94/13, 8 Sep. 1652.

69. ML 67/93, from Tom (? signature missing) to John Goldsmith, 29 Oct. 1650.

70. Payne, *The Baptists*, p. 31.

71. ML v78/6-8, a draft of *Justice Would-bee, that made himself a Ranter Last week in opposition to those hee calls QUAKERS*, n.d.

72. Other suggestions of a pamphlet to which Marten might have replied are given by Williams, 'Career', Appendix C, no. 4.

73. Examples both for and against the idea that the Quakers constituted a new wave of catholicism were Daniel Lupton, *The Quaking Moutebancke, or the Jesuite turn'd Quaker*, 24 May 1655, E840(4);

Henry Denne, *The Quaker no Papist, in an answer to the Quaker Disarmed* an attack on the Quakers by Thomas Smith, 16 Oct. 1659, E1000(13); William Brownsword, *The Quaker-Jesuite, or Popery in Quakerisme*, 5 Jan. 1660, E1013(4).

74. *Justice Would-bee*, f. 7.

75. Words inverted.

76. *A Dialogue of Polygamy, written Originally in Italian* (London, 1657), and dedicated to Francis Osborne.

77. ML v93/19–20, a fragment, badly water damaged; see listing in HMC Report 13, p.394.

78. Tuck, *Philosophy and Government*, p. 9.

79. ML v93/20.

80. ML b53/1–20.

81. ML v94/3. Burton died in 1631.

82. ML b65/189, 4 July 1618.

83. See chapter 5; ML v85/10; ML v85/9.

84. ML b55/unfol, 3 Nov. 1632.

85. ML b67/35, 20 Apr. 1635; ML b67/27, 7 Nov. 1635

86. ML b67/33, 1633.

87. Marten did not set up the school at Longworth, which was already in operation in 1622, when Andrew Weston was paid for work done to the building: ML 85/9. His father may have done.

88. ML v88/14, 3 May 1654.

89. Nevertheless, Henry's son, William, went to Merton College, Oxford. This Henry may have subsequently been the rector of Ipstone and Cuxham, Oxfordshire: Joseph Foster, *Alumni Oxonienses 1500–1714* (London and Oxford, 1892), p. 981.

90. *A&O*, ii, p. 257, 26 Sep. 1649. The Commons declared itself to be 'zealous to continue and establish all Works and Foundations tending to the advancement of learning'.

91. ML v89/7, to Marten in the Rules, Southwark, 27 Apr. 1657; ML v89/19.

92. ML v88/27, 22 Dec. 1656.

93. ML b67/53, n.d.

94. ML b67/42, 'Reasons for and on behalfe of the Poore Pet^{rs} why the ordenance of the 3rd of June should be confirmed and putt in Execution and why the other pet^{rs} menc̄oed in the Petic̄on should not have the 27400^l or any part thereof'; Gentles, 'London Levellers', p. 305, which shows that in their editions of *Flying Eagle*, Samuel and Katherine Chidley were interested in this issue and that of tithes.

95. ML b8/116.

96. William Kneale and Martha Kneale, *The Development of Logic* (Oxford, 1962), p. 300ff.; Pierre Gassendi, *Pierre Gassendi's Institutio Logica, 1658* trans. and ed. Howard Jones (Assen, 1981); Lynn Sumida Joy, *Gassendi the Atomist* (Cambridge, 1987).

97. ML 78/1–2v, f. 1.

98. For a full transcription of the document in the Brotherton Collection, see Williams, 'Career', Appendix C, no. 2.

99. ML v78/8.

100. C.R. Morris, *Idealistic Logic: A Study of its Aim, Method and Achievements* (London, 1933), pp. 34–9.

101. ML b8/116, a list of books (possibly incomplete) in the library of Sir Henry Marten, in his hand.

102. The author of *De Rebus Naturalibus*, published in 1590.

103. Sheffield University, Hartlib Manuscripts, 6/4/79A-80B, a letter from John Dury to Sir Henry Marten, written from Hamburg, 4 Sep. 1640.

104. Aubrey, *Brief Lives*, p. 265.

105. Brailsford, *Levellers*, p. 676.
106. Berman, *A History of Atheism*, chapters 1 and 2; J.J. Macintosh, 'Robert Boyle on Epicurean atheism and atomism', in Margaret J. Osler (ed.), *Atoms, Pneuma, and Tranquillity: Epicurean and Stoic Themes in European Thought* (Cambridge, 1991), pp. 197–219.
107. J.M. Rist, *Epicurus: an introduction* (Cambridge, 1972), pp.132, 138, 'Epicurus has no interest in statues which may be erected in his honour but wishes his friends to remember him . . . Statues, like crowns, are the marks of vain popularity and its concomitant dangers. Friends, and private life where friendship is possible, provide security'.
108. Pierre Gassendi, *Syntagma philosophicum*, 'Of happiness', reproduced in J.B. Schneewind (ed.), *Moral Philosophy from Montaigne to Kant: an anthology* (2 vols.) (Cambridge, 1990), ii, pp. 355–68.
109. Jones (trans. and ed.), *Institutio Logica*, p. xi.
110. Tuck, *Philosophy and Government*, p. 250. Tuck refers here to the son, not the father, who has inadvertently been knighted.
111. ML v93/63, n.d.
112. John Hedley Brooke, *Science and Religion: some historical perspectives* (Cambridge, 1991), pp. 122, 170. Marten never came to the point at which he admitted, in a way that would have serious implications for religion, that all that existed was matter, but that all that could be perceived or known was matter.

Chapter V The Lord of the Manor

1. Jasmine S. Howse, *Longworth through the Centuries* (2 parts) (privately published, 1982), pt 2 traces Sir Henry's lineage as the son of Anthony of London and the grandson of William Martyn of Wokingham and Margaret Yate of Charney.
2. ML b17/unfol, confirmed at b51/unfol.
3. ML b14/unfol.
4. ML b12/unfol and b35/1108.
5. ML b66/51, a petition by Fisher to the Lord Chief Baron.
6. ML b39/22, 15 June 1624.
7. ML 3rd ser./vol. 12, n.d. (*c.* 1618).
8. 4 nobles was worth £1 6*s.* 8*d.*, the whole being valued at £15 10*s.*
9. The total mead land was worth £106 0*s.* 6*d.*
10. A practice carried out by Marten father and son, which needed the co-operation of neighbours, whose land might be affected. Former High Constable John Southby, rehabilitated at the Protectorate, complained to Marten about the new wears that he and his father had cut in the Thames at Barcot, which denied him 'afterfeeding' on his land: Oxon RO Misc.we. I/i/1, 23 Jan. 1654/5.
11. In 1622 Sir Henry Marten employed Richard Stone to be fisherman in Hinton at an annual rent of £14: BRO D/ELS E8.
12. Punctuation has been added to most of the contemporary material to render it intelligible, but the dialect, spelling and idiosyncracies of speech have been retained.
13. ML b35/1103, 10 July 1619.
14. ML b28/529.
15. ML b48/unfol, 14 Nov. 1626 and b56/unfol, 8 May 1629.
16. ML b58/unfol.
17. ML b9/unfol, 12 May 4CI; b58/unfol, 12 May 4CI; b62/unfol, 11 May 4CI.
18. Finally confirmed in Sir Henry's hands on 1 Aug. 1634: licence of alienation: ML b31/1204.

19. ML b61/unfol; ML b38/892.

20. In 1631 George granted tenements in Longworth to citizens of London: ML b62/unfol.

21. Courts baron dealt with issues arising from the landholding of free tenantry, as opposed to the customary court, for matters relating to copyholders, and the court leet, for more serious criminal matters.

22. ML b44/unfol; *Historians' Guide to Ordnance Survey Maps* (HMSO, 1964); K.J. Allison *et al*, *The Deserted Villages of Oxfordshire* (Leicester University Occasional Papers 17, 1965); R. Muir, *The Lost Villages of Britain* (London, 1982). Inglesham had been decimated by plague in the fourteenth century.

23. ML v85/17. Inglesham was aided by its proximity to Lechlade and the demand for stone that could be transported down the Thames from Radcot bridge. Nevertheless, the sums to be raised by the hundreds of Faringdon and Shrivenham towards the supply of the Cromwellian army and navy, indicate that the land of Inglesham was of relatively low value: BRO D/EWa 02, 1 Jan. 1655/6; D/EX 1053/1/1–2, 26 June 1658.

24. ML b66/17–18v.

25. *CSPD* 1641–3, p. 126.

26. ML v85/19. If the collector of the tax, William Dyer, was related to the other Dyers on the Hinton/Longworth estate there was further evidence of an uneasy relationship between personal obligation and political loyalty. Henry Dyer was in charge of the workmen who refurbished Marten's estate, but Thomas Dyer was unable to pay the rent on his cottage: ML v87/17, 30 Jan 1641(2).

27. John Cox may have been the one who had Pendarves' sermons printed, see chapter 4.

28. ML box of loose MSS/unfol, incumbrances on Eaton.

29. ML v88/6.

30. ML b68/unfol.

31. ML v89/29.

32. By 1650 these debts amounted to over £140: ML v85/32.

33. Ian Roy (ed.), *The Royalist Ordnance Papers, 1642–1646* pt I, (Oxfordshire Record Society, 1963–4), pp. 41, 222.

34. ML b4/137.

35. Such as encumbrances owed to Anne Richmond in Ashbury, Berks.: 'There hath been disbursed in repairing of ye houses which were almost destroyed by Gunpowder blowne up in the howse by ye souldiers in ye Warre above [£]060-00-00': ML v88/10; the frustrating to-ing and fro-ing of first parliamentary and then royalist troops is evident from ML v92/35–38v, Thomas Clarke's accounts from December 1642 to Lady Day 1646.

36. R. Whitlock, *Agricultural Records AD220-1977* (London 1978), p. 50.

37. Robert Loder (b.1587, d.1640) was contemporaneous with Sir Henry Marten: G.E. Fussell (ed.), *Robert Loder's Farm Accounts 1610–1620* (London, Camden Society, 3rd ser., vol. 53, 1937).

38. Ibid., pp. xii, xviii.

39. Ibid., p. x; Loder's uniqueness is championed by Chris Durston, 'Berkshire and its county gentry 1625-1649', Ph.D., Reading, 1977, pp.13–14.

40. ML v75/991.

41. ML v90/2. Francis Reade was by no means the most diligent in this regard, but this is an example of the pains that agents took to send multiple copies of letters to minimise the risk of them being lost in carriage. Reade replaced Thomas Tuckwell as bailiff, ML v85/30: A. Kussmaul, *Servants in Husbandry in Early-modern England* (Cambridge, 1981).

42. In 1652 John, Lord Lovelace petitioned the Commons that £400 of his fine of £7,372 be abated and that he be given more time to pay: *CJ*, vii, p. 123, 16 Apr. 1652.

43. ML v90/1, 5 May 1650. Ashdown Park was the grand residence that the Earl of Craven had dedicated to the Winter Queen, and a victim of royalist composition.

44. ML v85/28, 5 Feb. 1650/1.

45. Or £657, if the figures in the left-hand margin are used.

46. ML b66/134 and b66/135.

47. ML b28/553 and b28/554.

48. ML v85/30, 16 Sep. 1650.

49. ML b66/70 and ML v85/29.

50. 3 July 1649: Whitelocke, *Memorials*, iii, pp. 22, 58, 74, 87; BL Add. Mss 34,326, f. 61; *CSPD* 1651, p. 49. Even as late as 15 February 1651 the Council of State was reminding him to make a list of his military arrears for 'good services to the Commonwealth'.

51. 28 Sep. 1650: *CJ*, vi, pp. 141, 196, 248, 300.

52. ML v86/39.

53. 20 March 1649/50, ML v85/24 and v85/25. Wetton was still holding court two years later: ML v78/72v.

54. ML v78/108, n.d.

55. Hill, from Weobley, a member of the Commonwealth sequestrations committee, was described by Aylmer as lesser gentry and a man who had been a bureaucratic force in the county during the war: Gerald Aylmer, 'Who was ruling Herefordshire from 1645 to 1661?', *TWNC* xl (1972), pp. 373–87, p. 381 and p. 386, n. 44.

56. G.E. McParlin, 'The Herefordshire gentry in county government, 1625–1661, Ph.D., Aberystwyth, 1981.

57. ML b33/135, letter from Miles Hill to Marten, 27 July 1650; ML b78/63, 10 Dec. 1651.

58. The 1651 survey gives closer to 25 acres.

59. ML v78/63, 10 Dec. 1651 and ML v78/61, 22 Dec. 1651.

60. ML v78/106, n.d.

61. ML v78/70, 1 Mar. 165½.

62. ML 78/71, 15 Mar. 165½.

63. ML v95/9, 12 Apr. 1652.

64. ML v95/11, 26 Apr. 1652. Charles Whistler was probably related to Marten's attorney, Gabriel Whistler. If this is the same Mr Ewer who was witness at Marten's trial in 1661 and who told the world of the frivolous way in which Marten approached the execution of his king, the malice that he felt towards Marten would provide a motive, but the fact that Marten cannot have known the Ewers until 1650 implies that the story was apocryphal. There were Ewers on the Berkshire estates, however, who had served Marten for much longer. Marten was also in debt to Ewer, though it was cleared in the first few days of 1655: see 'Almanack' BRO D/ELS F18 A4d.

65. ML v95/13; I have added punctuation here. It is not necessarily a full-stop in this sentence and the meaning is subtly different if there is, for example, a comma between 'lawe' and 'though'. Nevertheless, it is felt that this reading is the most plausible.

66. ML v95/15, 27 Apr. 1652.

67. ML v78/71; v95/9; v95/11; v95/15. There was a warning about the attorney, Mr Powle of Stagbach, John Norgrave's brother-in-law, who, as foreman, had swung a jury against Marten's interest (ML v90/37). Deane advised that Marten retain a non-local attorney, certainly not Powle, who was also related to the sheriff's bailiff, and although he had local knowledge of Marten's rights, yet Deane did not think Marten would get the better of him (ML v95/9, Deane to Marten, 12 Apr. 1652). Powle was, nevertheless, employed to survey the estate and paid £6 18s. 4d. (ML v90/51, accounts for Mich.53 to

Mich.54). Infighting was a characteristic feature of the Welsh marches. The Crofts were in armed dispute, together with their kinsmen, the Wigmores, Scudamores and Warncombes, as late as 1590, and Deane complained that the administration of justice there was much like that in the Council of the Marches: ML v78/81.

68. ML 95/15.

69. 'An act for removing of Obstructions in the Sale of the Honours, Manors and Lands of the late King, Queen and Prince', 18 Feb. 1650, *A&O*, ii, pp. 338–42.

70. ML v90/37; ML v95/15. Baskerville was to be proposed as a Whig Member for Weobley in 1675, see Joseph Hillaby, 'The parliamentary borough of Weobley, 1628–1798' *TWNC* xxxix (1967), 104–47, p. 118. McParlin describes him as a squire of an income of £100–250 p.a., 'Herefordshire gentry', Appendix I.

71. ML v95/11.

72. BRO Craven Papers, D/EC/E1, unfol., the purchase of Uffington between 1620 and 1623, a total of 10,575 acres, with an interesting reference, in view of the difficulties involved in tracing the early Marten family, to a half yardland in Sparsholt called Martens.

73. ML v95/2; Craven was a major creditor of Marten's: vML 78/63. The sequestered estates of William, Lord Craven were purchased by Thomas, Lord Grey of Groby.

74. HRO A63/I/305, 'Boke of Survey', 1651.

75. G.F. Townsend, *The Town and Borough of Leominster* (Leominster, 1861), p. 119. The fee farm rents had been sold by the parliamentary commissioners to the town bailiff and the burgesses. Metheglin was similar to mead.

76. ML v95/21; v95/23; v95/30, 27 Jan. 1653/4. The attempt to seize the priory was a week prior to Deane's moving in.

77. ML v95/32.

78. Gentles, 'Sales of Crown lands'; S.J. Madge, *The Domesday of Crown Lands* (London, 1938); *A&O*, ii, pp. 358–62, An act for the selling Fee-farms rents belonging to the Commonwealth of England, formerly payable to the Crown of England, Dutchy of Lancaster, and Dutchy of Cornwal, 11 Mar. 1650.

79. Aylmer, *The State's Servants* p. 151.

80. ML v95/5; v95/28v (misfiled backwards); v95/27; v95/30; v78/77; v95/33; v78/76.

81. *A&O*, ii, p. 916, 9 June 1654.

82. More is known about other members of the Croft family. James' elder brother, Sir William, was MP for Malmesbury, a commissioner of array for Herefordshire and was killed at the skirmish of Stokesay in 1645. Sir James succeeded his brother, but died unmarried in 1659, and was succeeded by his younger brother, Herbert, the future Bishop of Hereford. The family connections went beyond Anglicanism, for their father, another Sir Herbert, embraced Catholicism and at the end of his life (d.1629) became a lay brother at the Benedictine monastery at Douai.

83. There was a warning against a Mr Rawlings: 'one of the Citty whose father is [and] hath bene sufficently mallignant against the prsent government but hath p[ro]cured many hands for yt reson of a brother of his that was in the Army but died a yeare agoe': Hill to Marten, 10 Dec. 1651: ML v78/63. Similarly, [Richard?] Wigmore was one who 'smeles so much of delinquency': ML v95/30.

84. Jacqueline Eales, *Puritans and Roundheads: the Harleys of Brampton Bryan* (Cambridge, 1990); Hillaby, 'Parliamentary borough'.

85. ML v95/30.

86. ML v78/79, Deane to Marten, 15 July 1654; ML 78/109, a fragment in Deane's hand, n.d.: ML v78/81.

87. ML v78/88, 27 June 1655, Deane to Marten: 'these greate troubles in lawe doe vexe mee especially . . . here is on learning of a nother'.

88. ML v112/62, Marten to Deane, 2 Dec. 1656.

89. Such as Mr Pike, from whom Norgrave rented land. By 1664 Norgrave was a wealthy man, a gentleman, assessed at a hearth tax of £27 10s. in the parish of Ivington: see M.A. Faraday (ed.), *Herefordshire Militia Assessments of 1663* (London, Camden Society, 4th.ser., x, 1972), p. 156.

90. ML v95/29; v78/77.

91. ML v95/33.

92. Faraday's study of the militia assessments of the Restoration period show that the Leominster area (Wolphey Hundred) contained a higher than the national average proportion of 'esquires': Faraday, *Militia Assessments* .

93. ML v76/61; Lotte Mulligan and Judith Richards, 'A "radical" problem: the poor and the English reformers in the mid-seventeenth century', *Journal of British Studies* 29.2 (1990), 118–46.

94. ML v90/37.

95. ML v95/15.

96. ML v95/24; v95/30.

97. ML v78/96.

98. ML v78/105. Prior was described as a gentleman of Middleton in 1664 and was in charge of a militia company after the Restoration: see Faraday, *Militia Assessments*, p. 162 and n. 51.

99. ML v78/014; ML v78/107v.

100. ML v78/107v, 14 Dec. 1658. The river Pinsley started at Shobden, to the west of Leominster, and flowed into the Kenwater about three-quarters of a mile from the town: Elizabeth Taylor, 'The seventeenth century iron forge at Carey mill', *TWNC* xlv.2 (1986), 450–68; D.G. Bayliss, 'The effect of Bringwood forge and furnace on the landscape of part of northern Herefordshire to the end of the seventeenth century', *TWNC* xlv (1985–7), 721–9. John Wildman was involved in iron extraction in the Forest of Dean area, a lucrative project given the state monopoly to buy the iron produced; John Hollond, *Two Discourses of the Navy, 1638 and 1659* (ed. J.R. Tanner) (London, Navy Records Society, 1896), p.232.

101. ML v95/30; v95/5.

102. ML v78/84, 25 Jan. 1654/5.

103. ML v78/90.

104. ML 3rd ser./ vol. 7, pp.13–14; v78/7; ML v78/105. Savaker was wealthy, judging from his Hearth Tax charge of 1664, £15 for Perbin (Pervin) farm in Hope, see Faraday, *Militia Assessments*, p. 154.

105. ML v78/81; ML v78/88.

106. ML v78/87.

107. Another wealthy family from Hope and Humber, see Faraday, *Militia Assessments*, pp. 154–5.

108. ML v78/81 and v78/82.

109. ML v89/32, Marten to Deane, around 14 Oct. 1656.

110. ML v89/9, Marten to Deane, 5 May 1657; v78/107v.

111. ML v78/87; ML v112/57; ML v78/91; ML v78/95.

112. ML v112/60, Marten to Deane, from Westminster, 17 Nov. 1656. Stiffe was the carrier of the letter.

113. ML b23/unfol.

114. Robert Somerville, *Office-holders in the Duchy of Lancaster and County Palatine of Lancaster from 1603* (London, 1972), p. 179, who identifies the barmasters of the High Peak as Rowland and William Eyre, royalists, also known to Marten on the Hartington estate, p. 174.

115. DRO 1235/3: the earliest recorded document signed by the triumvirate of administrators, Wetton, Petty and John Hedges is dated 5 Apr. 1650. John Hedges was also a native of Berkshire, a churchwarden for Shrivenham in 1641 (Churchwardens presentments, BRO D/A2/c132, f. 262, 4 Oct. 1641).

According to Wildman, Petty was a relation of the Duke of Buckingham, whose lands he was administering on Marten's behalf, (see the interrogation of Wildman at the Restoration, BL Egmont 2543, f. 66).

116. ML b2/unfol; b8/82; b65/1; b65/172.

117. ML v88/8; b65/186; b65/172; v98/17; 8/79; John Langdon, 'Water-mills and windmills in the west midlands, 1086-1500', *Economic History Review* xliv.3 (1991), 424–44.

118. ML v98/17.

119. ML v98/12; BL Add. Mss 34,326, ff. 59–60v, 'Moneys recd by Collonell Martyn'. Peters received a total of £179 14s. for swords, belts, poleaxes and carbines. By 1649 Peters was in charge of the armaments of the regiment: BL Add. Mss 34,326, f. 65.

120. ML v98/14; v98/15; v88/16.

121. ML v88/16; v98/13.

122. ML v88/18, Heathcote had lent Peters £22 to pay the fee farm rents, of which Peters had only repaid £4. Heathcote had been forced to borrow from George Naden and asked for his rent to be abated to make up his debt: ML v88/19.

123. ML v78/66; v98/10; v98/6.

124. The Derbyshire tenants preferred to treat for lives, rather than years.

125. HM v88/17, Samuel to Peters, from Wilmot House, Whitehall, 9 Oct. 1655.

126. ML v89/2; v89/4.

127. ML b25/1149, 7 Oct. 1656, financed with Richard Blackwall of Hackney. Blackwall was one of the collectors and commissioners for prize goods and the commissioners were renting a house for which William Wetton was the agent: BL Add. MSS 5500, f. 18.

128. ML b40/unfol; 'Almanack', BRO D/ELS F18, f. 5.

129. ML v98/31, 15 Nov. 1655.

130. ML b65/172, as of Lady Day 1654; 1st ser./vol. 1/8, inquisition into the estate, 24 Aug. 1657; v98/16, 30 July 1655. There are approximately 25,000 sites of lead mines in the Derbyshire Peak District and the coal seams are to the north and west of Hartington, see Alan Roberts and John R. Leach, *The Coal Mines of Buxton* (Cromford, 1985).

131. ML v98/76, 27 Feb. 1658/9.

132. ML v98/92, 14 Dec. 1658. Peters was restrained from acting as vigorously as he might for Marten during the last quarter of 1658 by a virulent fever that hit his whole family but kept him confined to his bed for four months.

133. ML Box of loose MSS/ unfol

134. ML v78/105, 7 Dec. 1658. For the moves to end MPs' immunity from prosecution for debt, see *CJ*, vi, p. 187; Williams, 'Career'.

135. ML 1st ser./vol. 1/12.

136. ML v88/9, 15 Mar. 1656/7; 1st ser./vol. 1/8.

137. ML v78/97; v78/98; v78/105; v78/107v.

138. DRO D2375/M/7/11, 4 May 1674: the rights of the tenants to the common land and to collect coal on the south-east side of Firestone brook.

139. HM b64/120; b64/122.

140. ML v89/13–15.

141. Lovelace had difficulty recovering his money since Charles had subsequently granted Marten's lands to the Berkeley brothers, and to Henry Brunster, in trust for the Duke of York.

142. This is particularly true, unfortunately, for Richard Peters from Shefford, the parish records for this period having been lost.

143. BRO D/A1/62/78a, microfilm 514, will dated 25 Sep. 1624, inventory dated 11 Oct. 1626.
144. Robert Ewer was another who found a place in Marten's regiment: BL Add. Ms 34,326, f. 59v.
145. BRO D/ELS, f. 2., 22 Feb. 1653/4.
146. Jasmine S. Howse (ed.), *Berkshire Probate Records 1653–1710*, vol. ii (British Record Society, 1975).
147. BRO D/EZ 7/59, aquittance for Shrivenham, Stalpitts, Salop, Cley Court and Beckett, 16 May 1657. In 1652 Beckett had been bought by Sir George Pratt of Coleshill, and apparently, shortly after this, by Wildman, see the listings of *Auction of Lordships of Manors* at Faringdon, 26 July 1966 (published Hobbs and Chambers, Abingdon, 1966).
148. Howse, *Berkshire Probate*: her 'housekeeper', her unmarried daughter Anne, followed her mother in 1681: BRO D/P70 28/3, high constable's book, 1696.
149. I am grateful to David Shotter for pinpointing the reference and thereby revealing the subtlety of the wordplay, which went beyond pun or paraphrase. The original, from Horace's *Epistles* I.16.24. reads: 'Stultorum incurata pudir malus ulcera celat' [A false sense of modesty hides the uncured sores of foolishness]. Marten's lines, which he may not have shared, come from his almanack of 1655: BRO D/ELS F18 unfol, after a memorandum to himself 'to gett Sr Tho: Hirton to extend Longworth in case Hampson [his biggest creditor] be peevish'.

Chapter VI Trade and the Sea

1. If the Martens were related to the Yates, there may have been Bristol commercial links but the backgrounds of both families are too obscure for certainty.
2. Kenneth R. Andrews, *Ships, Money and Politics: Seafaring and naval enterprise in the reign of Charles I* (Cambridge, 1991), p. 193.
3. ML b67/22.
4. J.R. Powell and E.K. Timings (eds), *Documents relating to the Civil War, 1642–1648*, vol. cv (London, Navy Records Society, 1963), p. 9: the ship at this point was still rated at 700 tons.
5. ML b40/24 and b40/36; ML b67/21.
6. An obligation to Ingram either for a further £1,000 or for half of the principal money appears at ML b40/55.
7. The figures for the crew are computed from the list of costs given by Marten. Since his figures never seemed correct, a certain amount of guess work is involved: ML b67/22, 'A Note of what debts I stand ingaged for concerning my Shipp 1642'.
8. ML b67/22.
9. Clarendon, *History*, i, p. 95; May, *History*, pp. 137–8. Andrews, *Ships, Money and Politics*, p. 184; Clarendon, *History*, ii, pp. 215–26.
10. Snow and Young, *Journals*, p. 92; Powell and Timings, *Documents*, p. 15; *CJ*, ii, pp. 495, 498–9.
11. *CJ*, ii, pp. 720–1; Powell and Timings, *Documents*, pp. 34, 39.
12. ML b78/5.
13. Clarendon, *History*, ii, p. 223.
14. *CSPD* 1641–3, pp. 555, 560; Powell and Timings, *Documents*, p. 70.
15. Bernard Capp, *Cromwell's Navy: the Fleet and the English Revolution, 1648–1660* (Oxford, 1989), p. 90.
16. *CSPD* 1651, 27 Aug.1651, p. 379; *CSPD* 1651–2, pp. 120, 195, 567. PRO SP 25/I/66, pp. 255–62; pp. 501–8.
17. ML 2nd ser./vol. 23. Ralph Ingram died on 29 Oct. 1644.
18. Signified by the well-worn 'pseudonyms' Richard and John Doe.

19. ML GML/2, 29 Dec. 1656.

20. Andrews, *Ships, Money and Politics*, p. 188. The other members were Lords Northumberland, Warwick, and Holland, and MPs Giles Greene, Sir Robert Pye, the two Sir Henry Vanes, and John Rolle. With the addition of the two Bences and Samuel Vassell in December 1642, the preponderance of Berkshire connections is remarkable.

21. Andrews, *Ships, Money and Politics*, p.189.

22. ML 1st ser./vol. 8.

23. Marten might have added or considered adding to the estate in Bray under the Commonwealth, when Charles Stuart's estates were sold by the commissioners for crown land. Some of the Bray land had been leased from James I by the Lovelace family: see ML103, the Parliamentary Commissioners' survey of Bray, 1 Apr. 1650.

24. ML b40/69, 3 Apr. 1642.

25. ML 63/unfol; ML v84/2.

26. [No author cited] 'Documents and letters in the Brotherton Collection relating to Barbados', *JBMHS* xxiv (1971) 175–90.

27. R.S. Dunn, *Sugar and Slaves: the rise of the planter class in the English West Indies, 1624–1713* (Chapel Hill, NC, 1972), p. 9.

28. ML v84/10, 5 Apr. 1656.

29. PRO SP Col 1/21/170; Jerome S. Handler and Lon Shelby, 'A seventeenth century commentary on labor and military problems in Barbados', *JBMHS* xxxiv.3 (1973), 117–21.

30. Gary Puckrein, *Little England: Plantation Society and Anglo-Barbadian Politics, 1627–1700* (New York, 1984), p. 11.

31. Hilary Beckles, *White Servitude and Black Slavery in Barbados, 1627–1715* (Knoxville, Tennessee, 1989), p. 17; Peter Campbell, 'Aspects of land tenure in Barbados, 1627–1660', *JBMHS* xxxvii (1984), 112–59.

32. Vincent T. Harlow, *Colonising Expeditions to the West Indies and Guiana, 1623–1667* (London, 1924), p. 69.

33. Beckles, *White Servitude*, pp. 23–6.

34. Marten's 'town house', on the southern banks of the river Carlisle, south east of Bridgetown, was portrayed on Richard Ligon's map that accompanied *A true and exact history of the Island of Barbados* (London, 1657), reproduced in Vincent T. Harlow, *A History of Barbados, 1625–1685* (New York, 1926); Beckles, *White Servitude*, pp. 16–17; BL Add. MSS 33,845, f. 7.

35. BDA, Deeds, RB 3/3/907.

36. BDA, Deeds, RB 3/2/609.

37. Darnell N. Davis, *The Cavaliers and Roundheads of Barbados, 1650–52* (Demerara, 1887).

38. ML v84/6.

39. P.F. Campbell, 'Two generations of Walronds', *JBMHS* 38.3 (1989), 253–85. Links between the families of Berkshire, Wiltshire and Somerset were close, despite political differences, and the parliamentary Prestons, Pophams and Martens may have known the royalist Walronds before they left for the Caribbean.

40. Puckrein, *Little England*, p. 110.

41. Ibid., pp. 111–13.

42. Nicholas Forster, *A Brief Relation of the late horrid Rebellion acted on the Island of Barbados in the West Indies* (London, 1657), p. 51.

43. ML v92/73; 'Documents and letters', pp. 178–80.

44. *CSP Col* 1650, p. 346. The King was proclaimed on Barbados in May.

45. Davis, *Cavaliers and Roundheads*, pp. 250–5.

46. Capp, *Cromwell's Navy*, pp. 67–8, 175–6.

47. *CSP Col* 1650, p. 345, 30 Oct. 1650.

48. PRO SP Col 1/11/25, *Humble proposals of several Barbadeans*; Harlow, *History of Barbados*, p. 63.

49. PRO SP Col 1/1/26; J[ohn] B[ayes], *Letter from Barbados* E777(?).

50. PRO SP Col 1/11/23, 20 Nov. 1650.

51. *CSP Col* 1650, p. 345, no.24.

52. Lord Portland to Henry Marten, 13 Nov. 1650, ML v92/74.

53. G.F. Steckley (ed.), *The Letters of John Paige, London Merchant, 1648–1658* (London, 1984), p. 31, dated 6 Dec.1650.

54. *CSP Col*, 1650, p. 346, no. 27.

55. Ibid., p. 346, nos 25/27.

56. Ibid., p. 347. The radical committee consisted of Marten, Thomas Chaloner, William Heveningham, Henry Robinson, Sir Henry Mildmay, Sir William Masham, Sir Henry Vane, Sir Peter Wentworth and Sir William Constable.

57. PRO SP Col 1/1/25, 22 Nov. 1650.

58. BL Egerton MSS 2395, ff. 55–6; Thomas Modyford, *Brief relation of the troubles of Barbados*, p. 210; Puckrein, *Little England*, p. 117.

59. Campbell, 'Two generations', Appendix C, p. 277, which says Marten 'switched his allegiance'. 'Documents and letters' (p. 176) describes George as 'one who ran with the hares and hunted with the hounds'.

60. ML v84/1, 29 Mar. 1651/2. The editor of 'Documents and letters' (p. 182), has 'crimes' transcribed as 'ruins', either of which makes sense.

61. ML v93/9, Deptford, 6 May 1652; Capp, *Cromwell's Navy*, pp. 50–1, outlining Hollond's consistent complaint that politicians were lining the pockets of their families. The groat – worth 4*d*. – was removed from circulation in 1662. The word was also used colloquially to refer to a small amount.

62. ML b67/46, n.d. There is no record of publication for something with this title.

63. An act of 3 Oct. 1650 prohibiting trade with Barbados, Virginia, Bermuda and Antigua because of the political disloyalty displayed by the islanders: *A&O*, ii, pp. 425–9.

64. *A&O*, ii, pp. 403–6.

65. Ibid., pp. 559–62; Crump, *Colonial Admiralty Jurisdiction*, pp. 92–6.

66. This account corroborates Pincus's revision of Brenner, for whom Henry Marten and his closest allies were supporters of the Navigation laws, though in fact it was contrary to their interests; Steven C.A. Pincus, *Protestantism and Patriotism: Ideologies and the Making of English Foreign Policy, 1650–1668* (Cambridge, 1996), p. 52; Brenner, *Merchants and Revolution*, p. 630.

67. David Watts, *The West Indies: Patterns of Development, Culture and Environmental Change since 1492* (Cambridge, 1987), p. 184.

68. The site of the plantation is marked on William Mayo's map of Barbados, surveyed between 1717 and 1721 and published in 1722.

69. BDA, Deeds, RB 3/5/51.

70. Ligon, *True History of Barbados* cited in Dunn, *Sugar and Slaves*, p. 62.

71. BDA, Deeds, RB 3/5/52.

72. Dunn, *Sugar and Slaves*, pp. 194–5.

73. ML v84/10, 5 Apr. 1656.

74. I am grateful to Professor Tom Loftfield, Laboratory of Coastal Archaeology, University of North Carolina at Wilmington, for archaeological advice on the position, status and nature of George Marten's plantation.

75. Beckles, *White Servitude*, p. 117.

76. Ibid. and *idem*, 'The concept of "white slavery" in the English Caribbean during the early seventeenth century', in John Brewer and Susan Staves (eds.), *Early-Modern Conceptions of Property* (London, 1996), pp. 572–84.

77. BDA, Deeds, RB 3/5/51; RB 3/3/11.

78. The male slaves were called Absa, Adam, Occo, Occaba, two called Jack, Dippodessa, Apia, Cropps, Burgnoy, Peter, Ossa, Harry, Desa, Bussa, Seeba, Tom, Samba, two Tommies, Dallaca, Heym, Ockro, Rumbullion (one of the seventeenth-century names for rum), and Gage. The women were Queene, Jaba, Ampusa, Deddye, New Janey, Jeane, Feba, Jabin, Sandy, Nan, Sue, Nanny, Ogbo, Jane, Besse, Mary, Arninda, Radman, New Besse, Cheboe Cheboe, Coughs New, Queenba, Acoota, Ita Accoota, Chule.

79. Beckles, *White Servitude*, p. 122.

80. A comparative table of numbers of slaves and servants – including Marten who was one of those who had no indentured servants – is given in Dunn, *Sugar and Slaves*, p. 68.

81. Beckles, *White Servitude*, pp. 126–7; the figures were drawn up in 1685 by the Barbados Assembly.

82. Ibid., pp. 98–114, 121.

83. BDA, Deeds, RB 3/3/13.

84. Cited in Campbell, 'Two generations', p.259. The information provided here about George Marten is not altogether reliable. Nevertheless, Walrond's fortune collapsed because he encouraged slave trading with the Spanish for captives direct from Africa: 'Governors' residences', *JBMHS* x (1943), 152–62, p. 157.

85. [No author cited] 'St John's vestry minutes', *JBMHS* xxxiii.1 (1969), 32–49.

86. [No author cited] 'Some records of the House of Assembly of Barbados', *JBMHS* x (1943), 173–87, p. 175.

87. ML v93/15, 'Att A Meeting of the Honble Colonell Daniell Searle Esqr and Go^r of Barbados: and the wor^ll his Council the 6th Day of octob^r 1652'.

88. Described as the leader of the 'moderate' faction: Harlow, *History of Barbados*, p. 60.

89. There were then ten parishes; that of St Joseph's was not established.

90. E.M. Shilstone, 'The evolution of the General Assembly of Barbados', *JBMHS* i (1933), 187–91; 'Some records of the House of Assembly of Barbados'.

91. ML v84/1, 29 Mar. 1652.

92. ML v84/10.

93. ML v84/9, 24 July 1653.

94. ML v84/4.

95. ML v85/8. In the realm of speculation, George kept a slave called Susan, still alive but in England in May 1657: ML v84/8; BDA, Deeds, RB 3/5/52. Susan was certainly not his lawful wife. Frances Weld remained in England, see 'Documents and letters', pp. 175–87.

96. ML v78/33, 4 June 1655.

97. Letter from Lord Portland to Henry Marten, ML v92/74, 13 Nov. 1650.

98. BDA, Deeds, RB 3/3/739.

99. BDA, Deeds, RB 3/2/609.

100. BDA, Deeds, RB 3/3/907.

101. ML v84/2, 29 Dec. 1656. Henry Marten was also sure that Ingram's debt had been cleared, ML v73/593v, n.d.

102. 'Some observations on the island Barbadoes', PRO SP Col 1/21/170.

103. Campbell, 'Two generations', p. 277.

104. Adriaan van Berbel, *Travels in South America, between the Berbice and Essequito Rivers and in Suriname (1670–1689)*, trans. Walter E. Roth (Georgetown, Guyana, 1925); written in Dutch and published as *Amerikaansche Voijagien* (Amsterdam, 1695).

105. Ibid., p. 117.

106. Ibid., pp. 122, 136.

107. Ibid., pp. 114, 131.

108. John Carter Brown Library, Providence, Rhode Island, *A description of the coleny of Surranam in Guiana. Drawne in the yeare 1667, the planters names as they are settled in their Plantations in the severall parts of the Cuntry* (1667). Some of the planters listed owned more than one plantation on different sites. This map is reprinted in F.C. Blubberman, A.H. Loor and C. Koeman (eds.), *Schakels met het verleden* (Amsterdam, 1973).

109. Richard Price, *The Guiana Maroons: a Historical and Bibliographical Introduction* (Johns Hopkins, Baltimore, 1976), p. 6.

110. This is snakewood: Lewis Hinckley, *Directory of Historic Cabinet Woods* (NY, 1960). My thanks to Sarah Medlam of the Victoria and Albert Museum for her help in tracing this reference.

111. Jerome S. Handler, 'Father Antoine Biet's visit to Barbados in 1654', *JBMHS* xxxii.2 (1967), 56–75, p. 65.

112. Cited in Joyce Lorimer, 'The failure of the English Guiana Ventures 1595–1667 and James I's foreign policy', *Journal of Imperial and Commonwealth History* 21.1 (1993), 1–30, p. 24.

113. *A description of the Colony of Surranam.*

114. Henry Marten's creditors, Isabell and Thomas Westropp, of Newham Hall, Cleveland, were sadly disillusioned at their friend's (in)ability to pay his debts, and were themselves imprisoned: ML b48/unfol, b40/32, b64/137, 145–7, 149. For Westropp's political connections to Chaloner, see Barber, 'English attitudes towards the Scots'.

115. [No author cited] 'The Lucan manuscript', *JBMHS* xxiii (1955), pp. 187–8.

116. According to Aphra Behn's account.

117. PRO SP Col 1/21/170, cited in Handler and Shelby, 'A seventeenth century commentary', p. 119.

118. Maureen Duffy (ed.), *Oroonoko* (London, 1986), pp. 27, 33; Kim F. Hall, '"I would wish to be a blackmoor": beauty, race and rank in Lady Mary Wroth's *Urania*', and Margaret W. Ferguson, 'Juggling the categories of race, class, and gender: Aphra Behn's *Oroonoko*', in Margo Hendricks and Patricia Parker (eds.), *Women, 'Race', and Writing in the Early Modern Period* (London, 1994).

119. Duffy, *Oroonoko*, p. 36.

120. Ibid., p. 62.

121. Ibid., pp. 73-4.

122. Van Berbel, *Travels*, p. 121.

123. Ibid., p. 125.

124. Duffy, *Oroonoko*, p. 85.

125. Ibid., p. 90.

126. Ibid., p. 99.

127. These details are accepted as true in the *DNB* but this account declares that she returned to England around 1658, before Marten reached Surinam; Maureen Duffy, *The Passionate Shepherdess: Aphra Behn 1640–89* (London, 1989); Angleine Goreau, *Reconstructing Aphra, a Social Biography* (New York, 1980).

128. Duffy, *Oroonoko*, p. 91.

129. Robert Sanford, *Suriname Justice in the case of several persons proscribed by certain usurpers of power in the Colony* (London, 1662).

130. Ibid., pp. 11, 23, and similar statements cf. pp. 19, 21, 26, 34.

131. William Byam, *An exact relation of the most execrable attempts of John Allin committed on the person of his excellency Francis Lord Willoughby of Parham, Captain General of the Continent of Guiana, and of all the Caribby-Islands and our Lord Proprietor* (London, 1665), p. 2. The copy held by the Barbados Museum is annotated on the frontispiece, agreeing with Byam that Allin was 'A villain y[t] hath scarce his paralel'.

132. Ibid., p. 4.

133. Ibid., p. 11.

134. Ibid., pp. 8–9.

135. Although Caesar was a common slave name, there were specific reasons why Behn's hero should bear the name.

136. Duffy, *Oroonoko*, p. 36.

137. Goreau, *Reconstructing Aphra*, p. 21; James Walker, 'The secret service under Charles II and James II', *Transactions of the Royal Historical Society*, 4th ser., xv (1932), 211–35.

138. BL Egerton 2395, f. 180, Thomas Povey to Daniel Searle, 20 Oct. 1659.

139. C.F.A. Bruijning and J. Voorhoeve, *Encyclopedie van Suriname* (Amsterdam, 1977); Jos Fontaine, *Zeelandia de Geschiedenis van een Fort* (Zutphen, 1972), pp. 18–37; William Byam, 'An exact narrative of the state of Guiana', Bodl., Rawlinson MSS A 175, f. 344, (transcribed by George Edmundson, 'Verhal van de Inneming van Paramaribo (1665) door Generaal William Byam', *Bijdragen . . . Historisch Genootschap* 19 (1898), 231–62.

Chapter VII 'An Ugly Rascal and a Whoremonger'

1. Howse, *Longworth*, pp. 77–8.

2. Hexter, *King Pym*, p. 125.

3. Ibid., p. 126.

4. Russell, *Fall*, p. 461 and n. 5.

5. Scott, *Algernon Sidney*, p. 94, although Scott's portrayal of Marten's vigour is more sympathetic than his unease at Sidney's sanctimoniousness.

6. Aubrey, *Brief Lives*, p. 265.

7. ML 1st ser./ vol. 27.

8. ML b39/25.

9. ML b40/82.

10. ML b64/198.

11. ML b67/83–84v.

12. ML b8/33.

13. Grey of Groby died aged thirty-four, with very bad gout. Perhaps he was a drinker too.

14. Clarendon, *History*, ii, p. 200, 1115.

15. William Parker provided deliveries of 'lemon ale' during Marten's imprisonment in the Tower in 1660: Waters, *Letters from the Tower* and *Familiar Letters*, x, p. 14.

16. Aubrey, *Brief Lives*, p. 265.

17. Whitelocke, *Memorials*, iv, p. 5, 20 Apr. 1653.

18. Bodleian Library, Oxford, Clarendon SP 30/2 2722, f. 290, 10 Feb. 1647/8.

19. In July 1642 Marten rented in St Anne's Street, Westminster: ML b40/19.

20. J.C. Cole, *Some Notes on Henry Marten, the Regicide, and his family*, p. 32.

21. On 27 October 1635 a Mr Chamberlain received £107 14s. from Marten and 'Margaret his wife' for their step-daughter: ML b64/10. 'Part of Mr Marten Marriage mony, put into the great Iron Chist [chest]' notes that, as of 26 Feb. 1634/5, there remained £1,200. This money was paid out on 20 March: ML b67/15. The tripartite agreement by which Sir Henry made a marriage settlement on his son is dated 9 Dec. 1634: ML b58/unfol. On 18 January following, however, Margaret was still named as Staunton and described as a widow: ML b40/unfol.

22. Howse, *Longworth*, p. 73; the will of Sir Henry Marten, BRO D/ELS F1; ML b64/110, in which Margaret is described as 'the daughter and orpane of the said William Staunton'. The payment to Margaret was to be made according to eight recognizances dated 11 Dec. 1632. The records reveal the marriage of Edward Onely and Margaret Staunton on 20 Feb. 1638(9) (BRO D/P 112/1/1/). Strangely, an indenture of 20 Feb. 1642, announced the marriage of Margaret, daughter of Margaret and William Staunton to Edward Hurley of Catesby: ML b42/unfol. Margaret and Edward's daughter, another Margaret, married a Vernon in 1661 (aged nineteen), thereby rejoining the aristocracy.

23. Aubrey, *Brief Lives*, p. 265.

24. Anna, baptised 5 June 1636; Henry, baptised 9 July 1639: BRO MF296, D/P 112/1/1.

25. Howse and Cole disagree on the number of children Margaret bore Henry. Howse calculates five and Cole, four.

26. Aubrey, *Brief Lives*, p. 265. Margaret went to live in the Marten house, Longworth Lodge, after the destruction of Beckett House, Shrivenham, and its sale to Pratt and Wildman. She was looked after by her daughter, Anne, who remained unmarried, and who complained to Henry that she was short of basic provisions. There are four letters from Anne to Henry in the Marten Loder manuscripts, in which the twenty-year-old Anne complains that 'I am not keephouse without mony'. She also revealed that she knew Mary Ward: ML v89/20–23.

27. *Familiar Letters*, lii, p. 43, and xc, p. 78.

28. Marten, *The Independency of England*, p. 10.

29. Marten referred to Mary's kin as 'cousin' although this postdated the time at which Mary was so much a part of Marten's life that she was referred to as his 'wife'. 'Cousin' could therefore have been part of the same phenomenon. See ML b4/156 'for my Cos: Tho Wardes use', as well as cousins Frances and Jane Warde, 1655.

30. Wiseman, '"Adam, the father of all flesh"'.

31. *Familiar Letters*, iii, p. 7.

32. *CJ*, ii, p. 863.

33. Such as a letter dated 27 Aug. 1657, 'For my Lady Rogers': ML v89/11. Mary Rogers also used her married name in a letter to Marten dated 2 Apr. 1648: ML v89/29. This letter refers to Marten's daughter, Elizabeth (Betty), to whom there seems to be no other reference, and to Jane, Rebeckey, and Hal.

34. HMC Report 5, Appendix, p. 192, cited in J.G. Muddiman, *The King's Journalist 1659–1698* (London, 1923), p. 38.

35. Amongst many references to Derby House, see BRO D/ELS F18 f.1: 'ask Gabriel [Whistler] for ye main deed of Derby house' (1655).

36. Southwark Local Studies Library, Rate Book 1635–1661; Survey of London (London County Council), vol. xxv, St George's Fields, parishes of St George the Martyr and St Mary Magdalene, Southwark.

37 Joanna Innes, 'The King's Bench prison in the later eighteenth century: law, authority and order in a London debtors' prison', in J. Brewer and J. Styles (eds.), *An Ungovernable People* (London, 1983). Among Marten's papers is a copy, annotated in his own hand, of 'an Act for the relief of creditors and

poor prisoners', 5 Oct. 1653: BRO D/ELs Z7/4, and an ordinance to the same effect of 1654: D/ELs Z7/5.

38. ML b64/127, 23 Mar. 1657/8, 'my owne sole . . . It did well pleas me to he[a]r so quickly from thee and I have obaiced [obeyed] orders as well as I can. My cosin gose [*sic*] away to day and I have be[e]n at ipsom and have locked upon roms – 3 roms for sixtin shilings a weke and no emty hous to be got'. Spellings have not been modernised or corrected, but the original contains no punctuation, which has been added to ease the sense.

39. ML b40/unfol. Indenture of 30 July 1657 between Henry Marten in the first part and 'Mary Ward of Southwark, spinster' in the second. The land in the parish of Hartington which was made over to Mary totalled 781¼ acres, much of which had previously been in the hands of Richard Peters, Marten's high bailiff and steward, including the house in which Peters had been living, Fern House, near Buxton.

40. *Familiar Letters*, xc, p. 78. Letter lxviii had talked of the sale of goods.

41. Ibid., lvii, p. 48.

42. ML v93/19–19v.

43. *Oxford English Dictionary*, II, p. 377, in which concubine is defined as 'a woman who cohabits with a man without being his wife'.

44. ML v93/20: only two folios of the manuscript survive, badly water damaged.

45. Whitelocke, *Memorials*, iii, p. 190.

46. Mark Noble, *The Lives of the English Regicides* (2 vols) (London, 1798), vol. ii, p. 45.

47. ML b23/1052, describing him as a native of Lambeth and there are frequent references in the *Familiar Letters* to 'Dick Pe:'. Bartolomew Pettingall was Marten's contemporary at Oxford, Jesus College, BA 9 Nov. 1622, MA 21 June 1625; Clark, *Register*, p. 412.

48. The introduction to Waters' edition by Robert A. Hume, links Gayton with the Southwark prison at the same time as Marten, and with the son of Marten's minister in Longworth, Dr Fell, which would seem to point to Gayton's prior acquaintance with Marten and his knowledge of the letters. I have no doubt about the authenticity of these letters. The style is unmistakably that of Marten and the small matters of family and household life are too detailed to have been known by outsiders.

49. *Familiar Letters*, ii, pp. 6–7; Richard Tuck identifies this reference to the snail as a borrowing from Montaigne; Tuck, *Philosophy and Government*, p. 250.

50. *Familiar Letters*, xl, p. 35.

51. Ibid., lxxx, p. 66.

52. Ibid., xxx, p. 27.

53. Ibid., ii, pp. 6–7; vi, p. 10; lxvii, p. 54.

54. Ibid., xlii, p. 37.

55. Ibid., lvii, p. 48.

56. Ibid., i, p. 1, *A copy of H. Martins Letter in justification of the Murther of the late King Charles*. This was composed whilst a prisoner in the Tower and described at letter lxxx as 'not quite ready'.

57. Ibid., xviii, p. 19.

58. According to 'Shrivenham at the turn of the Century', p. 257, a locally written piece provided by Peter Durston of the Royal Military College of Science, Shrivenham.

59. Samuel Dunch from Pusey was sheriff of Berkshire in the later 1620s and '30s.

60. ML b4/146; BRO Ms Archd.pprs. Berks d.7, f. 145.

61. *Rump: or an exact Collection of the choycest Poems and Songs relating to the later Times, by the most eminent Wits* (London, 1662, reprinted 1874), pt I, p. 162; pt II, pp. 22, 187.

62. Ibid., II, 342, *A Quarrel betwixt Tower-hill and Tyburn*.

63. Ibid., II, 48–9, *Arsy Versy, or the Second Martyrdom of the RUMP*.

64. Ibid., II, 69, *The Rump Carbonodo'd*.

65. Ibid., II, 344. The erroneous award of a knighthood was a common mistake made by contemporaries and historians alike.

66. Ibid., II, 15, *Chipps of the Old Block; or Hercules Cleansing the Augaean Stable*.

67. *The Man in the Moon*, no. 25, 10–17 Oct. 1649, cited by Joad Raymond (ed.), *Making the News* (London, 1993), p. 151. There are several lists of apothecaries' remedies among the Marten papers, mainly for clisters and cordials, and, although there is some mention of hartshorn and mercury, there is insufficient evidence to prove that he was being treated for syphillis. He also lived to be seventy-nine, and in view of the agonised early death of the Earl of Rochester, it seems remarkable and unlikely, if the scale of Marten's whoring was as widespread as the balladeers implied, that he would have escaped the same fate.

68. Bertram Schofield (ed.), *The Knyvett Letters, 1620–1644* (London, 1949), pp. 42–3. Knyvett is referring to *The Parliaments Proceedings Justified*.

69. Barber, '"A bastard kind of militia"', pp.133–50.

70. *Mr Henry Martin his Speech*, p. 3. Lenthall was an unpopular landlord and Marten disliked him: ML b16/164.

71. All references to this pamphlet are to *Mr Henry Martin his Speech in the House of Commons before his Departure thence*, dated 8 June 1648, anonymously written, published and printed, E446(19).

72. 'A Speech in answer to Mr Martyn who railest against ye king Lord & Comons. Said to be Sr John Maynards for ye wch he was turned out of ye house'. In manuscript in Thomason's hand, E422(32).

73. W[illiam] Turvil, *Terrible and bloudy Newes fromt he disloyall Army in the North*, 11 Sep. 1648, E462(28) p. 1. Turvil's letter was dated 7 Sept.

74. Ibid., p. 2.

75. ML b48/unfol.

76. ML b67/14.

77. ML b68/(10)

78. *A List of all the Prisoners in the Upper Bench Prison*, 12 May 1653, E213(8), calculated a total debt of £976,120 held by 393 prisoners; *A List of all the Prisoners of the Upper Bench Prison, who have taken the Benefit of the Act of Parliament for the Relief of Poor Prisoners*, 12 May 1653, E213(9).

79. ML v84/4.

80. ML v84/3, written 29 Dec. 1656.

81. *Familiar Letters*, iii, p. 43.

82. ML v93/(Brotherton folio 24); ML v88/39–40v+2–4v; HMC Report 13, Appendix, pt 4, pp. 390–1; Williams, 'Career', transcribed in Appendix c, no. 3, ff. 547–8.

83. There is no evidence he was in prison in 1659, and was probably living in his own house in the Rules of Southwark.

84. H[enry] M[arten], H[enry] N[evill], I[ohn] L[ambert](?), I[ohn] W[ildman], I[ohn] I[ones], S[amuel] M[oyer], *The Armies Dutie or Faithfull Advice to the Souldiers*, [2 May] 1659, E980(12), p. 9.

85. Aubrey, *Brief Lives*, p. 266.

86. Marten, *Independency of England*, p. 10.

87. Ibid., p. 23.

88. Ludlow, *Memoirs*, ii, p. 325.

89. Ibid., p. 22. Both Marten and Marchamont Nedham liked to use Proverbs 26.11 –'As a dog returneth to his vomit, so a fool returneth to his folly' – to describe the Scots.

90. Marten, *The Parliaments Proceedings Justified*, pp. 7–8. The number of references to fire is graphically striking.

91. *The true Character of the Educations, Inclinations and several Dispositions of all and every one of those Bloody and barbarous Persons* (London, 1661, though in fact, 1660), [14 Dec.] 1660, E1080(15), p. 3.

92. Noble, *Lives*.

93. Ibid., p. 41.

94. Ibid., p. 45.

95. Baxter was confused with Bagster, but it was ruled that since both names were pronounced the same, this was sufficient reason to conclude that they were the same person.

96. Noble, *Lives*, p. 48.

97. Ibid., p. 49.

98. There were Ewers in the Berkshire villages on Marten's estates and Ewers on the estates that he took over in Herefordshire. If the former, this Mr Ewer was a previously loyal servant who had turned on his master; if the latter he was a yeoman who had previously been hostile to Marten, but who had not encountered him before 1650. See chapter 5.

99. Ludlow recalled the time when Cromwell threw cushions down the stairs after him, *Memoirs*, i, p. 184.

100. Noble, *Lives*, p. 53.

101. Aubrey, *Brief Lives*, p. 267.

102. O. Airy (ed.), *Burnet's History of my own Time* (2 vols) (Oxford, 1897), I, pp. 282–3.

103. Aphra Behn, *The Younger Brother; or, the Amorous Jilt*, in Montague Summers (ed.), *The Works of Aphra Behn* (6 vols) (?), iv, pp. 327–8.

104. BL Add. MSS 71532, f. 15, part of a draft of a reply to *Oceana* written from the Rules.

105. Behn, *Younger Brother*, p. 317.

106. Ibid., p. 331.

107. Ibid., p. 332.

108. Ibid., p. 335.

109. Ibid., p. 333.

110. Mercurius Menippeus, *The loyal satirist or Hudibras in prose* (London, 1682), pp. 14, 18. I am grateful to Nigel Smith for this reference.

111. By 1692 Codrington was a major landholder in Barbados, had defended the Leeward Islands from the French (and was to become governor of the Leewards in 1698), owned 725 acres at Betty's Hope, Antigua, and with his brother, John, leased Barbuda from the Crown. The majority of the Codrington papers are still held by the family at Dodington House, Gloucestershire.

112. Noble, *Lives*, p. 58.

Postscript The Immortality of Fashion

1. Coxe, *Historical Tour*, p. 304.

2. Ibid., p. 307.

3. P. Karsten, *Patriot-Heroes in England and America* (Wisconsin, 1978); Scott, *Algernon Sidney*.

4. Southey's revolutionary outbursts had been tempered by 1802: compare the work cited here with his essay on revolution in England, in J. Simmons (ed.), *Letters from England* (London, 1961), Letter lxi, pp. 372–80.

5. Robert Hume, in his forward to Waters' edition of Marten's letters from the Tower, asks whether Byron might have been reading Marten's letters when he wrote to Countess Teresa Guiccioli as 'my last and only love'. Marten's line to Mary Ward was one of his most literary and poignant: 'My last

and onely Love, though I were sure to live an hundred years longer, and thou not half so many hours'; Waters, *Letters from the Tower*, pp. ix, 1.

6. Thomas Hutchinson (ed.), *Shelley: Poetical Works* (Oxford, 1905, 1989 edn), pp. 338–9.

7. *Monthly Review*, 1:8, 20 Nov. 1797; Lionel Madden (ed.), *Robert Southey: The Critical Heritage* (London, 1972), pp. 5, 55–6. In 'nature's fair varieties' and 'the sun's delightful beams', Southey is paraphrasing Milton's *Paradise Lost*, bk 3.

8. *Anti-Jacobin*, 2:15–16, 27 Nov. 1797:

> For one long Term, or e'er her trial came,
> Here BROWNRIGG linger'd. Often have these cells
> Echoed her blasphemies, as with shrill voice
> She scream'd for fresh Geneva. Not to her
> Did the blithe fields of Tothill, or thy street,
> St. Giles, its fair varieties expand;
> Till at the last in slow-drawn cart she went
> To execution. Dost thou ask her crime?
> SHE WHIPP'D TWO FEMALE 'PRENTICES TO DEATH,
> AND HID THEM IN THE COLE-HOLE. For her mind
> Shap'd strictest plans of discipline. Sage Schemes!
> Such as LYCURGUS taught, when at the shrine
> Of the Orthyan Goddess he bade flog
> The little Spartans; such as erst chastised
> Our MILTON, when at College. For this act
> Did BROWNRIGG swing. Harsh Laws! But time shall come,
> When France shall reign, and Laws be all repealed!

9. Kineton Parkes (ed.), *The English Republic* (London, 1891).

10. W.J. Linton, *Claribel and other Poems* (London, 1865), pp. 67–74.

11. Ibid., p. 71.

Bibliography

Manuscript Sources

Barbados Department of Archives, St James, Barbados
Deeds, transcriptions of land transactions, baptisms, marriages and burials:
RB 3/3/907; RB 3/2/609; RB 3/5/51; 3/5/52; 3 3/5/51; 3/3/11; RB 3/3/13; RB 3/5/52; RB 3/3/739; RB 3/2/609; RB 3/3/907

Berkshire Record Office, Reading
D/A2 Berks. d.6., presentments to livings; Archdeaconry Papers, Ms Archd.pprs. d.7 f.143; D/A2 c.185 f.123 and f.124; D/A2 Berks. d.7. f.145; D/A2/c.160 f.345; D/A2/c.186 ff.13–14, 21 Sep.,1634; D/A2/c.185 ff.123–4; Henry Marten's Almanack D/ELs F18 A4d BRO; Craven Papers, D/EC/E1 unfol.; D/ELs f.2.; wills D/A1/62/78a and D/ELs F1; Churchwardens' presentments, D/A2/c132 f.262, 4 Oct.,1641; acquittance D/EZ 7/59; High Constables' book, D/P70 28/3; marriage of the Onelys, D/P 112/1/1; baptism registers, MF296, D/P 112/1/1

Bibliothèque Nationale, Paris
Fonds Français, 6716, ff.102–5

Bodleian Library, Oxford
Tanner MSS 57 f.197; Rawlinson MSS 57 William Byam, 'An exact narrative of the state of Guiana'; Rawlinson MSS A 175 f.344; Clarendon SP 30/2 2722 f.290

British Library, London
Additional MSS 71532–6, the papers of Sir Henry and Henry Marten, formerly in the possession of Lord Fairfax; Stowe MS 743 f.116; Add MSS 34,326 f.61 the interrogation of Wildman at the Restoration; Egmont 2543 f.66; Add. MSS 5500 f.18; Add MS 34,326 f.59v; papers dealing with colonial affairs, Egerton MSS 2395 ff.55–6; Egerton 2395 f.180

Derbyshire Record Office, Matlock
D1235/3, administration of Hartington; D2375/M/7/11, coal mining rights, Firebrook

Gwent Record Office
Kemeys Document M000(282.5), M120 5476 and M120 6119

Herefordshire Records Office, Hereford
A63/I/305, Commonwealth 'Boke of Survey', 1651

House of Lords Record Office
Manuscript copy of the Commons Journal

Oxfordshire Record Office, Oxford
Signature of Maximilian Petty, Li/XIII/ii/1 and Li/XIII/vii/b/1

Public Record Office, London
State Papers Colonial 1/21/170; 1/11/25, *Humble proposals of several Barbadeans*; 1/1/26; 1/11/23; 1/1/25, 'Some observations on the island Barbadoes'; 1/21/170

Scottish Record Office, Edinburgh
Hamilton Papers, GD 1/406/1/8277

Sheffield University Library, Sheffield
Hartlib Manuscripts, 6/4/79AÑ80B, a letter from John Dury to Sir Henry Marten

Southwark Local Studies Library, London
Rate Book 1635–1661

University of Leeds, Brotherton Collection
The Marten Loder manuscripts, being the papers of Sir Henry and Henry Marten, and John Loder. These items are too numerous to list individually and reference is made to respective items within the text (ML)

Westminster Local Library, London
Rate Book, Westminster St Margaret's, MF E165; H435; H438; H440; H441

Worcester College, Oxford
The Clarke Manuscripts, being the records of Sir William Clarke, Secretary to the New Model Army, vol. cxiv

Printed Sources

Printed Primary Sources
Abbott, W.C. *The Writings and Speeches of Oliver Cromwell* (4 vols) (Harvard, 1927–47)
Airy, O. (ed.). *Burnet's History of my own Time* (2 vols) (Oxford, 1897)
Articles of Treason and high Misimeanours [sic], *committed by John Pine of Curry-Mallet*, [2 Apr.] 1649, 669.f.14(15)/669.f.13(94)
Aubrey, John. *Aubrey's Brief Lives*, ed. Oliver Lawson Dick (Penguin, London, 1987 edn)
Ball, William. *Constituio Libreri Populi, or the Rule of a Free-born People*, 18 June 1646, E341(1)
Ball, William. *The Power of Kings Discussed*, 30 Jan. 1649, E340(21)
Ball, William. *State-maxims or certain dangerous positions destructive to the very nature very natural Right and Liberty of mankind*, [5 Aug.] 1656, E886(6)
Behn, Aphra. *Oroonoko and other Stories*, ed. Maureen Duffy (London, 1986)
Blencowe, Robert Willis. *Sydney Papers: consisting of a Journal of the Earl of Leicester, and original Letters of Algernon Sydney* (London, 1825)
Byam, William. *An exact relation of the most execrable attempts of John Allin committed on the person of his excellency Francis Lord Willoughby of Parham, Captain General of the Continent of Guiana, and of all the Caribby-Islands and our Lord Proprietor* (London, 1665)
Cockayne, William. *The Foundations of Freedome Vindicated*, 7 Feb. 1648(9), E341(25)

Cook, John. *King Charls his Case*, [Feb.] 1649, E542(3)

A declaration of the parliament of England, expressing the grounds of their late proceedings, and of setling the present Government in the way of a Free State, [22 March] 1649, E548(12)

de Gondi, Jean Francois Paul. *Memoirs of the Cardinal de Retz written by Himself*, ed. Ernest Rhys (London, 1970)

Denne, Cornet Henry. *The Levellers Designe Discovered*, [24 May] 1649, E556(11)

Faraday, M.A. (ed.). *Herefordshire Militia Assessments of 1663* (London, Camden Society, 4th ser., vol. x, 1972)

Firth, C.H. (ed.). *The Clarke Papers: Selections from the Papers of William Clarke* (4 vols) (London, Camden Society: vol. i, 1891; vol. ii, 1894; vol. iii 1899; vol. iv, 1901, with vols. i and ii reissued by the Royal Historical Society, Woodbridge, Suffolk, 1992)

Forster, Nicholas. *A Brief Relation of the late horrid Rebellion acted on the Island of Barbados in the West Indies* (London, 1657)

Fussell, G.E. (ed.). *Robert Loder's Farm Accounts 1610–1620* (London, Camden Society, 3rd.ser., vol. 53, 1937)

Gardiner, S.R. (ed.). *Reports of Cases in the Courts of Star Chamber* (London, Camden Society, 1886)

Gassendi, Pierre. *Pierre Gassendi's Institutio Logica, 1658*, trans. Howard Jones (Assen, 1981)

Grey of Groby, Lord Thomas. *Old English Blood boyling afresh in Leicestershire men*, [28 Aug.] 1648, E461(7)

Grotius, Hugo. *The Law of War and Peace: de Jure Belli ac Pacis Libri Tres*, trans. F.W. Kelsey (Bobbs Merrill Co., 1925)

Harrington, James. *The Commonwealth of Oceana*, ed. J.G.A. Pocock (Cambridge, 1992)

Hollond, John. *Two Discourses of the Navy, 1638 and 1659*, ed. J.R. Tanner (London, Navy Records Society, 1896)

Hyde, Edward, Earl of Clarendon. *The History of the Rebellion and Civil Wars in England* (6 vols) (Oxford, 1707)

Ley, William. *A Buckler for the Church of England against certaine queries propounded by Mr Pendarvis . . . called Arrowes against Babylon* (Oxford, 1656), 12 June 1656, E882(1)

[Lilburne, John]. *Regall Tyrannie discovered: or, a discourse shewing that all lawfull (approbational) institutied power by God amongst men, is by common agreement*, [6 Jan.] 1647, E370(12)

Lilburne, John. *Rash Oaths unwarrantable and the breaking of them inexcusable*, 31 May 1647, E393(39)

Lilburne, John. *A Copy of a Letter written to Col. Henry Marten*, 20 July 1647, 669.f.11(46)

Lilburne, John. *Two Letters written by Lieut. Col. John Lilburne*, 13 and 15 Sep. 1647

Lilburne, John, Overton, Richard, and Prince, Thomas. *The Picture of the Councel of State*, 11 Apr. 1649, E550(14)

Lilburne, John, Overton, Richard, Walwyn, William, and Prince, Thomas. *A Manifestation*, 16 Apr. 1649, E550(25)

A List of all the Prisoners in the Upper Bench Prison, 12 May 1653, E213(8)

A List of all the Prisoners of the Upper Bench Prison, who have taken the Benefit of the Act of Parliament for the Relief of Poor Prisoners, 12 May 1653, E213(9)

Ludlow, Edmund. *The Memoirs of Edmund Ludlow*, ed. C.H. Firth (2 vols) (Oxford, 1894)

Maltby, Judith (ed.). *The Short Parliament Diary of Sir Thomas Aston* (London, Camden Society, 4th ser., vol. 35, 1988)

[Marten, Henry]. *A Corrector of the Answerer to the Speech out of Doores*, [26 Oct.] 1646, E364(9)

[Marten, Henry]. *An Answer to the Speech without Doores: or Animadversions*, [16 Nov.] 1646, E362(9)

[Marten, Henry]. *An Vnhappie game at Scotch and English*, 30 Nov. 1646, E364(3)

Marten, Henry. *The Independency of England Endeavoured to be Maintained*, 11 Jan. 1648, E422(16)

Marten, Henry. *The Parliaments Proceedings Justified*, [7 Feb.] 1648, E426(2)

[Marten, Henry]. *A Word to Mr Wil. Prynne Esq*, 6 Jan. 1649, E537(16)

H[enry] M[arten], H[enry] N[evill], I[ohn] L[ambert](?), I[ohn] W[ildman], I[ohn] I[ones], S[amuel] M[oyer], *The Armies Dutie or Faithfull Advice to the Souldiers*, [2 May] 1659, E980(12)

Marten, Henry. *Coll. Henry Marten's Familiar Letters to his Lady of Delight* (London, 1662)

May, Thomas. *The History of the Parliament of England* (London, 1812)

Naylier, John, Ellergood, Richard, Marshall, John. *The Foxes Craft Discovered*, [2 Apr.] 1649, E549(7)

Ogle, Revd O. and Bliss, W.H. *Calendar of the Clarendon state papers in the British Library*, vol. i (Oxford, 1872)

Pendarves, John. *The fear of God: what it is and exhorted to*, a sermon preached to the Church of Christ meeting in Petty France, 10 June 1656 (London, 1657), 3 Apr. 1657, E907(3)

Pocock, J.G.A. (ed.). *Harrington: The Commonwealth of Oceana and A System of Politics* (Cambridge, 1992)

Raymond, Joad (ed.). *Making the News* (London, 1993)

Roy, Ian (ed.). *The Royalist Ordnance Papers, 1642–1646*, part I (Oxfordshire Record Society, 1963–4)

Rump: or an exact Collection of the choycest Poems and Songs relating to the later Times, by the most eminent Wits (London, 1662, reprinted 1874)

Schofield, Bertram (ed.). *The Knyvett Letters, 1620–1644* (London, 1949)

Coates, Willson H., Steele Young, Anne, and Snow, Vernon F. *The Private Journals of the Long Parliament* (2 vols) (Yale, 1982–7)

Steckley, G.F. (ed.). *The Letters of John Paige, London Merchant, 1648–1658* (London, 1984)

Stow, John. *A Survey of the Cities of London and Westminster* (London, 1755)

Summers, Montague (ed.). *The Works of Aphra Behn* (6 vols) (New York, 1967)

The true Character of the Educations, Inclinations and several Dispositions of all and every one of those Bloody and barbarous Persons (London, 1660), [14 Dec.] 1660, E1080(15)

Turvil, W[illiam]. *Terrible and bloudy Newes from the disloyall Army in the North*, 11 Sep. 1648, E462(28)

van Berbel, Adriaan. *Travels in South America, between the Berbice and Essequito Rivers and in Suriname (1670–1689)*, trans. Walter E. Roth (Georgetown, Guyana, 1925)

Walker, Clement. *Relations and Observations, hisatorical and politick, upon the Parliament begun . . . 1640* (London, 1648–1660)

Warner, G.F. (ed.). *The Nicholas Papers: Correspondence of Sir Edward Nicholas* (London, Camden Society, new ser. no. 40, 1965)

Whitelocke, Bulstrode. *Memorials of the English Affairs* (London, 1682)

Wither, George. *The Speech without Doore, delivered July 9 1644 in the absence of the Speaker and in the hearing of above 0000003 persons then present*, E4(30)

Wood, Anthony. *Life and Times* (5 vols) (Oxford, 1891)

Woodhouse, A.S.P. *Puritanism and Liberty: being the Army Council Debates (1647–9)* (London, 1986)

Wootton, David (ed.). *Divine Right and Democracy: an Anthology of Political Writing in Stuart England* (Penguin, London, 1986)

Printed Secondary Sources

Allison, K.J., *et al.*, *The Deserted Villages of Oxfordshire* (Leicester University Occasional Papers 17, 1965)

Andrews, Kenneth R. *Ships, Money and Politics: Seafaring and Naval Enterprise in the Reign of Charles I* (Cambridge, 1991)

Ashley, Maurice. *John Wildman, Plotter and Postmaster: a Study of the English Republican Movement in the Seventeenth Century* (London, 1947)

Ashton, Robert. *Counter-revolution: the Second Civil War and its Origins, 1646–8*, (Yale, 1994)

Auction of Lordships of Manors at Faringdon, 26 July 1966 (published Hobbs and Chambers, Abingdon, 1966)

Aylmer, G.E. *The State's Servants: The Civil Service of the English Republic, 1649–1660* (London, 1973)

Beckles, Hilary. *White Servitude and Black Slavery in Barbados, 1627–1715* (Knoxville, Tennessee, 1989)

Berman, David. *A History of Atheism in Britain: from Hobbes to Russell* (Croom Helm, Beckenham, 1988)

Blitzer, Charles. *An Immortal Commonwealth: the Political Thought of James Harrington* (New Haven, 1960)

Blubberman, F.C., Loor, A.H., and Koeman, C. (eds). *Schakels met het verleden* (Amsterdam, 1973)

Bradney, Sir Joseph. *A History of Monmouthshire*, pt 1, vol. iv, 'The Hundred of Caldicot', (London, 1929)

Brailsford, H.N. *The Levellers and the English Revolution* (Nottingham, 1961)

Brenner, Robert. *Merchants and Revolution: Commercial Change, Political Conflict, and London's Overseas Traders, 1550–1653* (Princeton, 1993)

Brett James, N.C. *The Growth of Stuart London* (London, 1935)

Brooke, John Hedley. *Science and Religion: Some historical perspectives* (Cambridge, 1991)

Bruijning, C.F.A., and Voorhoeve, J. *Encyclopedie van Suriname* (Amsterdam, 1977)

Capp, Bernard. *Cromwell's Navy: the Fleet and the English Revolution, 1648–1660* (Oxford, 1989)

Clark, Andrew. *The Life and Times of Anthony Wood* (5 vols) (Oxford, 1891–2)

Clark, Andrew (ed.). *Register of the University of Oxford* II (1571–1622) part iii (degrees) (Oxford, 1888)

Cousin, Victor. *Madam de Longueville pendant la Fronde, 1651–1653* (Paris, 1859)

Coxe, William *Archdeacon Coxe's Historical Tour through Monmouthshire* (Brecon, 1904)

Davis, Darnell N. *The Cavaliers and Roundheads of Barbados, 1650–52* (Demerara, 1887)

Duffy, Maureen. *The Passionate Shepherdess: Aphra Behn 1640–89* (London, 1989)

Dunn, R.S. *Sugar and Slaves: the rise of the planter class in the English West Indies, 1624–1713* (Chapel Hill, NC, 1972)

Eales, Jacqueline. *Puritans and Roundheads: the Harleys of Brampton Bryan* (Cambridge, 1990)

Eccleshall, Robert. *Order and Reason in Politics: Theories of Absolute and Limited Monarchy in early-modern England* (Hull/Oxford, 1978)

Fink, Z.S. *The Classical Republicans: an essay in the Recovery of a Pattern of Thought in seventeenth-century England* (Northwestern UP, 1962 edn)

Firth, C.H., and Davies, Godfrey. *The Regimental History of Cromwell's Army* (2 vols) (Oxford, 1940)

Flew, Antony. *A Dictionary of Philosophy* (London, 1979)

Fontaine, Jos. *Zeelandia de Geschiedenis van een Fort* (Zutphen, 1972)

Foster, Joseph. *Alumni Oxonienses 1500–1714* (London and Oxford, 1892)

Gardiner, S.R. *History of the Great Civil War* (4 vols) (reprinted London, 1987)

Gardiner, S.R. *History of the Commonwealth and Protectorate* (4 vols) (reprinted, London, 1988)

Gaskin J.C.A. (ed.). *Varieties of Unbelief: from Epicurus to Satre* (New York and London, 1989)

Gentles, Ian. *The New Model Army in England, Ireland and Scotland, 1645–1653* (Oxford,1992)

Gentles, Ian, Morrill, John, and Worden, Blair (eds). *Soldiers, Writers and Statesmen of the English Revolution* (Cambridge, 1998)

Goreau, Angleine. *Reconstructing Aphra, a Social Biography* (New York, 1980)

Gregg, Pauline. *Freeborn John: a Biography of John Lilburne* (London, 1961)

Harley, J.B. *The Historians Guide to Ordnance Survey Maps* (HMSO, 1964)

Harlow, Vincent T. *Colonising Expeditions to the West Indies and Guiana, 1623–1667* (London, 1924)

Harlow, Vincent T. *A History of Barbados, 1625–1685* (New York, 1926)

Havelock E.A. *The Lyric Genius of Catullus* (2nd edn, Russell, 1967)

Hexter, J.H. *The Reign of King Pym* (Harvard, 1941)

Hinckley, Lewis. *Directory of Historic Cabinet Woods* (New York, 1960)

Howse, Jasmine S. (ed.). *Berkshire Probate Records ii 1653–1710* (British Record Society, 1975)

Howse, Jasmine S. *Longworth through the Centuries*, 2 parts, pt. 2 (privately published, 1982)

Hutchinson, Thomas (ed.). *Shelley: Poetical Works* (Oxford, 1905, 1989 edn)

Jones, Howard (ed.). *Pierre Gasendi's Institutio Logica 1658: a Critical Edition* (Assen, 1981)

Joy, Lynn Sumida. *Gassendi the Atomist* (Cambridge, 1987)

Karsten, P. *Patriot-Heroes in England and America* (Wisconsin, 1978)

Keeler, Mary Freer. *The Long Parliament, 1640–1641: a biographical Study of its Members* (Philadelphia, 1954)

Kelsey, Sean. *Inventing a Republic: the Political Culture of the English Commonwealth, 1649–1653* (Manchester, 1997)

Knachel, Philip A. *England and the Fronde: the Impact of the English Civil War and Revolution in France* (Ithica, NY, 1967)

Kneale, William, and Martha. *The Development of Logic* (Oxford, 1962)

Kussmaul, A. *Servants in Husbandry in Early-modern England* (Cambridge, 1981)

Laurence, Ann. *Parliamentary Army Chaplains 1642–1651* (RHS, London, 1990)

Levack, Brian P. *The Civil Lawyers in England, 1603–1641: a political Study* (Oxford, 1973)

Linton, W.J. *Claribel and other Poems* (London, 1865)

Madden, Lionel (ed.). *Robert Southey: The Critical Heritage* (London, 1972)

Madge, S.J. *The Domesday of Crown Lands* (London, 1938)

Matthews, A.G. (ed.). *Calamy Revised* (Oxford, 1934)

Matthews, A.C. *Walker Revised* (Oxford, 1948)

Morris, C.R. *Idealistic Logic: A Study of its Aim, Method and Achievements* (London, 1933)

Muddiman, J.G. *The King's Journalist 1659–1698* (London, 1923)

Muir, R. *The Lost Villages of Britain* (London, 1982)

Noble, Mark. *The Lives of the English Regicides* (2 vols) (London, 1798)

David Norbrook, *Writing the English Republic: Poetry, Rhetoric and Politics, 1627–1660* (Cambridge, 1999)

Parkes, Kineton (ed.). *The English Republic* (London, 1891)

Payne, Ernest A. *The Baptists of Berkshire* (London, 1951)

Pearl, Valerie. *London and the Outbreak of the Puritan Revolution: City Government and National Politics, 1625–43* (Oxford, 1964)

Pincus, Steven C.A. *Protestantism and Patriotism: Ideologies and the Making of English Foreign Policy, 1650–1668* (Cambridge, 1996)

Pocock, J.G.A. *The Machiavellian Moment: Florentine political thought and the Atlantic republican Tradition* (Princeton, 1975)

Pocock, J.G.A. *The Ancient Constitution and the Feudal Law: a Study of English historical thought in the seventeenth century* (Cambridge, 1957)

Powell J.R., and Timings, E.K. (eds). *Documents relating to the Civil War, 1642–1648* (Navy Records Society cv, London, 1963)

Preston, Arthur E. *The Church of St Nicholas, Abingdon* (Oxford, 1895)

Price, Richard. *The Guiana Maroons: a Historical and Bibliographical Introduction* (Johns Hopkins, Baltimore, 1976)

Puckrein, Gary. *Little England: Plantation Society and Anglo-Barbadian Politics, 1627–1700* (New York, 1984)

Quinn, Kenneth (ed.). *Catullus: The Poems* (London, 1970)

Raab, Felix. *The English Face of Machiavelli: a changing Interpretation, 1500–1700* (London, 1964)

Ranum, Orest. *The Fronde: A French Revolution, 1648–1652* (London, 1993)

Rist, J.M. *Epicurus: an introduction* (Cambridge, 1972)

Roberts, Alan, and Leach, John R. *The Coal Mines of Buxton* (Cromford, 1985)

Rowe, V.A. *Sir Henry Vane the Younger* (London, 1970)

Russell, Conrad. *The Fall of the British Monachies, 1637–1641* (Oxford, 1991)

Schneewind J.B. (ed.). *Moral Philosophy from Montaigne to Kant: an anthology* (2 vols) (Cambridge, 1990)

Scott, Jonathan. *Algernon Sidney and the English Republic, 1623–1677* (Cambridge, 1988)

Shapiro, Barbara J. *Probability and Certainty in Seventeenth-Century England: A Study of the Relationships between Natural Science, Religion, History, Law, and Literature* (Princeton, 1983)

Sheppard F.H.W. (gen. ed.). *Survey of London* (London County Council and the Royal Commission on the Historical Monuments of England)

Sinclair, T.A. *A History of Greek Political Thought* (London, 1951)

Smith, Nigel. *Perfection Proclaimed: Language and Literature in English Radical Religion, 1640–1660* (Oxford, 1989)

Somerville, Robert. *Office-holders in the Duchy of Lancaster and County Palatine of Lancaster from 1603* (London, 1972)

Sommerville, Johann. *Politics and Ideology in England, 1603–1640* (London, 1986)

Southey, Robert. *Letters from England*, ed. J. Simmons (London, 1961)

Southgate, Beverley C. *'Covetous of Truth': the Life and Work of Thomas White, 1593–1676* (Dordrecht, 1993)

Stanley, John. *The Church in the Hop Garden* (London, c. 1920)

Summers, W.H. *History of the Congregational Churches in the Berkshire, South Oxfordshire and South Buckinghamshire Association* (Newbury, 1905)

Townsend, G.F. *The Town and Borough of Leominster* (Leominster, 1861)

Tuck, Richard. *Natural Rights Theories: Their Origin and Development* (Cambridge, 1979)

Tuck, Richard. *Philosophy and Government, 1572–1651* (Cambridge, 1993)

Underdown, David. *Royalist Conspiracy in England 1649–60* (New Haven, 1960)

Underdown, David. *Pride's Purge: Politics in the Puritan Revolution* (Oxford, 1971)

Walcott, M.E.C. *Westminster Memorials of the City* (London, 1849)

Wallace, James M. *Destiny his Choice: the Loyalism of Andrew Marvell* (Cambridge, 1968)

Waters, Ivor. *Henry Marten and the Long Parliament* (Chepstow, 1973)

Waters, Ivor (ed.). *Letters from the Tower of London, 1660–1662* (Chepstow, 1983)

Watts, David. *The West Indies: Patterns of Development, Culture and Environmental Change since 1492* (Cambridge, 1987)

Westrich, S.A. *The Ormée of Bordeaux: A Revolution during the Fronde* (Baltimore, 1972)

Wheatley, H.B. *London Past and Present* (London, 1891)

Whitlock, R. *Agricultural Records AD220–1977* (London, 1978)

Woolrych, Austin. *Commonwealth to Protectorate* (Oxford, 1982)

Woolrych, Austin. *Soldiers and Statesmen: the General Council of the Army and its Debates, 1647–1648* (Oxford, 1987)

Worden, Blair. *The Rump Parliament, 1648–1653* (Cambridge, 1974)

Articles

Aylmer, Gerald. 'Who was ruling Herefordshire from 1645 to 1661?', *Transactions of the Woolhope Naturalists Club*, xl (1972), 373–87

Barber, Sarah. 'The Engagement for the Council of State and the establishment of the Commonwealth government', *Historical Research*, 63.150 (1990), 44–57

Barber, Sarah. 'Irish undercurrents to the politics of April 1653', *Historical Research*, 65.158 (1992), 315–35

Barber, Sarah. '"A bastard kind of militia": localism and tactics during the second civil war', in Ian Gentles, John Morrill, and Blair Worden (eds), *Soldiers, Writers and Statesmen of the English Revolution* (Cambridge, 1998)

Barber, Sarah. 'The attitude of the people of Northern England towards the Scots, 1639–1652: "the lamb and the dragon cannot be reconciled"', *Northern History*, xxxv (1999), 93–118

Bayliss, D.G. 'The effect of Bringwood forge and furnace on the landscape of part of northern Herefordshire to the end of the seventeenth century', *Transactions of the Woolhope Naturalists Club*, xlv (1985–7), 721–9

Beckles, Hilary. 'The concept of "white slavery" in the English Caribbean during the early seventeenth century', in John Brewer and Susan Staves (eds), *Early Modern Conceptions of Property* (London, 1996), pp. 572–84

Burgess, Glenn. 'Usurpation, obligation and obedience in the thought of the Engagement controversy', *The Historical Journal*, 29.3 (1986), 515–36

Campbell, Peter. 'Aspects of land tenure in Barbados, 1627–1660', *Journal of the Barbados Museum and Historical Society*, xxxvii (1984), 112–59

Crawford, Patricia. 'Charles Stuart: that man of blood', *Journal of British Studies*, xvi.2 (1977), 41–61

Davis, J.C. 'Pocock, Harrington, grace, nature and art in the classical republicanism of James Harrington', *The Historical Journal*, 24.3 (1981), 683–97

Davis, J.C. 'Radicalism in a traditional society: the evaluation of radical thought in the English Commonwealth, 1649–1660', *History of Political Thought* III.2 (1982), 193–213

[No author cited]. 'Documents and letters in the Brotherton Collection relating to Barbados', *Journal of the Barbados Museum and Historical Society*, xxiv–xxvi, 175–83

Durston, Christopher. 'Henry Marten and the High Shoon of Berkshire: the Levellers in Berkshire in 1648', *Berkshire Archaeological Journal*, 70 (1979–80), 87–95

Ferguson, Margaret W. 'Juggling the categories of race, class, and gender: Aphra Behn's *Oroonoko*' in Margo Hendricks and Patricia Parker (eds), *Women, 'Race', and Writing in the Early Modern Period* (London, 1994), pp. 209–24

Firth, C.H. 'Thomas Scot's account of his actions as intelligencer during the Commonwealth', *English Historical Review*, xii (1897), 116–26

Gentles, Ian. 'The sales of Crown lands during the English Revolution', *Economic History Review*, xxvi (1973), 614–35

Gentles, Ian. 'London Levellers in the English Revolution: the Chidleys and their circle', *Journal of Ecclesiastical History*, 29.3 (1978), 281–309

Gleissner, Richard A. 'The Levellers and natural law: the Putney debates of 1647', *Journal of British Studies*, 19–20 (1979–80), 74–89

[No author cited]. 'Governors' residences', *Journal of the Barbados Museum and Historical Society*, x (1943), 152–62

Hall, Kim F. '"I would wish to be a black-moor": beauty, race and rank in Lady Mary Wroth's *Urania*', in Margo Hendricks and Patricia Parker (eds), *Women, 'Race', and Writing in the Early Modern Period* (London, 1994), pp.178–94

Handler, Jerome S. 'Father Antoine Biet's visit to Barbados in 1654', *Journal of the Barbados Museum and Historical Society*, xxxii.2 (1967), 56–75

Handler, Jerome S., and Shelby, Lon. 'A seventeenth-century commentary on labor and military problems in Barbados', *Journal of the Barbados Museum and Historical Society*, xxxiv.3 (1973)

Hill, Christopher. 'The Norman Yoke', in his *Puritanism and Revolution* (London, 1958, reprint 1969), pp. 50–122

Hillaby, Joseph. 'The parliamentary borough of Weobley, 1628–1798', *Transactions of the Woolhope Naturalists Club*, xxxix (1967), 104–47

Innes, Joanna. 'The King's Bench prison in the later eighteenth century: law, authority and order in a London debtors' prison', in J. Brewer and J. Styles (eds), *An Ungovernable People: the English and their Law in the seventeenth and eighteenth Centuries* (London, 1983), pp. 250–98

Langdon, John. 'Water-mills and windmills in the west midlands, 1086–1500', *Economic History Review*, xliv.3 (1991), 424–44

Lorimer, Joyce. 'The failure of the English Guiana Ventures 1595–1667 and James I's foreign policy', *Journal of Imperial and Commonwealth History*, 21.1 (1993), 1–30

Macintosh, J.J. 'Robert Boyle on Epicurean atheism and atomism', in Margaret J. Osler (ed.), *Atoms, Pneuma, and Tranquillity: Epicurean and Stoic Themes in European Thought* (Cambridge, 1991), pp. 197–219

Mulligan, Lotte, and Richards, Judith. 'A "radical" problem: the poor and the English reformers in the mid-seventeenth century', *Journal of British Studies* 29.2 (1990), 118–46

Norbrook, David. 'Lucan, Thomas May, and the emergence of a republican literary culture', in Kevin Sharpe and Peter Lake (eds), *Culture and Politics in early Stuart England* (London, 1994), pp. 45–66

Richards, J. 'The Greys of Bradgate in the English Civil War: a study of Henry Grey, first earl of Stamford and his son and heir Thomas, lord Grey of Groby', *Transactions of the Leicestershire Archaeological and History Society*, lxii (1988), 32–52

Scott, Jonathan. 'The rapture of motion: James Harrington's republicanism', in Nicholas Philipson and Quentin Skinner (eds), *Political Discourse in early–modern Europe* (Cambridge, 1993)

Shilstone, E.M. 'The evolution of the General Assembly of Barbados' *Journal of the Barbados Museum and Historical Society*, i (1933), 187–91

Skinner, Quentin. 'Conquest and consent: Thomas Hobbes and the Engagement controversy' in G.E. Aylmer, *The Interregnum: the Quest for Settlement, 1646–1660* (London, 1974), pp. 79–98

Smith, Nigel. 'The charge of atheism and the language of radical speculation, 1640–1660' in Michael Hunter and David Wootton (eds), *Atheism from the Reformation to the Englightenment* (Oxford, 1992), pp.131–58

[No author cited]. 'Some records of the House of Assembly of Barbados', *Journal of the Barbados Museum and Historical Society*, x (1943), 173–87

[No author cited]. 'St John's vestry minutes', *Journal of the Barbados Museum and Historical Society*, xxxiii.1 (1969), 32–49

Taft, Barbara. 'The Humble Petition of several Colonels of the Army', *Huntington Library Bulletin*, xlii (1978), 15–41

Taft, Barbara. 'Voting lists of the Council of Officers, December 1648', *Bulletin of the Institute of Historical Research*, lii (1979), 138–54

Taft, Barbara. 'The Council of Officers' *Agreement of the People*, 1648/9', *The Historical Journal*, 28.1 (1985), 189–97

Taylor, Elizabeth. 'The seventeenth century iron forge at Carey mill', *Transactions of the Woolhope Naturalists Club*, xlv.2 (1986), 450–68

Underdown, David. 'Party management in the recruiter elections, 1645–48', *English Historical Review*, 83 1968, 235–64

Underdown, David. '"Honest" radicals in the counties, 1642–1649', in D. Pennington and K. Thomas (eds), *Puritans and Revolutionaries* (Oxford, 1978), pp. 186–205

Walker, James. 'The secret service under Charles II and James II', *Transactions of the Royal Historical Society*, 4th ser., xv (1932), 211–35

White, B.R. 'John Pendarves, the Calvinistic Baptists and the Fifth Monarchy', *Baptist Quarterly*, 25 (1973–4)

Williams, C.M. 'The anatomy of a radical gentleman: Henry Marten', in D. Pennington and K. Thomas (eds), *Puritans and Revolutionaries* (Oxford, 1978), pp. 118–38

Wiseman, Susan. '"Adam, the father of all flesh", porno-political rhetoric and political theory in and after the English civil war', *Prose Studies*, 14.3 (1991), 134–57

Worden, Blair. 'The bill for a new representative: the dissolution of the Long Parliament, April 1653', *English Historical Review*, lxxxvi (1971), 473–96

Unpublished dissertations

Chris Durston, 'Berkshire and its county gentry 1625–1649', Ph.D. Reading, 1977

Ian Gentles, 'The debentures market and military purchase of crown land, 1649–1660', Ph.D. University of London, 1969

G.E. McParlin, 'The Herefordshire gentry in county government, 1625–1661', Ph.D. Aberystwyth, 1981

C.M. Williams, 'The political career of Henry Marten, with special reference to the origins of republicanism in the Long Parliament', D.Phil. Oxford, 1954

Index

References to place-names shown on maps are given in italics. References to Henry Marten are limited to those of his writings that appear in the main text.